FROM ENGLAND TO THE ANTIPODES & INDIA 1846 to 1902

WITH

STARTLING REVELATIONS,

OR

56 Years of My Life in the Indian Mutiny, Police & jails

FROM ENGLAND TO THE ANTIPODES & INDIA 1846 to 1902

WITH

STARTLING REVELATIONS,

OR

56 Years of My Life in the Indian Mutiny, Police & jails

I. TYRRELL

GYAN

Published by

GYAN

Gyan Publishing House
5, Ansari Road
Daryaganj, New Delhi-110002
Phone: 011-47034999, 9811692060
E-mail: books@gyanbooks.com

Distribution Network
gyanbooks.com
India, USA, Canada, UK, Australia

ISBN: 978-93-6433-361-0 (PB)

First Published, 1904

2nd Impression 2024

Printed at: Gyan Press, Delhi.

FROM ENGLAND TO THE ANTIPODES & INDIA 1846 TO 1902:
With startling revelations, or 56 years of my life in the
Indian Mutiny, Police & jails
Author: I. TYRRELL

From England to the Antipodes & India—1846 to 1902,

WITH

STARTLING REVELATIONS,

OR

56 Years of My Life
in the Indian Mutiny, Police & Jails

BY

I. TYRRELL.

MADRAS:

PRINTED AT THE A. L. V. PRESS, 149, POPHAMS'S BROADWAY.

1904

CHAPTER I.

I.—Chatham in 1846-47.

Looking back now through the dim Vista of my 54 years' absence from dear old England, there seems to me to be no doubt, that the dream of my life had been to visit foreign lands, and that the country most mysteriously attractive to my youthful imagination was "the gorgeous East" with all its wealth and grandeur, its glamour, and sunshine, all of which I had read of in books, and heard of from old soldiers of my acquaintance, which had taken a powerful hold of my youthful fancy. Moreover, I belonged to a roving family, all my brothers being in the army, and the only avenue by which I could realize my aspirations appeared to me to be the one which they had entered, hence I resolved to do as they had done and take the Queen's shilling.

Fifty-five years ago in my native town in Suffolk, there were no railways, no gas, no lucifer matches. Photography was in its infancy, and the new police had only just been introduced. At night the thoroughfares were, in most parts, dimly lighted with oil lamps, while watchmen patrolled the streets, and shouted out the hours. If you wanted to light a candle it was necessary to use a tinder box, and strike a light with flint and steel. Newspapers were few. "Punch" had only lately come into existence, and "Truth" whose mission in life is to expose shams and to take a paternal interest in all that concerns "a British soldier" and his welfare, was not even dreamt of. My first railway journey was from Ware to London, a distance of 21 miles, and my first sight of a policeman was in my own native town, in 1846 where police were just then appointed under Sir Robert Peel's Act. Very little was known about India, at the time, in country places, and most of the people still believed it to be the land of gold mohurs and of liver complaint. His Grace, the Duke of Wellington was Commander-in-Chief, and life in the army as a private soldier was not many degrees removed from penal servitude. Notwithstanding all the drawbacks of service in the ranks, my desire to enter was undiminished, and I accordingly enlisted at Chatham in the 46th Regiment of Foot, now the 2nd Battalion D. C. L. I. on the 25th August 1846. I venture to state however that if some of our soldiers of the present day were compelled to submit to the conditions of service in vogue in those days, they would find soldiering very different from what it is now. All enlistments were for unlimited service, though of course this generally meant 21 years. On enlistment each man received, to the best of my recollection, a bounty of £ 4 from which deductions were made for his kit, &c., so that the recruit enjoyed very little of his so-called " bounty " money. His regimental clothing consisted of cloth trousers with red side stripe ; a red tunic, or *coatee* as it was then styled, with yellow facings ; a red shell jacket ; boots, leather stock, and " shako, " in lieu of the helmets and bearskins of modern days ; and a round woollen forage cap which seemed to me the embodiment of ugliness. The tight fitting tunic, leather stock, and cross-belts, gave the soldier a stiff, ramrod-like appearance which was then considered the acme of military smartness ; but I leave the reader to imagine the torture it was to the unfortunate man who had to wear them on a broiling summer day. The pay of the rank and file was nominally the same as it is now, only that stoppages were much heavier, and if a man was well behaved, he could clear four pence per diem. In the matter of rations, each man was allowed daily a pound of meat, a pound of bread, and a pound of vegetables ; a pint of tea without milk for breakfast and the same for " tea."

There was an eternal sameness in the cooking which would appal the British soldier of the present generation. The meat would be cooked with the vegetables, and a little barley added, to make *soup*, and this constituted the old-time soldier's *menu* from January to December. The bread was black and heavy, a four-pound loaf being no larger in appearance than an ordinary two-pound loaf of white bread, and I have known a man of my depôt to eat an whole four-pound loaf at one meal. This was an exceptional case, and occurred once when I was cook of the depôt. Two Irishmen, Crummey and Duffey, by name, had been driven to enlist by the Potato Famine in Ireland in 1846-47, and were both in the depôt the evening prior to the incident I am about to mention. Crummey was a simple minded, generous fellow, but Duffey was the reverse. He had a "lean and hungry look" like *Cassius*. His hair was erect and bristly, as if he were in a perpetual fright, and his general appearance was anything but mild. I had drawn the ration bread, and had left the loaves in the room, while I went out for a few minutes. On my return, I discovered that I was deficient of a four-pound loaf, and it was with some difficulty that I ascertained that Duffey had come in from an adjoining room, seized a loaf, and devoured it Of course Duffey was marched off to the guard-room, but was subsequently released after pleading ignorance on consenting to make good the loss. The bread used to be most unpalatable, and those, like myself, who could afford it, purchased white bread, and other dainties out of our own pockets. Good-conduct pay to the young soldier of those days loomed too far off, for him to calculate with any certainty, upon receiving it, considering that he had to "be good," that is to say, his regimental defaulter sheet had to be clear of all entries for the space of two years, and must have served five years before he obtained his first "good-conduct badge," and had to serve a further term of five years of like service for his second, and so on, to the end of his service. The chances of a man obtaining good-conduct pay may be fairly judged by the following incident which occurred to me about seven months after my enlistment, On St. Patrick's day, 1847, I obtained a pass up to midnight, and, in the course of the evening, went to a public house known as "the Belle of the Brook," where a number of men of the 88th Connaught Rangers and other Irish corps had already congregated. I had taken but one half-pint of beer, and seeing that there was going to be a disturbance, I prepared to leave, but just at the door which was about four feet higher than the roadway below, I received a blow at the back of my head, which sent me headlong into the street where I lay unconscious until found by the Picquet at 11 P. M., carried to barracks, and while stil unconscious, thrown into the guard-room for being drunk. In the morning, however, I was taken to the Hospital where I remained 17 days, and on being discharged, I was taken back to the guard-room where I remained another seven days, owing to the Easter holidays intervening. When eventually brought before the Commanding Officer, Colonel Weare, he asked the Sergeant-Major, whether I was one of the men who had broken out of barracks on St. Patrick's day. Sergeant-Major Menzies informed him that I had not been one of them, but that I was a man of good character, and had had a pass for the night. "Six to barracks" said the Colonel "Right about face" said the Sergeant-Major, and that was the end of it. Needless to add that I was wise enough to hold my tongue, for had I attempted any explanation, or indeed to have uttered a single word, I should have been adjudged guilty of an *additional* crime and sentenced to seven days "cells." In those days, no soldier was allowed to smoke in the streets, or carry a cane, neither was he permitted to leave barracks, except on duty before 5 P. M. and "Tattoo," sounded at 8 P. M., daily in winter, and 8-30 P. M. in summer. There were no "married quarters," and I have often seen three, and sometimes four families, accommodated in the four corners of the single men's barrack rooms, with only a blanket or counterpane to screen them from observation and ensure privacy. The heating and lighting arrangements were miserable in the extreme, all lights being put out at 9 o'clock, but we, young soldiers, did not feel this a hardship, as we usually got an older comrade to tell us his experiences. I remember a man in my room, of the name of McGovran, an Irishman who afterwards got 20 years' penal servitude for an unmentionable crime, who used to earn enough money to pay for his beer daily by telling us of his exploits in sheep stealing, moonlight-raiding, and other devilries, while he was in Ireland. In the matter of amusements, regimental libraries of a sort there were, but reading and recreation rooms, such as now exist, were conspicuous by their absence, and as for Army Temperance Association Rooms, and Soldiers' Homes, there was no "Gelson Gregson" in those days. Here and there, there were a few officers who did their best, with more or less success to stem the tide of drunkenness, but soldiers generally were looked upon by their officers and indeed by the general public, as more or less drunken and disreputable, and treated accordingly We had many garrison duties to perform at Chatham, but the most fatiguing were the " coal fatigues," *i.e.*, carrying coal to the officers' quarters. Of the garrison duties, the most important was the Main Dockyard Guard, which consisted of two officers (a Captain and Lieutenant) two sergeants, three corporals, and 40 men. Well do I remember the first time I mounted with this guard. I was only a young soldier, in fact, a mere boy, and very nervous about the responsibility, for it was the simplest thing imaginable to get into trouble. At 11 P. M. some one shouted " guard turn out " and one man, in leaping off the guard bed, overturned the table on which stood over forty empty canteens (mess tins, in which dinners had been brought for the guard). The noise which followed baffles description and was such as I had never heard before. After some delay, the guard formed up when it was ascertained by the Captain, that the alarm was given by one of the men inside, who did so in his sleep. It would appear that he had heard the man next to him, one of the 78th Highlanders, groaning and making an unearthly noise, drumming with his feet at the same time. This, to those who were lying next to the Highlander, appeared to be the " Grand Rounds " approaching and hence the alarm, but who the individual was that had actually shouted out the alarm was never discovered ! At any rate the Captain came inside and saw for himself " Sandy," still on the guard bed, in the throes of a nightmare, and drumming away merrily with his feet !

I took part in only one " Field Day " while at Chatham, and on this occasion, His Grace the Duke of Wellington was present, and inspected the troops. My depôt formed part of the attacking force which was to capture the fort and garrison by a *Coup de Main*, and this we did most brilliantly, with all " the pomp and circumstance of war " and much expenditure of blank ammunition, the use of scaling ladders, and attacking in close order. This was the only occasion on which I had the honor of being present when the " Iron Duke visited Chatham. The only *contretemps* in my depôt on this memorable day, was that the man who was next to me in the attack, shot away his ram-rod in his excitement, and got into trouble over it! After this, there was the unvarying round of guard-mounting, fatigue and other garrison routine, but even guard-mounting sometimes, has its excitements, as instance the following. The post at the Spur hospital in rear of the officers' quarters was said to be haunted by the spectre of a lady, and as it was some 300 yards away from the " guard," the lot of the Sentry, if he happened to be ignorant and superstitious, was not a happy one, as practical jokes were sure to be played upon a nervous man. I remember a private of my depôt who actually bolted back from this post to the guard-room in a fright, swearing that he had seen the ghost of a lady crossing the Spur-battery bridge. This plea, however, did not avail him with the Court-Martial which tried him, and he received a severe sentence of imprisonment Some months after this occurrence, I was on this very same post, and soon, observed the figure of a woman, and not being superstitious, I was determined not to be outwitted and therefore challenged the figure. There was a low chuckle for an answer, and I quickly went up to the object which turned out to be a woman of the town. I detained her till my relief came when I handed her over to the corporal-of-the-guard, by whom she was detained in the guard-room until the next morning, but not as a prisoner. No doubt she was a " light of love." At any rate she helped me to pass away about an hour of my " sentry go " pleasantly. Another post that was much dreaded on account of its isolation, and the fact that a Marine sentry had shot himself, and had been buried close by some years before, was the one at St. Mary's Barracks, at the back of Brompton barracks. The post was a very lonely one, and to a young and nervous soldier, uncanny, and fraught with unknown terrors. It was in the trench facing the Magazine, close to which, the sentry, who had shot himself, was interred. On one occasion, at this post, I was on sentry from 10 to 12 midnight, and from 4 to 6 A.M. I marched up and down, and on to the road on the ramparts, but saw nothing for some time, until I observed a bright object, which I thought was approaching me. I went up to see what it was, when it suddenly darted between my legs and disappeared. It happened to be an intensely dark night, and it appeared hardly possible to distinguish what the object was. It was not surprising, therefore, that I should have been somewhat startled at first. However, I soon pulled myself together, and swore at myself for being so easily frightened by what perhaps might have been a cat, or a *will-o-the Wisp*, after all.

A journey in those days, even a comparatively short one by coach, was not undertaken without careful preparation against all eventualities; but one by steamer was regarded by the untravelled as a fearsome thing and a temptation of Providence. I remember a Revd. Mr. Grimwood at a prayer meeting in my father's house relating of the fearful voyage made by himself and family, from London to Yarmouth! The Revd. Gentleman evidently thought it, and so did his hearers, as something astounding. When therefore my mother journeyed by steamer from Yarmouth to London on her way to Chatham, on a short visit to my brother and myself, she was on her return home, considered by her friends to have done a most perilous thing! A curious incident occurred during my mothers's visit which struck me as rather singular at the time. During one of our walks out together one evening, we heard the "Dead March" being played by the depôt band, and as I was anxious that my mother should see a military funeral, we joined in the procession. On arrival at the cemetery gate, and while the coffin was being carried up a slope into the gateway, the dead man's "Shako" fell off the coffin and rolled down to my mother's feet. Subsequent enquiries elicited the fact that the deceased was my cousin, Fitzpatrick, of the 24th regimental depôt, who was ailing, but of whose death we had had no intimation of, and whom we intended seeing the next day. My brother was at this time serving in the 65th Foot now the 1st Battalion York and Lancaster Regiment, and I applied officially to be transferred to that Regiment. This was at first refused, as my commanding officer wanted to keep me, but on its being subsequently represented to the Duke ot Wellington that I was the youngest of six brothers serving Her Majesty the Queen, my transfer was sanctioned. The next few months of my stay at Chatham passed by uneventfully; but towards the end of August 1847, about a year after my enlistment, and when I had become a fully developed soldier, I embarked on the convict ship "Marion," a sailing vessel of 800 tons bound for Hobart Town in Van Dieman's Land, as one of a guard of fifty men, under two officers, Captain Pierce of the 96th and Lieutenant Grant of the 58th Foot. Before the vessel left the Thames, we took on board 200 convicts, "Lord Stanley's exiles" as they were termed, by reason of their being the first batch of convicts transported under the new Act, and at Portsmouth, we took on board 100 Reformatory boys from the Isle of Wight, all bound for Van Dieman's Land.

For the information of those unacquainted with the provisions of the Act, I may mention that it was a humane measure introduced by the Government with the object of giving well behaved convicts, an opportunity of settling down in a new country, and beginning life under fresh auspices. The convicts, as a matter of course, had not completed their full term of penal servitude, but were allowed their freedom, on landing, on ticket-of-leave, on condition that they reported their movements to the authorities at their port of destination every month. I may as well here state that while a good many settled down and led respectable lives, becoming the founders of what is, I believe, now termed "good old convict families," a large proportion, however, relapsed into their old ways and were again laid by the heels. One of the convicts was an Irishman, a fine built fellow, who became mutinous while we were lying in Portsmouth harbour, and was immediately sent on shore to undergo a further term of penal servitude n England. I may also mention that Her Most Gracious Majesty, with the Prince Consort, and her two eldest children, one of whom is at present, H. I. M. King Edward the VIIth passed close to us, in the Royal Yacht, on their way to the Isle of Wight, in September 1847. We could distinctly observe the Royal party standing on the poop of their vessel. Royal salutes were fired from the batteries on shore, as well as from the men-of-war in harbour. All vessels were decorated with bunting and the yards manned.

It was a stirring spectacle and the first time I had seen the Queen whom I have since had the honor of serving in active service for nearly 49 years—" a record service"—and it was also the last glimpse I had of my dear native land.

CHAPTER II.

THE VOYAGE, HOBART TOWN, VAN DIEMAN'S LAND IN 1847-48.

On the whole the convicts were a quiet lot and gave but little trouble. They were barricaded down and allowed on deck in batches, at intervals during the day, for the purpose of obtaining fresh air. Sentries were posted at the foot of the ladder and at the doors of the different barriers, and the stench arising from the lower deck was at times so overpowering, that during my two hours duty at night, I had often to knock my head against the battens to keep myself awake. We had the misfortune to be in a storm in the Bay of Biscay, and half of the guard as well as the convicts were sea-sick. I was horribly ill and asked one of the crew what was the best thing I should take for it " Take a bit of fat pork" said he, but I did'nt. The mizzen mast was struck by lightning, but there was no further damage done. The weather was delightful when we arrived in warm latitudes, and it was pleasant to see the gambols of the dolphins which followed the vessel in shoals in their chase after flying fish, many of which dropped on deck in their efforts to escape. We had a sick man on board of the name of Moore—" Roary O'Moore " as he was called, on account of a roaring kind of noise he made while coughing, and a very large shark followed the vessel for days, a sign we were told that there would be a death on board, but it was the shark that died first, for he was hooked by means of a 4-lb. junk of salt-pork and despatched by the ship's company, several days before poor " Roary" handed in his checks. The shark was a very large one, and one of the officers kept its back-bone for a walking stick, while the sailors made a meal of the flesh. In spite of the superstition about killing "Mother Carey's chickens," a number of these sea-birds, as well as albatrosses were shot, and porpoises harpooned by the sailors. On crossing the equator the usual frolic, so graphically described by Captain Marryatt in one of his stories, took place. The officers took good care to keep out of the way by remaining in their cabins, but many of us red coats, I among the number, had to undergo the process of lathering and shaving at the hands of Neptune's courtiers. Poor Duffey, the hungry one's ostrich-like appetite got him into trouble again on board. He walked off with a large piece of cooked salt junk from the cook's galley, and, being caught *in flagrante delicto*, was sentenced to 48 hours' confinement in an extemporized "cell" fastened to the bulwark on the main deck, close to the cook's galley. I may say here that soldiers going on board in charge of convicts had all their rations found and so cleared their shilling a day, but as each man was provided with a sea-kit before leaving, which he was expected to pay for and which cost nearly £2, there was very little saved by him after all. The first land which we sighted after leaving England was the Cape-de-Verde Islands at which we anchored for water and fresh provisions. It was a blessed thing to us when the boats came to the vessel with all kinds of tropical fruit. The oranges I remember, although perfectly green to look at, were delightfully sweet and palatable, and the best I had ever eaten. On weighing anchor, I remember seeing the peak of Teneriffe for nearly fifty miles as I thought. We spent Christmas day 1847 on board, being then about twenty days' sail from Van Diemans' Land where we duly arrived on the 13th January 1848, Captain Pierce, our Commanding officer, very kindly paid for the plums, flour, suet, &c., for our Christmas pudding, but as the stock of plums on board was very limited, the plums, in our pudding were very few and far between. At Hobart Town, the convicts were landed. Here another brother of mine was serving in the 96th Foot, now the 2nd Battalion Manchester Regiment. He applied to have me transferred, and I was attached to the regiment, pending the sanction of the General officer commanding at Sydney. At this time, Sir William Denison was Governor of Van Diemans' Land, and his brother Captain Charles Denison, was his Private Secretary. I make mention of these officers here, as years after, I had the pleasure of seeing both of them in Madras, when one was Governor, and the other the Adjutant-General of the Queen's forces of the Madras army. Hobart Town was at this period a small, but prosperous town, the population being chiefly composed of ex-convicts and their descendants. The houses were of brick with shingle roofs, and the streets were wide and macadamised. The four principal buildings were, the Court House, the Church, Government House, and the Jail. I saw very little of the aborigines, although a few used to be brought from inland every year to see the Governor, and these I saw. The island was remarkably healthy and deaths were few among the military. As a consequence, promotion was very slow in the ranks. It was a common thing for a lance-corporal to have to wait five years for his stripes as a corporal, and five years more, as a sergeant. Society was very much mixed in Hobart Town. One evening, shortly after my arrival, my brother took me for a walk, and going down Liverpool Street, we met a fine, stalwart, well-dressed man who accosted my brother in a familiar tone. I said to him you appear to be acquainted with some respectable people in the place. "Yes" answered he dryly. "Do you know who that is?" "That is Solomon Blay, the hang-man." My brother then related to me how he "Solomon" became public executioner. It seemed that he (Blay) was one of a gang of convicts who were being taken on board the brig "Governor Phillips" from Sydney to Norfolk Island where the worst lot were sent, when the convicts mutinied and seized the ship. They were eventually overcome by the officers and crew, not however without loss of life on both sides, and on arrival at Norfolk Island, they were tried by a special judge, a barrister, who had been sworn in at Sydney and sent down for the purpose, and he sentenced them in dozens to be hanged. There was a difficulty, however, as to the executioner, and Solomon Blay volunteering for the work, was reprieved, and being sent back to Hobart Town, was released on "ticket-of-leave," and was for years afterwards public executioner there. There was much lawlessness, and executions were of frequent occurrence, while stirring and startling were the experiences we at times met with while on guard over the convicts. In the event of an execution, the hang-man used to come to the gaol the day before, and remain there over night, and many a blood-curdling tale would he relate to the guard, of his experiences, whilst making calico caps, and greasing the ropes for his victims next morning. An indent would be sent to the Government stores for "rope, soap, and calico" for three; or whatever the number was, that were awaiting death. One particularly gruesome experience I remember, which, I think, is worthy of mention as instancing the rough and ready methods adopted with the convicts. A ticket-of-leave man, called Happy Jack, who belonged to the Harbour Master's boat's crew, was condemned to death, for the murder of one of his companions, who had threatened to report him and have him turned out of the crew. The Harbour Master's boat's crew was composed of selected ticket-of-leave men, and the position was considered a sort of catch amongst the men. Happy Jack, one night, seized an opportunity, when he and his companion were together near the stone quarries on Kelly's steps, close to our Barracks, to dash his brains out with a stone. Happy Jack was a tall man and Solomon Blay allowed him too much rope with the result that the unfortunate man came down on the lid of his coffin which was in accordance with the then practice kept below the drop, and smashed it. As life was not extinct, Happy Jack had to be finished off by Solomon Blay clinging to his body and strangling him. It was a most revolting sight, but I have seen something just as bad some years afterwards during the Indian Mutiny. Although the convicts were closely guarded at the different convict settlements, yet there were many who succeeded in breaking out from durance vile, and effected their escape, some of them to the mainland of Australia. All took to bush-ranging, and "black-faced" robbery, as it was then termed, that is to say, the robbers used to wear a black mask. One night I was on sentry over the condemned ward at the back of the jail in which were six men under sentence of death; three for black-faced robbery and three for bush ranging. These men had committed a murder, combined with an attempted outrage on a young lady, a farmer's daughter in the neighbouring colony. They were caught and brought back, but the principal culprit, one Rogers, escaped the gallows by jumping over board in Hobart Town harbour, and one of the men escaped with penal servitude, having prevented the outrage on the young lady. One would have thought that these men would have shown a spirit of contrition during the last few days of their earthly existence—not a bit of it! They all kept up a lively conversation about men of their acquaintance who had shared a similar fate, describing each one as a "pebble" or a "sandstone" according to the degree of hardihood he had shown at his execution. Many of the convicts were most desperate characters. In one case, two men were breaking stones at a settlement, called "the mines." One of these men was chewing tobacco which had been dropped for him by one of the sentries, a crime that would have got the sentry a court-martial had he been caught. The other man asked for a chew, but being refused, he seized his hammer, beat out his companion's brains, and then deliberately took the tobacco out of the dead man's mouth, and put it into his own, but the most gruesome of all was that of three convicts, one a mere boy, who had escaped from the penal settlement and were making their way across the island to the sea-shore, but being unable to secure any food the two men murdered the boy and ate his flesh. A few days afterwards one of the other convicts was obliged to give in on account of want of food when he was butchered by the other convict in the same manner as the boy had been and a great quantity of his flesh was eaten by the remaining convict who eventually gave himself up to justice through sheer starvation and was hanged. The truth of this may be ascertained from "Geoffrey Hamlin," one of Kingsley's works. One individual I remember, a married man with a family, had been transported for seven years from my native town in England for breaking into a store-room, and stealing two sacks of apples. He was then a farm labourer, and left behind him a wife and nine children. He was a small contractor to Government, and comparatively in affluent circumstances. Apparently, his theft was a turning point in his career, and the best thing that could have happened to him for had he remained in England he would still have been a poor man. What I at that time considered one of the sights of Hobart Town was the slaughter-house close to our barracks. Here the butcher armed with a spear seated himself on a beam which ran across the building several feet from the ground, and as the cattle were driven into the building, the animals to be killed were promptly speared, and the remainder driven out. The best beef and mutton could be purchased for two pence per pound at Hobart Town, while fish, oysters, and potatoes were in abundance, and very cheap. Many of our men were very loth to leave when we received orders to proceed to India. Two men of my company, Howand and Howarth, I remember, committed serious burglary in a jeweller's shop in the town in order that they might remain behind, but as the regimental authorities had got an inkling of their reason for committing themselves, they were tried by court-martial and made an example of, but had, nevertheless, to go to India. Notwithstanding this, a Yorkshireman, named Metcalfe, deliberately broke out of barracks, smashed a jeweller's window, and did a lot of other damage. He was tried by the military authorities and got twelve months, but for years afterwards while in India this unfortunate man was under stoppages of pay for this folly. The guard-room was close to Government House, and the Governor, Sir William Denison, who used to wear a white hat had the habit of going out to the Government gardens for his " consitutional, " nearly every morning at day-break, and I remember an unfortunate sentry got into trouble for not saluting him. There was another individual who used to wear a white hat in the town, an half-mad Irishman, an ex-convict, called MacCarthy, who carried a shillelagh and used to fling his arms about and dance in the street, just for fun—for he never gave offence. A sentry, who had not seen the Governor before, enquired one morning, how he was to recognize His Excellency. " You will know him by the white hat he wears" said one of the guard. Poor Paddy came dancing along the street, and swinging his shillelagh about, " guard, turn out" shouted the sentry, and the guard turned out, and poor Paddy was nearly receiving an unexpected honor. The sentry was quickly brought to book, but his plea of ignorance did not avail him and he got seven days' cells for his little joke.

Our regiment shortly after this received orders to proceed to India, but we got into bad odour with the towns-people owing to an unfortunate disturbance which occurred before we left. A man of ours, named Jonathan Smith, who belonged to the grenadier company, had a quarrel with one of the towns-people an ex-convict and pugilist, named Hunt, at a cricket match between the military and the civil population. Smith had the habit of keeping his mouth open, and his tongue partly hanging out, and, in the scuffle which ensued, it was nearly cut in two. This caused a bitter feeling amongst the Military element, which was still more excited by the jeering terms in which the local newspaper alluded to the incident. The result was a challenge for £25 a side, the stakes being deposited at a public house in the town, and some of the officers were present in mufti, at the fight, which took place at Point Pure, across the water, opposite Hobart Town, and when the military arrived on the ground, Hunt and his friends wanted to know if the soldier's coffin had been brought, but contrary to their expectation, Smith knocked out his opponent after a fight of twenty three rounds. Some time later when Smith and his friends called upon the publican for the money, they found that they had been duped by Hunt, and his friends who had been beforehand with them, and had claimed the stakes and made off with the money. The publican who had been imposed upon by their assurances that Hunt was the winner, repudiated all responsibility, but this did not satisfy the military, who turned out in a body at night, many with their side-arms, ransacked the house, carried the barrels of beer into the street, and stove them in. This, of course, brought great discredit on the regiment, especially as we were about to leave for India, and I remember Colonel Cumberland, the officer commanding the regiment, in addressing the men, told them that he would rather have had his Regiment defeated on the battle-field, than have had them disgraced in such a manner. The men took this, of course, for what it was worth.

On Sundays, church parade was invariably held at 10 A.M., and by 10-30 we would be seated in church. The Chaplain, a clergyman of the old school, who had attended scores of men to the gallows, would ramble along in his sermon with his firstly, secondly, thirdly, and lastly, at such a length, that I never remember our leaving the church before the dinner bugle had sounded at quarter to one o'clock. Our feelings can be better imagined than described, when we marched back to a cold dinner. In February 1849, we were relieved by the 99th Foot from Sydney, which was then the last regiment in the service, and they brought with them the new fire-arm, the percussion musket; our regiment being the last corps that was armed with the old flint-lock, which we took to India with us. Methinks even now, I can hear the word of command "open-pans" "shut-pans." Loose powder was of course put in the pan from the cartridge, and if any man carelessly put in a little over and above, the man on his right would get the benefit of it full in the face. No Lee-Metford's with wind-guages and "patent sights" in those days. No shooting at 900 yards either, for I remember being company's shot that same year, with a score of ten centres out of ten rounds, at 100 yards distance.

CHAPTER III.

The Voyage to India, 1849.

In February 1849 we embarked on the "Duke of Newcastle" for India, and the voyage passed without any particular note. One morning, however, the command "All hands to shorten sail" sounded throughout the ship. We had been overtaken by a squall and doubtless, had this squall struck the vessel at night, the writer would not have been alive to relate his reminiscences. Our principal amusement during the voyage consisted of impromptu concerts got up by the non-commissioned officers and men. I remember a Private Norris of No. 2 Company who used to sing a loyal and patriotic song, the refrain of which ran

> "Well may she gain a soldier's heart,
> A soldier's gratitude."

This was always received with enthusiasm by officers and men alike.

On the 19th of April 1849, we landed at Calcutta and marched to Fort William. The regiment was highly elated at the prospect before us. The change from Van Diemans' Land to India was a great one. In those days the natives of the country treated the British soldier with the greatest respect and deference. But better than all was the marked change in food. Everything was cheap and for a few pice daily men could live most comfortably and even have hot joints for breakfast. Our elation, however, was of short duration. One day shortly after our arrival in India four men of my company reported sick and were taken to the hospital by the sick orderly Corporal, Corporal Blanchfield, an Irishman, and a facetious individual. One morning at the breakfast table I remember one man asking, "Corporal, how is my chum Vardon"? "Dead and buried" was the abrupt reply. We were greatly surprised at this, but were informed that all four men who had gone to hospital the day before were not only dead, but actually buried without our knowing a word about it. To many of my readers this may seem incredible, but not more so than to us at the time. On enquiry however we found that a staff of natives were maintained at the general hospital for the purpose of burying cholera patients off hand as soon as they expired. Then it was that our men began to think how short was life in India. Literally, it put the fear of God into their hearts, and scores of men turned religious, and began to say their prayers regularly every night. In course of time, however, when they grew accustomed to seeing their comrades being carried to hospital and buried within a few hours, their good feelings soon evaporated, and the men were as bad as ever.

In those days commissions amongst officers were to be had by purchase, which meant that comparatively poor men grew old whilst still Lieutenants and Captains. One of our officers, a Captain MacGregor, had been in India before with the 26th Cameronians, and on landing at Calcutta was met and recognized by his old butler who asked him where he had been since leaving India. On being told that he had been to Europe, the native said " Europe plenty good country, master in India no hair ; now got it plenty hair. Master no teeth ; now got it plenty teeth. Europe wonderful country." The Captain needless to add had invested in a wig and false teeth.

Our pay in those days would hardly do for the up-to-date soldier of to-day. A sergeant-major's pay was Rs. 46 per month ; a color-sergeant's 29 ; a sergeant's 22, while a private got Rs. 10-6-4, with no prospect of an increase except when he was 200 miles from a presidency town when field batta was allowed at the rate of about Rs. 2 per month. Out of his pay each man had to pay on his arrival in India for four white suits —no " Khaki." Other stoppages were annas 8 per month for dhoby, annas 10 for cook, annas 4 for the shoe black, and annas 4 for barber. At this time the Marquis of Dalhousie was Governor-General, and about a month after our arrival in Calcutta, the Regiment formed a guard-of-honor to meet General Sir Charles James Napier, who had come out to relieve Lord Gough after the battle of Chillianwallah. General Napier reviewed the regiment in the Fort prior to his departure from Calcutta. When we were formed up on the parade ground, standing at ease, awaiting the arrival of the General, an incident occurred which interested us very much at the time. An adjutant crane was strutting about in front of the regiment, and several crows, whose displeasure, the crane had aroused by a robbery, which he had committed on a crow's nest, were flying about his head pecking him and worrying him generally. Suddenly however he snapped a crow in his immense beak and swallowed it down when the crows left him severely alone. After a most minute inspection and walking down the ranks of each company, Sir Charles addressed the regiment. He spoke of having reviewed them many years before in Manchester, and especially warned them now that they had come to India, against indulgence in alcoholic liquor. He knew he said many of them would laugh and think him an "old fogey," but he spoke of two regiments which had served under him in Sindh where the hard drinkers were literally swept off the face of the earth.

In July 1849 we received orders to proceed to Ghazipore. In those days, I should inform my readers, all orders read out on parade invariably concluded with the words: By order John Weir Hogg and other Directors;

From Calcutta we travelled up the river in flat-bottomed barges towed by a river steamer. We were frequently delayed on account of the paddles becoming choked by dead bodies floating down the river. We lost a few men through cholera, but we had become accustomed to take little notice of this; nor is it to be wondered at, for the only water we had to drink was that drawn from the river. No Macnamara filters, or Permagnate of Potash in those days. A little alum was supposed to render the water fit to drink. We had 200 men on each barge and did not land till we reached Ghazipore. Crocodiles were numerous all the way up the river.

In August 1849 we reached Ghazipore, and were marched to barracks which were large thatched buildings. Shortly after our arrival we furnished a guard-of-honor for Lord Gough, who was then on his way to Calcutta after being relieved by Sir Charles James Napier. Here also a party of the 24th regiment on their way to England were attached to us for some time, and terrible were the tales they told of Chillianwallah's dread day. Near the banks of the Ganges stood the tomb of Lord Cornwallis who had been killed by a fall from his horse.

This was of particular interest to me from the fact of my having been born and brought up in the same country as this well known officer; but I remember that the sight, at once the most pathetic and the most interesting in Ghazipore, was the grave-yard, and terrible was the tale it told in those days of many a brave and stalwart mother's son, who had left his English home only to be laid low by fell disease on the banks of the great and mighty Ganges. At Ghazipore in October 1849 I received my first step on the ladder of promotion. I was made lance-corporal. I was particularly elated at this because Lieutenant John Shipp, another native of Suffolk, had received his first stripe at the same place many years before. My readers may not understand the allusion to Lieut. John Shipp, but in those days his name was familiar to every soldier, and "The Life and Adventures of Lieut. John Shipp" might have been found in every regimental library. He rose from the ranks to a commission, got into trouble at Cawnpore over a racing affair and was cashiered. He enlisted a second time and again rose to a commission, and I believe, at the time of his death was Governor of Liverpool gaol. During the Mahratta war, he served in Lord Lake's army, and I was much struck with an act of bravery related of him. He was in the Quarter-master-General's department at the time, to which he was appointed on account of his linguistic attainments, and while the British force was encamped and in touch with the Mahratta Army, a native chief came out, and in front of the whole combined forces, challenged the British, as Goliath of Gath of old did the armies of the living God. Lieut. Shipp begged and obtained permission to meet the man in combat, went out with only a sword and cut him down. In these days of Lee-Metford's, and repeating rifles, such a thing would not be possible as his challenge would have been at once stopped by a bullet. About the time I was made lance-corporal, I first tried to smoke and never shall I forget the penalty I paid. So ill did I become that I solemnly vowed never to attempt the like again and strange to relate it was exactly twenty years afterwards when I was keeper of the Penitentiary of Madras that I made my next and more successful attempt.

We were joined at Ghazipore by Lieut. Archer of the 24th, who exchanged into the 96th. He was said by his men to have brought what was left of them out of action at Chillianwallah.

The largest crocodile I ever saw in my life was caught on the bank of the river at Ghazipore. It was roped down in the judge's compound where it took ten days to die. The station was well known for its attar of roses; but it was also a very unhealthy place, and none of us were sorry when in December 1849 we started off by road to Cawnpore.

Cawnpore in 1850.

On our way to Cawnpore, we camped for two days at Benares, the Holy City of India, and saw the sights of the place. It looked to me an old-world city, with narrow streets and high houses. Fruit could be had very cheap, and was in abundance. The guavas especially, were the largest and finest I had ever seen, and could be obtained for an anna a dozen. We halted also for two days at Allahabad, known for its large fort, and for its being the junction between the Ganges and Jumna, but it was also known for its being a famous place for cholera. In February 1850 we arrived at Cawnpore, where we were located in the old thatched buildings facing the church, known as the "old barracks." We relieved the 75th regiment of foot, who had suffered terribly from sickness during its stay in Cawnpore. The station was pleasant enough during the cold weather, but in summer, the heat was almost unbearable. Suicides, and deaths from disease, were almost of daily occurrence. Sanitary arrangements were of the most primitive kind, and what with vermin, and mosquitoes by night, and flies by day, life was not worth living. I have often seen the mess-tables literally black with flies, and as for the beds, they used to swarm with vermin, so much so, that we had to pay a man two annas to have them cleaned, but this was hardly of much use, as they were soon full again. A benevolent Government supplied each man with a "vermin trap," a rectangular piece of wood with holes drilled on two sides of it, to admit of the vermin creeping into them; but this was not of much benefit in exterminating these pests. It was at this time that I first took part in amateur theatricals in India, and one of the first pieces we played here was "Ella of Rosenberg." Our scene painter, poor fellow, a bandsman, died in the theatre of heat apoplexy. In the matter of food, Cawnpore was particularly cheap. Forty-six pound loaves of bread could be bought for a rupee, pigeons could be had for three pies each, and wild fowl of all kinds were plentiful. Indeed, the station was a sportsman's paradise.

About this time, two companies of the regiment were sent to take over the famous Lalla Moolraj, ex-governor of Mooltan, who, after the surrender of that city, was tried for the murder, in cold blood, of Mr. Vans Agnew, a Bengal Civilian, and Lieut. Anderson of the Bombay army. He had been condemned to death, but the sentence was commuted to imprisonment for life, and he was on his way to his place of incarceration. He was a sort of "mad mullah" of his time, and regarded as possessing supernatural powers by the natives, who firmly believed that it was impossible to keep him a prisoner, and their belief came very near being realized, for, shortly after taking charge of him, our men were at night enveloped in one of the most terrific dust storms ever known in southern India, and all the men's tent's Moolraj's included were blown down. To those in Madras and Southern India who have not experienced a dust-storm, I may explain that it is generally the precursor of a thunder-storm, and while it lasts, every living creature has to fly for shelter under the nearest roof and all doors and windows have to be shut, and securely fastened, notwithstanding which, the fine sand effects an entrance, and the furniture in the bungalows is covered with dust. The most violent of these sand storms I have known to occur in Lahore, but Cawnpore is, I know, not far behind in this respect.

Perhaps to us the most exciting event of the year 1850 was the Cawnpore Race meeting. Captain MacDonald of the regiment had a very beautiful Arab which was heavily backed to beat anything, but our adjutant Lieut. Cumberland (son of our commanding officer) had a big black waler on which he simply carried everything before him.

Of course there was the usual private betting amongst the members of the local jockey club, but happily for the noble sport, there were no bookmakers, and everything was "O. K." I may say here, however, that this Captain MacDonald was somewhat of a sportsman, and had once brought in from the jungle a tiger cub, which was playful enough when young. He used to have it in his quarters, and when it was half-grown, it grew ferocious, and few dared to approach. It once severely mauled a man and had to be destroyed.

Cawnpore at this time had a large garrison, and Colonel (afterwards Brigadier-General Sir Henry) Havelock was on the staff at the station. During the Christmas festivities of that year, the afterwards notorious Nana Sahib gave a grand dinner and ball to the officers of the garrison, in the Assembly rooms, and I recollect hearing the band play "The Roast Beef of Old England." We had frequent opportunities of seeing this perfidious wretch during our stay in Cawnpore. He was very popular with the officers and used frequently to drive in from Bithoor to listen to the band, which played twice a week at the band-stand near the church, and I may here observe that he was up to that time the first native I had seen riding in a carriage of English manufacture, since my arrival in India. He was undoubtedly "as mild a mannered man as ever cut a throat or scuttled ship" and must have possessed the heart of a fiend, but in outward appearance he showed nothing of all this, and little did we think at that time that he would in the near future be the instigator of the terrible atrocities which are now a matter of history. My brother Jim, with his wife and two children, was, seven years later, butchered at the instigation of this incarnate demon. I had many a time stood and watched him as he sat listening to the Band, little imagining what the future had in store. Often and often in after years have I thought how differently written might have been the succeeding pages of history had any of us at that time been able to look into the near future, and yet the coming revolt was, even at that time, common talk amongst the natives, but the authorities evidently did not realize the grave nature of the approaching storm, until it had fairly burst upon them. The man who used to shave the men of my company every morning, and was known as "Barber Tom" could speak English fairly well. Many a time this fellow told us that "we would all get our throats cut some day" and although we only laughed at him, plotting was even then going on at Lucknow, but those in authority failed to notice the signs of the times.

With the New Year of 1851 we started on the march to Lahore, and a lively three months we had of it. There were of course no railways in India, then, and as each regiment had its own regimental bazaar, etc., a regiment on the march with its camp followers, women, etc., would extend quite two miles along the road. This was interesting march, for, on several occasions we camped on battlefields where our brave men had been shot down and buried, during the campaign against the Sikhs in 1845. At Moodki where Sir Robert Sale, the hero of Jellalabad fell, I, as well as many others of us, slept on the battlefield, with the mounds over the graves of fallen comrades for pillows.

At Ferozeshah, where a terrible battle had been fought under Sir Hugh Gough, and at Sobraon where the Sikhs in 1846, had been routed prior to the capitulation of Lahore, we picked bullets out of the trees near the camping ground.

At Paniput, where, as all readers of Indian History know, the fate of India was twice decided, we were overtaken by a terrific thunderstorm, and the ground on which we camped became so sodden that we were compelled to strike camp, and in obedience to the commanding officer's orders we had to proceed to the next camping ground. On we trudged through that terrible downpower till we came to a nullah through which we waded up to our arm-pits in water while the Colonel kept shouting out to us in midstream "Keep your cadence men! Keep your cadence." It was with the greatest difficulty that we kept our arms and equipment from being swept away, for one man lost his musket and a bandsman his clarionette, and the wonder is that none of us lost our lives. After crossing we had still to march three miles to the next camping ground, in many places up to our knees in water. By the time we arrived at the next camping ground, which was at 2 o'clock in the afternoon, the rain had ceased and the sun shone forth hot and fierce, but our baggage and stores were far behind. The "Gawd forsaken oonts" (camels), as Kipling calls them, had lain down and nothing would induce them to move. We were all soaked to the skin and without any sort of protection from the sun, while as for food, we got our breakfast next day. However, we stripped off, every man of us, and laid our clothes out to dry, presenting meanwhile the unique spectacle of a regiment entirely innocent of any covering for our bodies and running wild. We remained a week at this camp, getting the baggage in, drying our tents, washing and drying our clothes, ourselves, and our transport, and generally pulling ourselves together again. Before we resumed our march, we built a raft of empty barrels and pieces of timber with which to cross another nullah (on the other side of our camp, which was unfordable.) We crossed in batches of fifty after getting our baggage, etc., safely over, and then continued our march to Lahore. Our march each day was always enlivened by songs sung by those of the men who had good voices, and we would all join in the chorus, if there was one to the song. A Private Morris of the regiment who had, I remember, a particularly good voice used to render the "Farmer's boy" in fine style and both officers (the colonel included) and men would join in. It seems a pity that this method of banishing the tedium of a march is not more cultivated in the British army, as it is I believe in other European armies.

At Lahore, we were located in the old Anarkali Barracks, the present barracks at Mian Mir being then in course of construction by order of the then Commander-in-Chief, Sir Charles James Napier. Opposite the Anarkali barracks was an old Sikh temple which we had used as a Protestant church. Before the Sutlej campaign, the same building was used by General Avitable (one of the Italian generals in Runjit Singh's service) as his head-quarters. Here also on the 30th of June 1851 I was married having attained the age of twenty one years on the 4th of the same month, and at the time of the ceremony, when the clergyman came to the prayer "as Isaac and Rebecca, etc." I was much struck with the coincidence of names, mine being Isaac and my partner's Rebecca.

Sir Henry Lawrence, afterwards of Lucknow fame, and known during this period as the "soldiers' friend" was Chief Commissioner of the Punjab and his brother John Lawrence, afterwards Governor-General, was his Secretary. Sir Henry, shortly before this had opened the Anarkali gardens for the benefit of the troops, and it was a great boon to the Military as all our sports were held here.

The regiment suffered much from sickness in this station, as many as 400 men being down at one time with fever, and during one month, the deaths totalled as many as 33. At the end of May, we were joined by a draft of 89 men from home, who had marched all the way up country. By the end of September, 42 out of the 89 had joined the great majority. This is sad reading for the soldiers of to-day who may chance to see these lines, but it should be remembered those were sad times for the British soldier in India. He led but a hard and weary life at best, and it was quite common to see a whole regiment decimated by disease in a few weeks. We had few opportunities for amusement, and but little in our routine of life.

Were I a Charles Lever or a Conan Doyle, I might romance after the style of "Charles O'Mally" or "Brigadier Gerard" but I would assure my readers that I am narrating my actual experiences without any attempt whatever at romancing.

CHAPTER V.

At Lahore we had one company located in the Dewan-i-Am-or the citadel. The walls, I remember, were decorated with paintings of richly caparisoned warriors, and grotesque figures of various kinds. One of the sights of Lahore was the Shalamah gardens planned and laid out three hundred years before, by order of the Emperor Jehangir. It was a capital place for pick-nicking and bathing, with its shady retreats and fountains.

In the Fort I made the acquaintance of a gunner, who, at an auction sale of the loot taken after the capitulation of

Lahore, had purchased an old Sikh shield, for I think, rupees two. It was battered and disfigured, but it was eventually found to be made of pure gold! During all the time I have been in India, never have I seen melons so plentiful and of such variety as in Lahore. Moreover, they were very cheap, and much appreciated by the troops. For those who liked sport, wild pig, duck, teal, and in fact all kinds of wild fowl were to be had only a few miles out of Mian Mir. Beer was a luxury in those days! neither could ærated waters of any kind be obtained, but at the canteen we could get toddy at the rate of a quart per man daily by paying for the same, while nominally, at any rate, we had no teetotallers in the regiment, for every man got the credit of drinking his quart, whether he drank it himself or gave it to some-one else. There was an old out-building, however, a short distance from barracks, where those in the secret used to assemble to play cards, and where the bheestie used to bring toddy as well as rum in "mussucks."

Our principal game used to be "Loo" with *nine pies* per head for stakes. Another officer of my company at this time committed suicide, and when his effects came to be sold by auction, there were six bottles of whisky, which now is common in India but extremely rare in those days, and on being sold, realized a very high price. The principal beverage of the troops was ginger beer, a bazaar-made decoction which was sold very cheap, and as no one ever thought about microbes, it was doubtless responsible for much of the sickness that prevailed amongst us. We contrived however to amuse ourselves fairly well in Lahore. Three nights a week we had amusements in barracks, one night being devoted to boxing competitions, one to a "free and easy" and another night to a "dance" up to tattoo only. For this last, we engaged the services of a bandsman of the corps at rupees ten a month, who acted as our dancing master, and many men, who had never seen a quadrille or a polka in their lives, soon became expert dancers. Our only refreshment at these entertainments was ginger beer. At the end of the year, we were ordered to the new barracks at Mian Mir, which to us soon became famous for snakes, tarantulas, and dust-storms, all of which we soon had more than enough. When these storms occurred the natives, if they happened to be away from any shelter, wrapped their faces in a cloth and lay flat on the ground, face downwards, until the storm had passed. In fact this was the only safe thing to do under the circumstances. A corporal, one evening, on his way to barracks, was overtaken by one of these storms, and there being no shelter near, the poor fellow lost his way and was suffocated. One man of my company repeatedly asserted that a snake was in the habit of sleeping in his bed every night. He was usually laughed at, but one day a search being instituted, the snake was discovered coiled up under some kit boxes and bed-boards which were stacked in the verandah opposite his cot. On another occasion, I was walking to Lahore when just at the entrance of the Lahore gate, a hawk dropped a snake close to me! I may explain for the information of those unacquainted with the fact, that this is the method which kites and hawks, as well as blue jays adopt in killing snakes prior to eating them. The last-mentioned in particular is a great destroyer and devourer of very small snakes which have no greater enemy. At Mian Mir, many of the men indulged in cock-fighting, and I have known one man of the regiment stake thirty rupees on his bird and win it too, but this was a common pastime with the natives, which the soldiers had taken to, and it was difficult to put it down.

My chief amusement at Mian Mir was amateur theatricals in which I took a great deal of interest. Prior to leaving Lahore, I had been made full corporal, and assistant schoolmaster, so that I was in a position to devote more time to this hobby of mine, than I could have done had I been at regimental duty. Our theatre was an old mosque about halfway between Mian Mir and Lahore. The first of the pieces put on the boards by the officers of the regiment was I recollect "Bombastes Furioso" in which Captain Rocke (of whom more anon) took the part of "Bombastes." Our posters were executed by hand and would now be regarded as curiosities. There were no printing presses in the station, and as the day of the type-writer was not yet at hand, I frequently had to copy out our theatrical bills myself. My share in the plays used generally to be a female character such as "Louisa Love-Trick" in a piece called the "Dead Shot," or an old man's character, such as *Matthew Esdale* in the "Charcoal Burner." The Captain Rocke I just mentioned had recently joined us at Mian Mir having come out from Home. As a Lieutenant in (I think the 32nd regiment) he had been tried and convicted of murder for his share in what was known as the "six-mile-bridge affair" in Ireland. To those of my readers who may not be acquainted with the particulars of this trial, I must explain that during one of the parliamentary elections which took place in Dublin about this period, a large mob had assembled to prevent the entry into the city of the voters for the opposing candidate for parliamentary honours, and as a natural result a riot ensued. A company of the 32nd under Lieutenant Rocke accompanied by a magistrate was sent out to quell the riot. A collision of course occurred between the military and the rioters, and a few of the latter, who were fired upon, were killed. Lieutenant Rocke, along with two or three others, had to stand his trial at the Dublin High Court, and was found guilty of the capital offence by Mr. Justice Perrins, who, if I remember rightly, based his decision on the fact that the Riot Act had not been read; but the conviction was set aside by a full bench. Years afterwards, when preparing for my examination in Law in Madras, I came across this very case in Norton's "Law of Evidence," a well known authority on such points and found his report of, and comments on the trial most interesting reading. Shortly after the occurrences I have mentioned, Lieutenant Rocke was promoted to a captaincy in the 96th Foot, and came out to join us. Subsequently I became his color sergeant in the 43rd regiment of foot and some years later, at Cannanore, while I was Superintendent of the Central Jail, Colonel Brereton, who commanded the station informed me, that this same Captain Rocke had died at Hyderabad while Postmaster-General in H. H. the Nizam's service, and previously Commander of His Highness' Reformed troops, and that he had been refused burial by the clergyman of the station on account of his religious views, and that he Colonel Brereton, performed the ceremony willingly. I had read of Captain Rocke's death in the "Deccan Times" of Secunderabad, and wrote a long letter to the "Madras Mail" concerning him, which was published. My brother, Jeremiah with his wife and two children joined us here. This was the brother who was serving in the 65th regiment at Chatham at the time of my enlistment and on whose account, I had transferred to that regiment. He had married a young woman from Manchester, but she poor woman had only come out to India to find her final resting place in the cemetery at Mian Mir. We twice experienced somewhat severe shocks of earthquake whilst in this station, and on the second occasion, which occurred at 10 A. M., many of our men were somewhat alarmed and rushed out of barracks but one rather facetious character, dubbed "Dr." Dearing on account of his drollery, on seeing the patients rush out of hospital shouted out "Ah ! there goes the last shake of the fever and ague." This same man on another occasion, during a cholera epidemic, loudly proclaimed that he wouldn't die while any other man lived, but I saw him go poor fellow all the same, with many more during the mutiny. Another notorious character was a man named O'Brien. A party of our men, who were invalided, and were going down country *en route* for England, arrived at Ferozepore, and going into the canteen of the 87th regiment which was stationed there, one of the men spotted O'Brien, and gave him into custody for having deserted from their corps at Norfolk Island. The facts were that O'Brien was in collusion with several convicts who contemplated escaping from the Island, and while on guard had unobserved removed the powder from the pans of the muskets of the soldiers on guard so as to cause a miss-fire in the event of the muskets having to come into requisition, oiled the pans, and escaped with the convicts in the Captain-Commandant's boat. When the alarm was given the guard turned out, and were ordered to fire upon the runaways, with the result already mentioned, and as there was no other boat available, pursuit was out of the question and the party successfully effected their escape. They had to undergo, however, some terrible experiences on the open sea before they were eventually rescued from death by a whaler; but they at last found their way to Spain where O'Brien found employment in the Spanish army in which he served for some years before he returned to England and re-enlisted. Had he been arrested while effecting his escape he would have been sentenced to transportation for life, as it was regarded as a most serious offence at the time to assist in the escape of convicts. He was brought from Ferozepore to Mian Mir, and tried by courtmartial; but as the only evidence adduced against him was the regimental records which merely specified the fact of his desertion from the corps, he got off with only eighteen month's imprisonment, and went home with the 96th in 1854. This man's life and adventures were so varied and interesting, that Captain Deighton of the grenadier company, to which O'Brien belonged, published them in the form of a book.

Cabul ponies could be had very cheap at this time at Mian Mir, a really good riding pony costing ten to fifteen rupees, while a racing one could be had for about rupees thirty-five. This provided lots of sport for our men, who also went in greatly for cricket; but foot-ball was not known amongst us.

In 1853, we started off for Dinapore leaving scores of our comrades in the graveyards of Lahore and Mian Mir. This terrible mortality was chiefly due to dysentery which was the scourge of European troops at the time. On our way we camped at Amritsar, where I visited the famous temple of the Sikhs, and saw and wondered at the "Grunth," the sacred law of this body of Hindus, which was constantly fanned by an attendant with a "chowree" (a horse hair whisk), to keep the flies off I suppose. Captain Rocke, to whom I before alluded, here made a wager with his brother officers, that he would walk fair heel-and-toe six miles in one hour for fifty gold mohurs,—and he won it. We met with any amount of sport on this march, and had some excellent shooting until one day's march from Delhi, where one of the men named Hunt got into a quarrel with some natives about shooting pea-fowl, and put a charge of shot into one of them. He was of course made a prisoner, but was not tried until six months after by a general court-martial at Dinapore when he was acquitted as he could not be identified. But this put an end to our sport for the remainder of that march. While it lasted, however, the permission to shoot game was fully availed of, and I have seen as many as thirteen pea-fowl together with other game in one tent alone. At Delhi we camped for a week. It was dangerous to go too near the city, and if any of us went into the trench which surrounded the walls the natives would turn out and stone us.

My brother Jeremiah, whose wife had brought him some money on his marriage, here purchased a goodly collection of Indian curios. So high a value was set upon these things then by people at home, that he was induced to exhibit them by his commanding officer who lent him a room in Beggar's Bush barracks, Dublin, for the purpose. When two days march from Cawnpore, we were inspected by the new Commander-in-Chief, Sir William Gomm. At Cawnpore where the 81st Regiment was then stationed, we halted for three or four days. My eldest brother, William, who had enlisted in 1830 was a color sergeant in this Regiment, when I was yet a child. On visiting their camp, I came across an old Corporal who had belonged to his Company. Near Allahabad we embarked on two decked flat bottomed river-boats, similar to those we had on coming up stream ; but on this trip we did not have occasion to use steamers to tow us along as we were drifting with the current. Passing Benares where the permanent way was then being laid for the railway, and our old station of Ghazipore, we at length reached Dinapore where I was shortly after promoted to the rank of sergeant. I often wonder what sergeants in India of to-day would think of our Sergeant's mess of those days. No matted floors, no comfortable chairs, no billiard tables, no tennis courts, and no whisky or ærated waters. Ordinary barrack room furniture within four bare walls constituted our mess room. The staple stock of our liquor bar was Bengal rum, and ginger beer, and inferior wine if any one cared to buy it. We could also obtain our daily allowance of toddy in the morning. Card-playing was not allowed in the mess, but only backgammon and draughts. Our chief amusement, however, consisted of shooting, or rather trying to shoot at (for we seldom could hit them) "flycatchers" on the walls, with bottles of "ginger beer" for guns, and corks for ammunition. So much has lately been written about mosquitoes, and malaria, that a few words from an old campaigner who had occasion to remember "The merry little cuss that sings while he works" would not come amiss here. I have known the mosquito of Madras and Southern India and the north-west, but for a sheer downright, unmitigated pest give me the mosquito of Bengal, especially the gentleman who has his habitat in the Sunderbunds; but I have never known that our men ever got malarial fever through being bitten by them. If anything it was the other way for it seemed a curious circumstance that there were fewer cases of fever among the men where mosquitoes swarmed most. Possibly none of those gentry belonged to the anopheles, or cocktailed variety of which so much has been written; but in my humble opinion, the "cocktail" that was most responsible for the ailments of my comrades was that taken internally in the shape of spirits. I have always slept without mosquito curtains, and have in the course of my service in India been bitten on my hands and feet thousands of times, and so have thousands of others of His Majesty's subjects, by myriads of these insects, without any further result than the irritation caused by their bites.

CHAPTER VI.

Dinapore in 1853-54.

Shortly after our arrival at Dinapore, my second son was born, and died a few days after his birth. As the child had not been baptized, I was compelled to perform the burial service over his remains myself.

We had several thunder-storms in Dinapore, one of which was of a rather uncommon character. Without any premonitary signs, there occurred two vivid flashes of lightning followed by two peals of thunder in quick succession, in the middle of the day. I had been standing talking to Sergeant Dunskin of "ours" at the back of the mess and had left him to proceed to my quarters which I just reached when the crash occurred. The lightning struck the globe end of the Wesleyan chapel, doing some damage to the building and killing an adjutant crane which was perched on the top; but strangest of all it knocked the pipe out of Sergeant Dunskin's mouth while he was standing at the back door of the mess-room about twenty yards from the chapel, looking at the bird, without doing any injury to his person. I girded up my loins to doubt this, as Mark Twain would say, but I knew Sergeant Dunskin to be a truthful man, and he gave the most positive assurance that such was the case.

We had more amateur theatricals at this station, our first piece being "The Happy Man" in which one of the doctors of the Regiment, a facetious son of Erin, took the leading part. Captain (afterwards General) Middleton, who died in London, about three years ago, and who at the time of his death was keeper of the crown jewels, also took part in this piece. I recollect having at his request to make out a copy of the play for General Wheeler afterwards commanding at Cawnpore during the Mutiny who was somewhat deaf, and had asked to be furnished with the words of the piece, as there was no second copy of the play. He was at this time in command at Dinapore, and with his daughter Ada was present at our first performance which proved most successful and was much appreciated by the audience. One of the most curious sights at Dinapore was the vast number of adjutant cranes. Immediately the dinner bugle sounded, these birds would come from across the Ganges in great numbers where but a moment before not one was to be seen. I have counted as many as eighty-seven strutting in front of the barracks, whilst the men were at dinner in the verandahs. In height when their necks were outstretched they would compare favourably with a man, and their length of beak was about two feet. They were very tame, and although we had strict orders against injuring them our men practised some acts of cruelty on them. One of these was to tie a large bone to one end of a length of rope and a brick at the other. The bird would greedily swallow the bone and then rise with the brick dangling several yards below him, until the weight and discomfort made him disgorge the bone. Some of these acts of cruelty, however, were not so harmless, and on one occasion a man named Joe Ward filled a large bone with gun powder and attached a lighted fuse to it, with the result that the bird, which swallowed it, had its head and neck blown off; but so much indignation was aroused among the men at this cruel act that it was never repeated. The powers of digestion possessed by these birds was something marvellous, and reminded one of those of a python combined with the digestion of an ostrich, as will be seen by the following instance which I can vouch for. There were three pet monkeys, a large and two small ones, belonging to the company, which used to be secured in the Bowl alley. One of these had bitten one of the quarter-master-sergeant's children, and on the matter being reported to the Captain of the company, the animals were ordered to be destroyed. This was done and the bodies were left for the cranes to dispose of. Several birds came down and quickly swallowed the two smaller monkeys, but the large one was beyond the powers of the ordinary sized birds, and it was left for a large sized crane to devour, which he succeeded in doing after several attempts, to the surprise of all who were looking on. One of the men, a lance-corporal met with his death in a somewhat strange manner by coming into collision with one of these birds. He was running around the corner of a barrack, and suddenly came into collision with a crane flying low towards him. The sharp beak of the bird pierced his chest, and he died shortly after from the effects of the wound. The adjutant is not choice in his diet. Everything that is possible to be eaten is acceptable to him; even old leather. One of the children of the regiment, Johnny Lynch, by name, was playing in the verandah of the Married Quarters, and dropped one of his shoes which was quickly seized and swallowed by one of these birds. Johnny got indignant, pulled off his other shoe, and threw it at the bird and it was promptly swallowed in the same manner and poor Johnny had to retire defeated and shoeless. He poor fellow with many of his playmates, was afterwards doomed to a cruel death at Cawnpore.

At this time in Dinapore, an attack of dysentery meant almost certain death, and so few were the recoveries that a man going into hospital with this complaint was regarded by his comrades as practically having received his death warrant. I had a severe attack at Mian Mir, but was lucky enough to recover. Here however I got another attack and while proceeding to hospital, I met an apothecary belonging to the battery of Royal Artillery, also stationed at Dinapore. He asked me what was the matter, and on my telling him, he bluntly remarked that if I went into hospital with that complaint, I would remain there until carried out feet foremost. On his recommendation, I went back to my quarters, sent to the Patna Bazaar, a short distance from barracks, for an earthen jar of Bael-fruit jam and took it on toast three times a day. This was the means that soon restored me to health, although scores of our men succumbed to the disease in hospital. I afterwards learnt that this apothecary had given similar advice to the men of the battery with marked success during the previous year, for not a single man of those attacked had died of dysentery, except one poor fellow, and he probably would have recovered also had he not insisted on going into hospital.

Some years later when I was in Madras, I read of a Lieut. Pogson who had been very bad with the disease at Dinapore, and had on the advice of his butler, cured himself with this remedy. He commenced its manufacture with a view to pecuniary advantage, and I believe Lieut. Pogson's Bael-Com. may still be obtained at some chemists'. As most Anglo-Indians are aware, this remedy is as "old as the hills" and was known to the natives of India, hundreds of years ago.

In September 1854, the regiment was ordered home, and a great number of men, including seventeen married soldiers whose families were all butchered at Cawnpore in 1857, volunteered for the 32nd foot. My brother James of whom I have already spoken, and who was a corporal, with his wife and two children were included among this number. When we reached Chinsurah where we stayed about two months, volunteers were again called for, and I with twenty-nine men volunteered for the 43rd, then in Fort St. George, while twenty-two men volunteered for the 74th Highlanders, also stationed in the Madras Presidency.

My brother Jeremiah, who was a private and whose wife had died at Mian Mir, decided to go home with the regiment, having nearly completed his twenty-one years in the Army. At Chinsurah our men commenced drinking heavily, and the regimental authorities were at a loss to know from where the liquor was obtained, but at length owing to an accident, the secret was discovered. The back of the men's latrine used to be barricaded to prevent the men going out, but the women's latrine had no such obstacle, and only outlets out of the barrack precincts were the apertures in the back wall of the latter, through which they were cleaned. The men used to make their way out at night through these holes, and proceed to the neighbouring French town of Chandernagore where all kinds of spirituous liquors could be had at an extremely cheap rate. One of these men in making his way back to barracks through one of these apertures, was detected at 4 A.M. by a woman, who had occasion to go there, but what followed will not bear publication, and I will draw a veil over the rest.

By this time the railway had been laid for a distance of twenty miles from Calcutta, and we completed our journey by rail. I embarked with the volunteers for the 43rd, and 74th regiments, while my brother Jeremiah embarked on another vessel with the head-quarters of the regiment and, about two or three hundred, of the 96th for home. Here on the Hooghly, I said "good-bye" for ever to my brother, and to many old friends in the regiment. The party I was with, was in charge of Captain Rocke who was also going to the 43rd, having exchanged with Captain the Hon'ble Mills (afterwards killed at Lucknow in the mutiny).

We left Calcutta, but when some distance down the Hooghly we dropped anchor to await the tide. Here we remained all night, and about 4 A.M., the following morning, I was on deck when the ship was hailed, a boat came alongside and a man came on board enquiring for Captain Rocke. I directed him to the latter's cabin and, a few minutes after, he sent for me to say that he was ordered back to Calcutta, and handed Rs. 500 to me, being the advance of pay for the men, together with a lot of baggage of his own which was in the hold of the vessel, and which he directed me to take on to Madras until he joined us later. It was no easy task to be in command of 52 men on board and I had to invoke the aid of the Captain a couple of times during the voyage in order to maintain discipline.

As Government had already paid for Captain Rocke's cabin, I with my wife and child took possession of it under his orders, and obtained our meals from the Captain's table. Thus was I made very comfortable during the voyage to Madras which we reached after ten days sail without any serious mishap.

There was no pier at Madras then and we had to go ashore in Masulah boats, many of us getting thoroughly drenched in the surf before we arrived on *terra firma*. I marched the party to barracks, where the men were posted to companies, and there was keen competition among the color-sergeants to get hold of some of the men for their own companies, for they were a fine lot of old soldiers above the average in height, sixteen out of thirty having belonged to the grenadier company of the 96th.

I was taken to the sergeant's mess which I found a considerable improvement on such institutions in Bengal, although not quite up in point of comfort to those of the present day. It was fairly comfortable and the members were as pleasant a lot of men, it has been my good fortune to have come across. Ale could be had *ad lib.* for those who indulged in it, and the mess even sported a bagatelle table.

CHAPTER VII.

Bangalore in 1855.

The morning after our arrival at Fort St. George, I received orders to parade the men in the verandah of the orderly room of the 43rd at 8 A.M., before Colonel Skipwith who was then commanding the regiment, and who, after inspecting the detachment, dismissed us to barracks, myself and the two corporals excepted, who had to appear before him in the orderly room. I should explain for the information of my military readers of the present day, that a soldier, volunteering to another regiment from his own, lost his army rank, and had to start afresh as a private in his new one, so that when I volunteered for the 43rd, and my transfer was sanctioned at Chinsurah, I reverted to private, but was, with the two corporals, re-appointed to our respective positions of which we drew the pay and allowances until the head-quarters and right wing of our new regiment, when we reverted automatically to the ranks again. We were called into the orderly room, and the Colonel after examining our papers appointed us lance-corporals in the 43rd, I by virtue of my having been a sergeant, taking precedence over the other two. This was a tremendous climb down for us, more especially for me who had been in command of the party during the voyage ; but it was strictly *en regle* and could not be avoided. We were then fitted with the uniforms of our new regiment, and sent to recruit's drill in accordance with the usual practice. At this period volunteers from one corps to another were looked upon in the light of fresh recruits in the service, and had to go through their military course *de novo* in their new regiments, and this we succeeded in doing in the space of one month. I may say that this was the third time I had gone through my course, the last occasion being at Hobart Town, Van Dieman's Land, when I was transferred to the 96th Foot. Theatricals were common in Fort St. George, and while the final rehearsals for the melodrama "Black-eyed Susan" were going on, one of the actors suddenly fell ill, and I volunteered at a day's notice to study and enact the part, which I am glad to say I did successfully, along with another part in the farce "Doctor Bolus" which immediately followed the melodrama. Draught-playing was greatly indulged in by the men of the 43rd, both the single and the double or Spanish game, and as I possessed some skill at the first, I played a match with a man of the regiment who had, or fancied himself to have, the reputation of a very good player, and I beat him easily. This led me to remark to him that if there were no better players in the corps than he was, I would be game to play the best man three games out of five for ten rupees, and this resulted in my playing a match with a Sergeant Morrison for Rs. 10 a side, which I won. Morrison then asked me if I could play the Spanish game, but as I did not know it, I declined. I promised, however, to learn it, and meet him on equal terms in three or four months time, and this I did, and won another Rs. 10 from him. The best player of the regiment was a Scotchman named Johnstone who came with me from the 96th and who was the only man who could beat me at both games. He was also an exceedingly good chess player, at which game I was in Military parlance a muff.

People who knew Madras in 1854 would hardly be able to recognize it at the present day owing to the unprecedented development the city has undergone during the last 47 years. I may, however, say that comparing the prices of provisions in this place at the present day, things were very cheap indeed in the "fifties." Soldiers of less than two years standing were not allowed outside the Fort in the evening without a pass, and perhaps, this was a wise regulation after all, as it prevented many a young fellow from getting into trouble. In the month of March 1855, we started on our march to join the left wing of the Regiment which was stationed at Bangalore. There was no railway, and we had to proceed by route march all the way. The march was pleasant, but uneventful, and wanting in the excitements of shooting and other little pleasures which we used to have on our marches in Bengal and the Punjab. At Chittore, however, a stage somewhere about midway en route, an agreeable incidentoccurr ed which broke the monotony of the journey. A bandsman of the regiment got up on one of the several hills near the camp while it was growing dark and with his cornet-a-piston started playing some very pretty tunes. The man was an exquisite player, and the music coming on the camp in the stillness of the evening, mellowed by the distance, was inexpressibly sweet and the whole of us listened enraptured. Two years later, however, our remembrances of this town were anything but pleasant, as we buried sixteen men of the left wing who had died of cholera at this stage; but of this more anon. We commenced each day's march about 3 A.M., and finished by 8 A.M. while midway between the stages native followers had coffee and ginger-tea ready for us. Neither of these preparations was "first chop" but coming as they did when the day's march was beginning to pall on us, they were thankfully received. The regimental bheesties as a matter of course always accompanied the column, but who would drink doubtful water when coffee and tea however inferior could be had. We were glad when we at length reached our destination.

Bangalore was then, as now, a place of importance from a military point of view, and the garrison, the largest I had ever belonged to, consisted of two batteries of European artillery, one regiment of European infantry, one native cavalry and three regiments of native infantry. There were only two churches in the station, "Trinity" and "St. Mark's," and with the exception of these, there were no public buildings at all worthy of mention. Even the barracks were not much to look at, as the magnificent buildings at Agram which the Cavalry and Artillery occupy now were non-existent. The Government buildings near Sir Mark Cubbon's statue had not then been erected, nor was the fine new market, now the pride of Bangalore, thought of. In short, both the civil and military portions of the station had not reached such dimensions as they have now, and there were more open spaces between the several localities. The arsenal was located in the Fort which was garrisoned by four companies of European infantry. Fruit and vegetables are known to be comparatively cheap and plentiful in this "City of Beans" at the present day; but my readers would scarcely believe me if I were to mention the absurdly low prices we had to pay for these things when I first went there. Of course English vegetables came later. As for food grains, an officer could feed three horses for the price he would have to pay for the up-keep of one at the present time.

These were the days when the value of the much depreciated rupee was 2 shillings 1¼d and sometimes as much as 2—2 and we were allowed refunds of Rs. 1-12 a month on account of what was termed "back rations."

An officer, who would now be styled "Cantonment Magistrate," but at this period was either called a "Commissary" or a Bazaar master," I forget which, was the chief civil power in the cantonment, and exercised something of the powers of an autocrat over the servants and camp followers. If an officer's servant gave offence to his master in any way, it was only necessary for the latter to send the culprit to the Bazaar master with a chit, when he would get two or three dozen lashes without any further enquiry. The incident of the butler who got flogged by mistake, one reads of in Aliph Cheem (Captain Yeldhams') "Lays of Ind" and of a somewhat similar case in one of Florence Marryatt's (Mrs. Ross Church's, tales, are by no means overdrawn.

CHAPTER VIII.

Bangalore in 1855.

(*Continued*).

At this time General Budd was in command of the garrison, and he was succeeded by Generals Beresford and Whitlock. We used to have many field days, those under the first two officers being the most harassing, and trying to one's patience that the men ever endured. Not only were the manœuvres unduly long, but they seemed to have been designed with the object of testing the abilities of the troops to undergo extreme fatigue. We were very glad therefore when General Whitlock assumed command, and altered this state of things completely, for, if I may so express it, his field manœuvres were a *multum in parvo*, and were a happy blend of instruction and amusement, combined with the minimum of fatigue to the soldiers. For example the troops would assemble on the South Parade, instead of marching all the way to the Arab lines as formerly and while the bands of the various corps would mass and play in the middle of the ground, the troops would perform their evolutions around the parade ground, all the while keeping time with the music. At a sham fight on one occasion, General Whitlock ordered a pontoon bridge to be thrown over the Ulsoor tank from the back of the barracks across to St. John's Hill. The idea was to dislodge a force (the 8th Madras Light Cavalry and three Infantry regiments) who were in possession of the hill, and contemplating an attack on the garrison. The pontoon was made of empty beer barrels and planks, and as soon as it was completed, we crossed, and were promptly charged by the enemy's cavalry, whom we received in square, with bayonets fixed and firing volleys into them. This sent the cavalry back helter skelter, and we then exchanged some volleys of musketry with the enemy's infantry, when we were ordered to retreat in consequence of being outnumbered. Our retirement was not so orderly as our advance, and two men were immersed in the tank, one dropping his musket which fell into rather deep water and was recovered next day.

General Whitlock made it a practice to ride into our barrack square, once a week, on a large mule which belonged to him. He was a kind-hearted man and was much loved by the children for whom he always brought some small change, and who always ran to see him. Kind as he was to the little ones he would not allow himself to be imposed upon. One little boy of the name of William Dempsey came up with the others, and after getting his two annas which was the amount usually given to each child, dodged around by the back gate, and came in by the front entrance for a second dole, making sure that he would not be recognized; but the General's eyes were keen, and detected the young lads manœuvre, and Master William Dempsey had his ears soundly boxed instead, the old General exclaiming "you would rob your General, would you?" Bangalore was very healthy at this period, and deaths among the European troops were very few compared with the stations I had been in, in the Bengal Presidency. I was here appointed an assistant schoolmaster in the regiment, which supplemented my pay by an additional ten rupees, and shortly after sent as schoolmaster to the Fort school. In this latter office, I was fortunate enough to obtain the fees paid by the men, *viz.*, four annas for a sergeant, three for a corporal and two for a private, as perquisites, and since men attending school were excused from all evening roll calls, the attendance was very good, which added materially to my income. My total allowances therefore was far superior to that of a non-commissioned officer in the regiment, inasmuch as I was not put to any outlay for paper, etc., for the pupils, these being furnished by Government free of charge. Florence Marryatt (Mrs. Ross Church) the talented authoress, was at this time in the station and was a frequent contributor to one of the local papers in Madras; but a good many of her sketches of character, although very entertaining, had to be taken with some reserve, as some of the persons alluded to in her contributions were known to many of the residents of Bangalore, whose opinion of the parties probably differed from Miss Marryatt's. The Bangalore theatre, if my memory does not fail me, occupied a site on the Church road and in 1855, Goldsmith's comedy " She stoops to conquer" was put on the boards, but where are the actors now? A gallant Major of artillery, who was in charge of the arsenal in the Fort, played the part of " Hardcastle." Captain Trafford de Trafford, 43rd L I., said to have been a descendant of the Welsh Kings, played the part of " Tony Lumpkin," and not long ago died a peer of the realm. Captain H. B. H. Rocke of whom I have already written in a previous chapter, and who joined us, and took charge of my company during the month of August preceding played " Marlow." He has, as I have already stated, since gone to his final rest at Chudderghat, Hyderabad, Deccan. Captain Glover played " Mrs. Hardcastle" and his brother, Lieutenate Glover played " Miss Hardcastle." Both these were killed in the storming of the Gate Pah in New Zealand, together with the officer commanding the Regiment, Colonel Booth,—while as to other officers, Lieut. Hore Hatchell was drowned in Dublin Bay, along with a comrade, by the capsizing of his boat.

In this play my part was but a minor one. There was some difficulty in the selection of a supernumerary for the part of the drunken servant, Jeremy, but at length a gunner was found who played the character to perfection, and no wonder, for he was on the verge of intoxication, when he made his first appearance on the stage.

A few days before the performance, we received tidings of the fall of Sebastopol, and the gallant Major of artillery I have just spoken of, wrote a song on the subject, for the occasion. This was sung at the conclusion of the piece and was received with enthusiastic delight by the audience who all remained standing while it was sung, there being many references to her late Most Gracious Majesty in the verses of the song. There are perhaps a few now living in Bangalore who remember that night, but of the actors, I fear I am the only one surviving. The Crimean war was in progress, while we were in Bangalore, and the excitement among the troops was so great, that we used to lie in wait for the individual who was detailed for the duty of bringing the letters and telegrams from the Post and Telegraph offices. Telegrams at this period were rare and not so common as they are now. During our stay in the station Captain Rocke had a walking match with Captain Colville. This was a six mile contest, and came off on the race course adjoining the Arab Lines. Contrary to our expectations, Captain Colville won, but most of the spectators were convinced that this officer's walk was not fair "heel and toe," and that Capt. Rocke should have been declared victor While on the subject of this last named gentleman, I may say that he always took an interest in the welfare of the men of his regiment. On two occasions, I have known him to condemn as unfit for consumption, 1,100 lbs. of bread and 1,100 lbs. of potatoes, when as "Captain of the day" and together with his subaltern, he had to inspect and pass the rations supplied by the Commissariat department. The bread and potatoes, I remember, he ordered to be buried, and this was done accordingly, close to the Quartermaster's stores, and many a laugh we had at the expense of the Commissariat department, when we passed the place where the bread and potatoes were buried.

CHAPTER IX.

The March to Fort St. George in 1857.

In March 1857, the left wing of the 43rd was ordered to Madras to relieve the 1st Madras Fusiliers (distinguished for its performances with General Havelock's Column for the relief of Cawnpore, which was ordered on active service to the

Persian Gulf, in consequence of the outbreak of the Persian War. The order was rather sudden, and Captain Rocke was placed in command of the wing. All went merrily as a marriage bell until we marched down the ghats, and arrived at the first camping ground, about four miles from the foot of the ghats, when four men were struck down by cholera, and were quickly buried.

In order to shake off the disease an evening march was made to the next stage, Chittoor, where we halted for two days. But this time the disease had taken firm hold of the wing, and we buried sixteen men here, in addition to a number of women and children and camp followers. I had to see Captain Rocke on duty in his tent, and in the course of conversation regarding the outbreak, I incidentally mentioned to him that I had a pamphlet with me written by Deputy Surgeon-General Maxwell of the Madras service, on the subject of the treatment of cholera, which I thought might prove useful under the existing circumstances. I may say here that the worthy doctor likened a human being when suffering from cholera to one of those little earthen oil lamps which flickers, and dies out for want of oil, or is suddenly extinguished if too much oil is put into it at one time. Similarly in the case of cholera patients, the medicines and nourishment usually administered soon extinguish the little vitality that is left in them.

His theory was opposed to the then accepted treatment of cholera, and although I do not profess to have much knowledge of the subject, it struck me as being worthy of perusal. Indeed I believe that the work might be read with advantage at the present day. As a matter of fact, a quarter of a century later, I spoke on the subject to Doctor Furnell, Surgeon-General to the Madras Government, who had occasion to visit the Penitentiary in connection with an outbreak of cholera, and our conversation turned to the subject of the pamphlet, and he admitted to me, that although he and the other young medical officers who knew Doctor Maxwell when they first came to the country, were amused at some of his theories, there was a good deal in what he (Dr. Maxwell) had written, and that the old man knew something worth knowing. Dr.

Furnell himself was of opinion that impure water was the cause of cholera, and this in many cases I found to be correct, although no doctor myself; or in other words "death often lay in the water pot."

According to Dr. Maxwell, the treatment adopted in cholera cases had caused the death of nine persons out of every ten of his patients, while with the method he subsequently employed the percentage of fatalities was only one in every ten. I ventured very respectfully to point this out to Captain Rocke, and to remark that up to then we had lost every man that took bad with the disease, but he only replied that Doctor Maxwell was not present to assist us, and that the men must take whatever the regimental doctor ordered. Lieut. Bligh came into the tent at this time and reported the death of four men of his company that day, and asked for permission to bury them near some rocks about three-quarters of a mile from camp as the men of the company were anxious that they should be interred alongside two of their comrades who had died and had been buried on the journey to Bangalore. Captain Rocke gave the permission, but he observed at the same time that it would give the burial party a lot of trouble, and the best and quickest way of disposing of the dead was to bury them outside the hospital tents. The truth of Captain Rocke's observations was soon verified, for a man belonging to this same fatigue party caught the disease while in the act of digging the graves, and died on the very spot before medical aid could be summoned to his assistance. On leaving Captain Rocke's tent I went out for a walk with a man named Holding who told me that he had had ten hard boiled eggs for tea that evening; eggs were cheap at the place and could be had for about an anna a dozen, or in English currency one and half pence. Holding was in a most cheerful frame of mind amusing himself by running after lizards, and I left him after a short walk, bidding him "good-bye" at his tent. I never saw him again, for he took bad and died in a couple of hours, and was buried before I knew anthing about it. At the next camp the disease, had assumed a still more virulent type, and there were more attacks and more deaths, several children succumbing to it that morning. I was with the married people, and travelled with my wife and child in the old style of common country carts covered with bamboo matting, and my little boy who was four years old at this time was attacked with cholera but it seemed to me hopeless to attempt to cure him with the hospital medicines. Nevertheless I did not wish to be thought heartless in neglecting any means to save his life and I accordingly went to the hospital tent with a small bottle in which Apothecary Spiers poured some opium and chalk mixture, the medical officer, Dr. Charles Madden, having himself reported sick with fever. This Dr. Madden, I may here remark, was years after Surgeon-General to the Queen's Troops in the Madras Presidency, subsequently holding a similar position in Bengal, and was said to have married a daughter of one of the Board of Directors of the East India Company. With the exception therefore of Apothecary Spiers, we were left without any medical man at all But I may say this of the apothecary, who in consequence of being minus the sight of one eye was nicknamed by the men "the one-eyed gunner," that he worked conscientiously, and was indefatigable in his attention to his patients. While I was returning from the hospital tents, many of our poor fellows were dying and one or two shouted out to me as I passed which probably was meant for a final farewell. I took the medicine back to the bandy, but as I felt convinced that the medicine would do more harm than good to my child, I poured it on the ground. There was a native woman, a camp follower, who spoke English remarkably well. This woman happened to pass my bandy, and as she was going by I handed her a rupee and begged her to get me a bottle of the cordial distilled from Bishop's weed seed, or Omum water, as it is commonly known in Madras, which I knew to be often efficacious in cholera cases, and this I am glad to say eventually pulled the child through; my wife broke out with a rash that was thought to be small-pox, and I was ordered to keep some distance away from the other families, and vividly does the remembrance come back to me of my journey into Arcot next morning with a sick wife and child in the bandy, and I following behind on foot. When the carts containing the Hospital tents passed me, a man of my company, named

Redding, who sat on the first bandy shouted out to me "Here you are, Corporal, I have got them here like herrings in a barrel." On enquiring from him what he meant, I ascertained that he was sitting on the bodies of four men (rolled up in the side walls of the tents) who had died at the last camp just before the wing marched, but who could not be buried for want of the necessary fatigue party to dig the graves, as the wing was in the act of moving, and would have been delayed Redding would, a week before this, have been horrified at his position. But the terrible and rapid mortality had rendered the man callous, and he was perfectly unconcerned, even cheerful, if I may say so. The four bodies had therefore to be brought on and buried at Arcot. The railway had been laid up to Arcot, 65 miles from Madras, and in response to a "wire" which had been sent from the previous camp, the Surgeon-General with two medical officers, and the Adjutant-General of the Queen's Troops serving in the Madras Command, came by train from Madras within an hour of our arrival at Arcot. With this array of medical officers every attention that could possibly be paid was given to to the troops. One of the doctors also examined my son and declared that the bright-eyed little fellow would get over it.

A morning order had been issued that we should proceed forthwith to Madras, and by 2 P.M., we were marched to the station and entrained, but not without burying, just outside the station, four men who had died during the short time we were in Arcot. The cholera however was with us, and the train had to be stopped four times on this journey of sixty-five miles to bury those who had succumbed in the train. In the carriages set apart for the married people, there was not a man or woman, except my wife and myself, who had not lost at least one member of his or her family. In some cases, a husband had lost both wife and children, and *vice versa*. My son got a relapse in the train, and one of the married women kindly gave me three bottles of cold tea for him which he kept drinking and bringing up, until the fit of vomiting ceased, when I administered the cordial, and he got better. By reason of the stoppages on the road, we did not reach the Railway terminus at

Madras (the old Royapuram station) till 8 P. M. We were marched to the Fort, and the sick were sent to the European General Hospital, which was not the palatial building it is now, but a miserable looking structure in comparison and an apology for an hospital, as one understands the term now-a-days. The cholera, however, had a tight grip of the wing, and was not to be shaken off so easily, for on the day after our arrival, sixteen funerals had moved out of hospital, of men women and children who had died since our arrival, and these were the first who had coffins supplied for them since the out-break, for on the road such a thing as a coffin was practically out of the question. On the 1st of April, or four days after our arrival, my wife gave birth to a daughter, and I was attacked with cholera in the female hospital, while on a visit to her, I immediately made my way to the men's hospital, and actually ran up against Dr. Blacklock, a Medical Officer well known to old residents of Madras, and whose name was a household word at one time. On the following day, I felt slightly better, but towards evening I got a relapse, and had I continued taking the iced water which some of the patients kept calling for I should probably have fallen a victim to the disease as others had done; but I succeeded in obtaining some omum cordial from a private source, and dosed myself with it. Remembering also Dr. Maxwell's opinion as expressed in his pamphlet, I called for warm soup or broth which I took in large quantities, and kept bringing up again until I was able to retain some, so as to sustain my fast receding strength. By means of this treament and the effects of a mustard plaster which remained on my stomach all night, blistering the skin completely and taking a quantity of it off, I eventually pulled through. Of course the cholera bacillus was not dreamt of at this period, and in all probability the Railway carriages were sent back the next day without any attempt to disinfect them, nor do I think, was anything done to fumigate the Hospital tents used on the journey. However "all is well that ends well," and in a few days the epidemic gradually abated and died away, and the convalescents (I among the number) were sent back in dhoolies to recuperate at Poonamallee.

When we were considered fit to return to duty, we were sent back to Fort St. George in the old springless hospital carts which for discomfort and inconvineuce could hardly be surpassed by any vehicle. Looking back, the experiences of the few days on which the epidemic ran its course seein even now to stand out vividly in my memory. In those few days we lost 48 men, 6 women and 26 children, or every tenth man, fifth woman, and second child, exclusive of the mortality among the camp followers. It is not to be supposed that such a matter as this would be allowed to pass unnoticed by the Press, and some scathing articles and letters appeared in the *Madras Athenæum*, prompted doubtless by some of those who had lost their relatives during the progress of the epidemic, and whose feelings were naturally much embittered against those who were chiefly responsible for neglecting the usual precautions, and more especially was their wrath directed against the officer commanding, for not keeping the men in camp, but I feel perfectly sure that had this been done, the men would have become discontented, and matters would have become serious, as the British soldier abhors being confined in camp. While I was in hospital, Colonel Denison, the Adjutant-General, came on a visit to it several times. I made myself known to him as one who had been serving in Hobart Town, while he and his brother were there, and that I had seen both officers frequently. After some conversation, he very kindly sent me some English papers to read.

I had just been appointed assistant orderly room clerk to the wing and recollect seeing an official letter from Army Head Quarters calling upon Captain Rocke for an explanation as to what had appeared in the papers, as well as to the events of the march generally. This was of course very annoying to Captain Rocke, but he was quite equal to the occasion. I am able to speak with certainty as to its purport, as it was I who copied his reply, Captain Rocke, after expressing his astonishment that unauthenticated communications to the Newspapers should be taken seriously by the Government, stated that the authorities were well aware that cholera existed on the road, and yet had ordered the march without making adequate provision for medical staff, dhooly bearers, water carriers, etc., and that instead of there being one medical officer less than the authorised establishment, there should have been one more, as well as a clergyman to bury the dead. Captain Rocke's reply was found to be unanswerable by the Head Quarters Staff and he was not troubled again over the matter.

In this connection, I may here say that at this very time the wife of a Coionel Stevens, if I remember rightly, with two children, and another lady, while on their way to Bangalore contracted the disease at Palmanair on the top of the Ghauts, and several of the party, including servants, died. Two medical officers were at once sent up to examine and report on the wells in the vicinity. I cannot conclude these remarks without adding a word in praise of Assistant Surgeon Kees (afterwards Principal of the Madras Medical College) whose name was so familiar to old Madrasees. This medical officer rendered the most valuable assistances to the wing, both in Madras and Poonamallee and his name was gratefully remembered by the survivors for many years after.

CHAPTER X.

Madras in 1857.

We had hardly been a month or two in Madras, when the Mutiny broke out in Bengal, and the Government of Madras took precautions against a similar outbreak in the Madras Presideney. Artillery was brought down from St. Thomas' Mount, and stationed in the Cathedral and Government House compounds, while a couple of companies of European infantry patrolled the road in the direction of Poonamallee. This duty devolved on the wing of the 43rd to which I belonged.

Most alarming reports were spread abroad, and some of the good people of Madras were in a state of fright. Some mounted troops were raised under the command of Mr. John Bruce Norton, the famous Barrister, and were reviewed by His Excellency the Governor (Lord Harris), and the Madras Volunteer Guards were enrolled for the defence of the City.

On the 17th of June I received a letter from my brother James at Cawnpore, who was with the 32nd, and who with seventeen others had volunteered for that regiment from the 96th at Dinapur. This letter was dated the 4th June and was probably in the last mail that left Cawnpore before the garrison was cut off. In it my brother spoke of the arrangements made by the General Officer Commanding, Major General Wheeler, for the protection of the Cantonment, and stated that they were occupying two of the barracks on the plains together with all their wives and families, as well as those of the officers, in anticipation of an outbreak. He spoke in rather hopeful terms of their ability to hold out until relief came from Allahabad.

Subsequent events, however, did not justify his hopes, for the native troops broke out next day. The results that followed, as well as General Wheeler's terms with Nana Saib, are now a matter of history. Of the whole garrison only two escaped, and of the seventeen I knew, every one fell a victim in the holocaust which followed General Wheeler's surrender.

The Commander-in-Chief (General Anson) had died, and Major-General Beresford of Madras, was ordered to Bengal to assume command of the Army. The 8th Madras Light Cavalry received orders to proceed to the seat of operations, but there was so much discontent and murmuring among the men regarding their pay and allowances, that it was thought advisable by the Government to disband them and accordingly two Companies of the left wing of the 43rd were sent down to Vellore for the purpose, by rail, which had been completed now as far as that Station. We encamped not far from the Railway Station, and after a few days' halt, we entrained for Arcot where the 8th Madras Light Cavalry was stationed, and here the disbandment of the regiment took place. The object of the move first to Vellore where Gillespie had distinguished himself during the Mutiny of 1806 was to allay any symptoms of discontent among the inhabitants of that city.

I was orderly room clerk for the detachment, and while with it, an order had been received from Army Head-quarters directing the examination in future of all men prior to their promotion to the non-commissioned ranks, and a few lance-corporals and corporals amongst us had to go through the test. It was the first time there had been any such examinations in the regiment, but it was done in obedience to orders from the Horse Guards, and was probably due to the large number of illiterate men who had been promoted without regard to their educational qualifications, and who were occupying positions as sergeants, while getting their clerical duties performed by privates, I was among those who were examined, and although the test was a simple one, there were a few who failed to pass it. It was the first and last time I went through the examination, and doubtless the results were satisfactory for me, for I was shortly after promoted to full corporal, then lance-sergeant at Nandydroog, next full sergeant at Kirwee, and finally color-sergeant at Madras without having to go through any further examination. We returned to Madras from Arcot in November, and early the following month, the left wing was ordered to rejoin the headquarters of the egiment at Bangalore. We went by train to Vellore, and thence by pony carts on to Bangalore, as orders had been received for the corps to proceed to Central India to aid in the suppression of the Mutiny. Preparations were made on a large scale for the march, and our regiment together with the 19th Madras native infantry, and some guns, all under the command of Brigadier McDuff, were ordered to join General Whitlock's column. After a lengthy march to Secunderabad, we halted there for a few days, as the city of Hyderabad was believed to be seething with rebellion, and an outbreak was expected.

Through the efforts, however, of Sir Salar Jung the first, the danger passed away, and some of our officers were enabled before our departure, to visit the city on elephants provided by that nobleman. Hyderabad was then, as it is probably now, anything but a safe and pleasant place to visit. The sergeants of the 43rd visited the sergeants' mess of the 12th Royal Lancers, and a pleasant spirit of *camaraderie* was established between us. The mess sergeant of the 12th Lancers was a droll and original character, and sang some very comic songs, "The Good Saint Anthony" being one of them. He always seemed to be nonplussed as to what change he had to give back when asked to change a rupee, as there were two other kinds of coinage (the Halli Sicca and the Shai) current in the station, but he managed some how to err on the right side. We fared pretty well on the march, so far as supplies on the road were concerned, for Captain Rocke, who was interpreter for the Regiment, would always go on in advance, and make the necessary "bundo-bast" with the village authorities, so as to prevent disputes, and we would have poultry, eggs, etc., waiting for us in any quantity. Coffee was also supplied to us half-way between each stage, by the regimental coffee shop. On the first stage out of Secunderabad, a Sergeant Birmingham of "ours" an enthusiastic Shikaree accidentally shot himself while carelessly loading his gun, and on the next day, the Master Tailor, a Sergeant O'Brien, was drowned in a tank, while going after a duck which he had shot. The roads here were very bad, in some parts mere jungle cart tracks, and very frequently the baggage carts were delayed till 3 and 4 o'clock in the afternoon. How often did I wish we had the Grand Trunk Road from Calcutta to Lahore. The dust was very fine and penetrating, and not only would our eyes and hair be full of it, but often there would be no tank at hand to have a good wash at the end of a march. Some of the marches were through thick jungle where wild animals abounded, and we passed hamlets surrounded by high bush faggots eight feet high to keep the wild beasts from getting at the people at night. I was Sergeant of the Baggage Guard when we crossed the Nirmul Ghat, and did not get into camp until sunset owing to the heavy gradients we had to traverse. I was in the rear and had plenty of time to look about me, and while crossing a nullah I searched for any rare and precious stones, I came across a piece of plain opal large enough for a signet ring and made a present of it to Captain Robinson who commanded my company, as a memento of the march. The Captain thanked me but while accepting it said "a labourer is worthy of his hire" and gave me a present of Rs. 10. Nothing further of any interest occurred until we reached Kamptee. Here we arrived on a Sunday morning, being welcomed by the sound of an old cracked church bell ringing for morning service. To our great delight, we found at Nagpore, fruits plentiful and cheap, particularly the oranges, and we had our fill of them. We then proceeded to Jubbulpore where we halted for three days.

CHAPTER XI.

The March to Central India.

At Jubbulpore there was a Battery of European Artillery as well as a Company of the 3rd Madras European Regiment (now the 2nd Battalion Royal Inniskilling Fusiliers), the remainder of the Regiment being with General Whitlock's column. Several of the officers of our Regiment visited the far-famed Marble Rocks, one of the sights of the place. Here I purchased a few moss agates, chiefly ring and brooch stones, at an extremely cheap rate. We then marched on to Saugor, and while on the road, I shot some partridges, and had a very narrow escape, through the accidental discharge of my gun, one of the old style of muzzle-loading fowling pieces. One of the birds had only been wounded, and while opening my haversack to show the game to an officer, the bird flew out and took refuge in some thick scrub. Here I tried to drive it out by means of the stock of my gun instead of putting the muzzle into the bush at first. The gun went off burning the sleeve of my coat. Had it gone off while I was putting the stock of the gun into the scrub, I should not have been alive to tell this story at the present day. I reproached myself for my carelessness and stupidity.

The day before we reached Saugor, I was again Sergeant of the baggage guard, and while going down the back of a rather wide water channel I was chased by an alligator which was desirous of making a closer acquaintance with me. Needless to say, I was up the bank again quicker than I went down. At the camp across the suspension bridge over the river, Sergeant Lavelle shot an alligator from the top of the bridge, and the reptile was secured with some difficulty. This Sergeant

Lavelle afterwards became noted for his discovery, of gold in Kolar, and subsequently in 1895, I followed the poor fellow to his long home at Bangalore, where he had made a name for himself before his death. On we marched, the heat becoming more intense the farther we proceeded on our journey, the sky at midday would be a canopy of fire, and we had some deaths from sunstroke. We had great difficulty in getting the baggage over the Punnah Ghat where the Punnah Rajah had a diamond mine, and the baggage was not got over till the evening of the second day. Our Paymaster, Captain Denton, who travelled with his cash chest in the bullock carriage over the ghats, was found dead of heat apoplexy, with his cash chest in front of him.

Some of the men also who unwisely helped themselves from a rum barrel belonging to the commissariat, which had broken on the way, died from the effects of the heat and drink. Below the ghats the heat was so intense that we buried, in addition to the poor Paymaster, Lieut. Elms of my company, a Brevet-Major of the 19th M. N. I., and 13 men of the 43rd, all of whom had died suddenly of heat apoplexy that day. At the back of the camp was a nullah in which half the men had bathed, and curious to relate scores of fish floated up dead afterwards. There being no bread obtainable, we had frequently to live upon old and worm-eaten biscuits which were not exactly appetizing. Often the only vegetables to be had were onions, but however wholesome the vegetable may be, we were soon satiated with it, when our daily ration consisted of a pound of onions together with a pound of meat, and the same quantity of weavilled biscuits. By this time we were only a few stages from Banda, and owing to the terrific heat a lot of the men became debilitated, and had to fall out of the ranks on the march, and I myself felt shaken and weak on the legs. We were therefore very glad indeed when we finally reached Banda which had, a little while before this, been captured by General Whitlock after an engagement with the rebels.

Executions of the mutineers were of daily occurrence, and hundreds of them were hanged for their misdeeds and for the murders of Europeans they had committed at that place. After a rest at Banda for a fortnight, the march was continued to Kirwee which surrendered without any fighting, on the 7th of June 1858. The Rajah of the place and his son, who refused to surrender when called upon by the General to do so, being tried by Court-martial, were transported for life and deported. A tremendous quantity of loot was captured, and, if I remember rightly, there were distributions years after of prize-money to the troops engaged in the operations. But £400,000 sterling in promissory notes of the Government of India, which was taken at the time, was never distributed, and although Colonel Doran and the Revd. Mr. Kinlock, Chaplain to the force, who were Prize Agents, brought the matter before the House of Commons, the troops were never granted their share of this money.

In consequence of the death, from small-pox, at Banda, of Sergeant George Martin of the 43rd, I was here promoted to a full Sergeant and was Sergeant of the European guard over the prize hackeries (country carts), there being a Havildar's guard over them as well. In addition to a large quantity of silver coinage, there was a large quantity of gold bricks, jewellery, and other valuables. The General rode up and inspected the loot, and I recollect turning out the guard and presenting arms to him.

A box full of rupees was broken open afterwnrds by some of the native guard, but the perpetrators were soon discovered and earned for themselves five years' imprisonment each.

Two Companies of the 43rd were left to garrison Kirwee, and occupied the Palace, while all the treasure was afterwards sent for security to the Fort at Allahábád. The troops were then marched on to Calpee, to which place General Whitlock had previously gone from Banda, leaving two companies of my regiment to garrison Hameerpore, while Brigadier-General MacDuff followed him a few days after with the remaining troops. On the second days' march from Banda we found the bodies of four rebels hanging to a tree in the middle of the village. These were the headman and three others who had raised the flag of revolt in the village, and refused to take it down when commanded. At the request of the Political officer who accompanied General Whitlock, the place was surrounded by the troops, and the ring-leaders received condign punishment. The bodies were still hanging when we halted at the place, but as the stench arising from them was unbearable the Medical Officer obtained the Commanding Officer's permission to have them taken down.

Hameerpore is situated on an Island formed between the Betwa and Jumna rivers, and two companies were left to garrison it, while the rest of the troops marched on to join General Whitlock at Calpee. The station at the time of the outbreak was the head-quarters of a Collectorate, and the Collector, together with other officers had been hanged by the rebels to a tree and shot, the only one escaping being a young East Indian girl, the daughter of a European pensioner, who had been rescued while lying concealed in a cave near the bank of the Betwa through the efforts of a friendly native of the place. The two companies were stationed in an old chuttram, and the station became notable for the number of trials and executions that took place in it. A bough of the tree on which the Collector and others had been hanged, was selected as the very place on which to carry out the executions. A table with a flap working on a hinge was placed beneath, and would act as a drop, and the mutineers, usually three or four at a time, made to mount, and the uprights on which the flap rested drawn away by ropes when all was ready. After life was extinct, the table was removed, the bodies cut down the next morning, dragged along the ground and thrown into the river Jumna. The tree was called by us "the tree of retribution" and I recollect sending a leaf from it in a letter which I wrote to my mother. On one occasion, two mutineers belonging to the Gwalior contingent were to be executed. The men were tall and the drop allowed was too long with the result that they came to the ground, and had to be re-hanged with shorter ropes.

Hameerpore was a delightful station in the cold weather, but snakes and scorpions were rather too common, one of the largest whip snakes I ever saw being killed here. There was excellent fishing, and bathing to be enjoyed in the river. Our men used to run up the bank and after jumping into the water, would let themselves be carried down by the stream, although on the opposite banks crocodiles could be seen basking in the sun. In the month of November 1858, the two companies marched back to Banda and were located in the Nawab's Palace. Major Booth who was in command of the two companies at Hameerpore, also took command of them at Banda. For our amusement, we played in a room improvised as a theatre in the palace, and soon erected a stage for the performance, which consisted of the melodrama "Black Eyed Susan," and a piece called "The Bengal Tiger"; I took part in both plays, "Sir Paul Pagoda" in the latter, and I recollect feeling highly gratified by being complimented on my performance by the commanding officer, Major Booth. Although the youngest sergeant in the three detachments of corps stationed at Banda, I was appointed sergeant-major, as well as writer to the Staff Officer of the garrison, which of course meant additional emoluments to me. It gave us a shock when in two of the rooms of the palace, we discovered the marks of sword cuts, where the Europeans had been cut at and killed by the mutineers. Indeed the tulwar marks were most plainly discernible in these rooms.

On Christmas Eve 1858, while the men were preparing their puddings for their next day's dinner, General Whitlock marched into Banda with the main body of the troops, by forced marches from Mashobra, and hundred men of the two companies of the 43rd were ordered to march to Kirwee, 51 miles from Banda, where the rebels were reported to be in some strength. Thus our poor fellows had to make a long march without their Christmas dinner. General Whitlock marched back to Kirwee, and afterwards caught the rebels and routed them on the heights of Panwaree. The mutineers evidently knew that a great quantity of treasure was still concealed in the precincts of the palace, and this was quickly verified. In the court-yard of the palace, at the back there were a number of fire places where the retainers used to cook their food in the open, as all Hindustanis usually do. In this backyard were a guard of one corporal and nine Europeans, and one havildar and twelve men belonging to a native regiment. The havildar while digging in one of these fire places with an old crowbar, with the view of searching for treasure accidentally unearthed an immense earthen pot filled with rupees. The havildar communicated the fact to the European corporal and the news soon became known to the rest of the guard, and both Europeans and natives helped themselves liberally to the money, and some even went away with six and seven hundred rupees stowed away in pouches, socks, etc., in fact all over their persons. The fact was also communicated to the relieving guards who also came in for a share of the spoil, and this was carried on for several days, the secret being well kept by each individual until a man for this Guard, named O'Brien, was selected for duty as Commanding Officer's orderly on account of his neat and tidy appearance, and thus lost his chance of sharing in the loot. O'Brien was much annoyed to think that he would be left out in the cold through no fault of his own, except in being too clean, while the others would help themselves freely, and in a fit of temper let the "cat out of the bag." The result was that the General himself came down along with an Officer of Engineers and took charge of the cash. A thorough search was instituted and six more pots of coin were found buried beneath the other cooking places. These were carried away in carts and while passing the front guard of the palace, each man was permitted to help himself to a handful. The companies of my regiment which garrisoned the place from the month of June 1858 to the December following, came in for a wind-fall in the shape of jewellery and other valuables secreted in the wood-work and other hiding places in the palace. Indeed some of them were lucky enough to come across some rich loot. As a matter of fact, the Pioneer corporal of the two companies which were garrisoning the place, not only succeeded in obtaining a lot of money, but also brought quantities of valuable jewellery back to Madras, which he had found buried in an old staircase of the palace. A Captain of one of the companies was also said to have done fairly well in this respect. I myself bought some oriental topazes and other precious stones for a few rupees which I subsequently sold at a good profit. Moreover at Banda I purchased some beautiful moss agates and carbuncles at an exceedingly cheap rate. Banda was famous for its lapidaries, and I have seen them cut and polish stones in beautiful style, all in one day for a mere eight annas.

CHAPTER XII.

THE MARCH TO SAUGOR.

Prior to leaving Banda, a column had been sent after Tantia Topee who was much in evidence at the time, and elusive as De-Wet of South African fame. How he was eventually caught and executed is a matter of history. The regiment was directed to march back to Saugor, and on reaching that station, we were located in the barracks there. After a short stay we received the order to form part of a Column under Colonel Primrose, with five companies of the 43rd, several companies of a native regiment, some "Shutar Sowars" or Camelry as they are called now-a-days, *i.e.*, mounted infantry on camels, and were sent to dislodge a body of rebels who were giving trouble in the valley of the Barunnah.

After marching through thick jungle surrounded by high hills, we reached the Barunnah valley. Before descending into the Valley, a Mahout went on his elephant to cut branches from a tall fig tree in the vicinity. While engaged in this work, a cheetah which was concealed in the long grass below, made a bound on to the elephant's neck, and would have undoubtedly pulled the Mahout down, had he not made a vigorous blow with his hatchet and cut into the beast's skull, killing it on the spot. The carcass was brought into camp and shown to Colonel Primrose who made a present of rupees ten to the Mahout, ordered the beast to be skinned and kept the skin as a trophy of the march.

On the 26th March 1859, we met a body of rebels at Dhooleypore, and dispersed them after a sharp engagement.

Our loss in this action was only two or three of the native infantry killed, a havildar of this Regiment meeting with his death in a strange manner. He was shot in the neck, and although the wound did not appear serious at first, on examination it was found that the bullet had driven the hook in the collar of his tunic into his gullet, and the unfortunate man bled to death. I saw the poor fellow after his death and could not help being struck with the calm and peaceful appearance he presented. It was difficult in the dense jungle to get any tidings of the whereabouts of the rebels, but on the 14th of April 1859, in consequence of receiving reliable information, we marched into the valley and attacked them opposite to a place called Puraha, wading through a deep stream before we could get at the place. The rebels did not wait to receive us, but made for a pass through the hills. They had been occupying a village on the other side of one of the streams; and Colonel Primrose directed some companies to proceed up the right of the ghat, and one up to the left, while a few men were left to burn the village. The part I played in this morning's manœuvre comes back to my recollection owing to an incident which nearly cost me my life. Half of the company I belonged to, under the command of Lieut. Hore Hatchell, was sent after the rebels on the left of the Ghat. It was a most difficult task, climbing up the hill, and we had gone only half up, I being a little in advance of the men, and the Lieutenant close on my right, when a ball struck a rock close above my head. The shot came from the directron of the village behind us and must have been fired by one of our own men. I mentioned this to Lieut. Hore Hatchell and remarked that although I did not mind meeting my fate in the cause of duty at the hands of the enemy, I did not at all relish the idea of being shot by one of our own men. Some rebels were killed while our men were ascending the Ghat, one shot taking effect on both a rebel and his wife, and killing them outright. A man of "ours" named Watt Tyler removed a large gold hoop nose ring from the dead woman's nose, in which was set a large rough ruby of a bead-like shape, and which he sold to an officer of the regiment for Rs. 20.

All these hills were covered with tall spear grass, three feet high, the needles of which went through one's clothing and caused us much discomfort. It was noon before we got into camp that day. The valley was a feverstricken locality, and fever of a malignant type prevailed there. I myself was laid up with a severe attack, my life being despaired of, and it was not till a month afterwards, when the wing marched into Saugor that I was convalescent. We passed the hot weather at Saugor, and had two or three field days under General Whitlock.

Brigadier Wheeler was in command of the station, and at the close of the hot season a column was formed under the command of the Brigadier, consisting of the left wing of the 43rd, a wing of native infantry and some Camel sowars, and left Saugor on the 20th November 1859. Our first march was a night one on the Fort of Rathgarh at a distance of 27 miles, and was a very trying one, many of us being exhausted when we got into camp the next morning. After a halt of one day, we made a march of 29 miles having to wade through two fordable rivers on the way. This was an all night march. Information regarding the whereabouts of the rebels was received in camp, and we were ordered to fall in and commenced our march at 4 o'clock in the afternoon. On the following night we had a much longer march, one of 33 miles, and while going through a jungle track the leading company under Captain I. C. Desbrow, to which I belonged, came to a halt, as the Bugler of the company came running back with the information that the rebels were in strength on our left. Day was just breaking at this time. The Brigadier was in the rear of the company and the information was given to him at once by Captain Desbrow. He came forward immediately, looked attentively through his field glasses and gave the order to Captain Desbrow to "form the company into line, kneel, and take careful aim at them." I could see a movement on the left in the direction of wherethe enemy was supposed to be. I thought I observed Dresser Hailsworth on his pony, recognizing him by the red blanket he used to wrap around him shouted out to Captain Desbrow "good God! Captain, that is our Dresser Hailsworth." The Captain at once informed the General and our movement against the supposed enemy was at once stopped. How the mistake happened was that the connecting files between the different companies had not kept in proper touch with the leading company, and thus missed their direction, getting on to another path in the jungle parallel with our own, and were a hundred yards on our left. Had we fired at the time, there would have been a serious catastrophe and we should have killed a number of our own men. After marching half a mile, we came close to the village of Gopalapoora where the rebels were believed to be in some force. Many of them were seen rushing into the jungle from the village, and shortly after a great crowd of them was seen moving off about 400 yards on our right. Had the wing been ordered to fire a volley at them we should probably have killed a great many, but instead, the order was given to "fix bayonets and charge." This coming after the march of 33 miles which we had made during the night was too much of a good thing, as we never could, tired and worn out as we were, hope to reach the enemy in time to make use of our bayonets. The result was that when we came to the place which the great crowd had just left, the enemy were discerned 400 yards away making for a hill which they succeeded in getting over without much difficulty and very little risk to themselves. Our men opened fire on the flying enemy, and a sharp fusillade was maintained for some time, but without doing any execution worth speaking of, although a few of the rebels while going over the hill, were killed. A good deal of baggage and a number of ponies and cattle belonging to the enemy were captured, and this was the only practical result of the morning's work, for the whole of the affair seems to me now to have been something of a blunder A shot was fired by a man of my company, who was some little distance away on my right, which I knew as a matter of fact to be directed against me, for it struck close to my feet and came from the direction of a small hill on which he was standing. I felt sure the shot never came from the rebels, but in the heat of an action it is almost impossible to bring home the fact to the individual concerned.

Being one of the actors, although an humble one, in the morning's work, it was with much surprise and amusement that I read the account of it which appeared in the General Officer's despatch, and was published in the Gazette of India. In it the General gave great praise to the 43rd which he eulogised for not throwing away their ammunition, but after all very little was done in the way of execution, and it was clear to all, the regiment certainly did waste its powder and ball on this occasion. The highly colored and exaggerated account of the morning's engagement, if such it can be called, certainly staggered those who were actors in it, and reminds one of the reports of some of the recent actions in South Africa. Of course absolute silence was maintained in it of the fact of one company very nearly firing point blank into another, but mistakes of this kind sometimes occur, as one or two incidents in the recent war against the Boers will show.

It was a standing joke amongst the men owing to the very long marches, that the Brigadier who was an inveterate smoker used to carry 25 cigars on his person before starting on each day's march, and that he would never think that a proper day's march had been done until all the cigars were finished. The men were rather sarcastic on the subject.

CHAPTER XIII.

Operations in Central India.

Continuing our chase of the rebels whom we followed from place to place, we encamped at the town of Garrispore situated at one end of a hill a mile long, forming a hog's back. Above the town is situated an old fort in which were a few native troops belonging to the Rajah who had remained loyal to the British Government. A ledge ran round from the foot of the hill on the east side and gradually rose as it encircled the hill. This ledge was merely a foot path with overhanging boulders of rock above, and a steep declivity on the offside, so that the greatest caution had to be exercised when either going up or descending the pathway. This explanation is necessary for what follows.

The first night in camp, a tiger was heard prowling about close to the camp, and the next morning, some of our men who went up this ledge on a ramble came across a dead tiger cub about the middle of the pathway, which they brought into camp, together with the news that there was the den of a tiger running into the rock close to the spot where they had found the cub. One of the men in my tent, an Irishman of the name of Enright, a plucky fellow, on hearing of this remarked to me. "Sergeant, you have got a double barrelled fowling piece, suppose we go out after the tiger." He had read or heard of Sir James Outram having crawled into a tiger's den without any harm to himself, as the beast usually makes a bolt out into the open under such circumstances, and he offered to do the same if I went with him. I consented, loaded my double barrelled gun with ball, and away we went. We got on the ledge which ran the whole length of the hill, Enright leading. It was not possible to climb the hill in a vertical direction on account of the beetling rocks that overhung the whole pathway, while below the narrow path on our left, the descent was sheer and precipitous down to the bottom of the hill two hundred feet below the spot where we were. The ledge was narrow and a fall from it meant certain death. About the centre of the hill, we came to the locality of the tiger's den and we could plainly discern our camp about half a mile away on the east. Enright asked me to cock both barrels of the gun, hold myself in readiness, and when the tiger rushed out, to give him both barrels at once, while he crawled into the den to root the beast out.

He went into the den, which was like going into a narrow tunnel, without any hesitation at all, and he was so long absent that the minutes seemed like hours to me, and I began to feel uneasy. He came out at length and said that the tiger was "not at home," and that the den smelt frightfully owing to the number of bones in it. We wended our way then to the other end of the hill where we got on to level ground again. Here there was a small building sheltering a colossal stone figure standing on a pedestal of solid masonry. It was fully fifteen feet high and was of exquisite workmanship and seemed to me a work of art, hundreds of years old. After admiring the workmanship for some time, we returned to camp. Some months after this occurrence, poor Enright was invalided along with others from Saugor, and on the march from that station to Calcutta to embark for Europe, he cut his throat with a razor, and died from the effects of the wound. I often thought of Enright afterwards, and it is my belief that he was scarcely answerable at times for his actions. But to return to Garrispore; that evening in camp, Sergeant Lockwood, an old shipmate of mine, who had been out for a walk in the jungle close by, came back in great haste, and with an ashen face informed us that while he was walking on one of the jungle paths, a tiger crossed his path not many yards from him, without however making any attempt to attack him. Sergeant Lockwood nevertheless had received a severe fright. This occurred only half a mile from the camp. On the day following this incident, an Irishman of E. Company named Sam Seeley brought into camp a dead python about 12 feet long, and about 18 inches in girth at the thickest part, and was holding forth to the crowd that had collected around him, how he had shot it while hanging by its tail from a tree and in the act of killing a bullock. Now I knew Seeley to be something of a romancer and addicted to "spinning yarns," and when I also joined the crowd and heard his story, I offered to bet him 10 Rs. that it was not a bullock the snake had killed. "Well then" said he a little taken aback "It was a young heifer." I offered to bet him the ten rupees that it was not even a young heifer. This staggered him, and then he admitted that it was a goat. Knowing Seeley's proclivities, I offered to bet him the ten rupees that it was not even a goat. He replied that he hadn't the ten rupees otherwise he would take my bet, as he stoutly maintained that the snake had killed the goat. Sergeant Morris of his Company having offered to lend him the money, I placed my ten rupees in

Sergeant Morris' hand, and asked [Seeley to mention where the affair happened. He said, "on the top of the hill opposite, in a shepherd's hut, while it was dragging the goat out of the compound." I declined his offer to accompany me and show me the spot, but took instead the Tindal of the tent lascars, who spoke English very well and to whom I gave a rupee to assist me in my enquiries. By going through Garrispore, we got on to the top of the hill where the shepherd's hut was and visited it. The snake it appeared from the account of the natives had come up from the other side of the hill, got into the compound of the hut, seized the goat and while making its way back, was hit on its back by a stone thrown by one of the natives, which retarded its progress, and hence it got near a tree surrounded by a bush. The natives surrounded the bush with thick grass, with the object of destroytng it by fire. Meanwhile Seeley with a comrade had come up, borrowed an old matchlock from a native soldier of the fort who was looking on, and shot the serpent. Of course, I returned to camp and told Sergeant Morris to pay Seeley the money as the snake had actually killed the goat. General Wheeler gave Seeley 10 Rs. for the snake and had it skinned.

Of course, a boa of this size is large enough to kill a half-grown bullock or even a man, if it got around him properly, but knowing Seeley's habit of drawing upon his imagination, I was induced to make the bet. He had been severely wounded in a jungle action some months before. A bullet had struck his left side, went all round the front of his stomach, came out on the right side, and then went through his right wrist. It was well for him that he had no breakfast that morning, and his stomach was pinched, for had the ball gone through his entrails, it would doubtless have been the cause of his death. His narrow escape, however, did not cure him of his inveterate habit of drawing the long bow. This wound of his was received in the Rewah jungle where some others of my regiment came to grief also in driving out a number of rebels who had escaped from Cawnpore and had sought refuge in the Rewah and Bundelkund jungles. Poor

Adams of the 43rd also met with a serious mishap here. Mr. Osborne, the Political agent, had been chased by a number of the rebels. Adams came across two, shot one and attacked the other with his bayonet. This one, who was a man of great size and strength, seized the bayonet and pulled the musket out of Adams' hand, and then came a hand to hand struggle in which Adams was overpowered and fell with the native on the top of him. He had the rebel by the throat, while the latter kept sawing at his (Adam's) legs with a tulwar. Poor Adams was on the point of succumbing through loss of blood, when foitunately for him two other men of the Regiment appeared on the scene, and shot the rebel while he was on Adams' breast. Adams was carried out to the edge of the jungle, and fortunately for him one of the Regimental doctors was close at hand, and amputated both legs on the spot. The poor fellow bore the operation bravely and only winced when the bones were being sawn through. Adams eventually recovered and got an enhanced pension for his services, besides which the Political Agent settled £ 20 a year on him for life. Adams was alive in Bangalore for years after this.

The tanks and rivers in this part of the country were full of alligators and some small alligators were caught and stuffed by our men. Some very large horned owls were also caught and taken back with us to Saugor.

CHAPTER XIV.

Last days in the Army.

We were ordered back to Saugor and remained there during the hot season of 1859. We were indeed glad to get back to Barracks again after the marches we had done. The 12th P. W. O. Royal Lancers were stationed along with us here, and we came across some old friends whose acquaintance we had formed at Secunderabad during our journey to Central India. One of their horses suddenly ran " amok ": after biting the arm of the syce, it actually chased a Sergeant of " ours," and had to be shot. We lost a few men from fever, which malady they had contracted in the jungles of Rewah and Bundelkund, while clearing out the rebels. I made a little money here by purchasing and selling precious stones. Being a judge of these things, I was commissioned to do this by Captain Morgan, the Paymaster, and Captain Richardson of E. Company and brought a number of uncut rubies for them. Small uncut rubies could be had for three or four rupees in the Saugor bazaar,—stones that would now sell for 15 or 20 rupees.

A horned owl that belonged to a man of my company, named Godfrey, used to leave barracks every night on a prowl for rats, mice, and bandicoots, and return to its perch very early in the morning, and on two occasions, it returned minus a lot of feathers, which was due no doubt to some of its nightly raids on rats and bandicoots. It was a very game bird and no amount of shouting or noise would startle it. The only object, which it seemed to have any fear of, was one of the small stuffed alligators that Godfrey had with him.

During our stay at Saugor, a dreadful thunderstorm occurred, and a tree between the barracks and town was struck by lightning. No less than eleven donkeys and five or six sheep, that had sought shelter beneath its branches were killed on the spot.

At the commencement of the cold weather, the dying embers of the Mutiny having been finally extinguished, the Regiment received orders to proceed to Madras. Our return march was not by the same route we had come up, but instead, we were ordered to proceed by way of Bengal, and marched from Saugor to two stages below Allahabad where we embarked on the usual river barges on the Ganges which were in readiness for us. We went round by the Sunderbunds to Calcutta where we halted for a few days.

The right wing embarked on a small steamer known as the "Duchess of Kent," while the left wing embarked on the old "Sesostris" which had the reputation of being an old cholera ship—Sir Charles Napier's troops had returned in this latter vessel on their way back from the campaign in Scinde, and it had then obtained its evil reputation, owing to the deaths from cholera that occurred on board. The "Duchess of Kent," a small paddle wheeled steamer, took the "Sesostris" in tow, and went merrily down the river, A few men had died from cholera on the way down from Saugor to Calcutta, but there were no cases when we embarked. On clearing the Sandheads, cholera broke out on the "Sesostris," and several men in addition to Sergeant Smith of my company, an old comrade of mine, died from it. There were no cases on the "Duchess of Kent," and those on board that vessel were not aware that we had the disease till they were informed of the fact by a most primitive method. A black board was erected on deck near the forecastle of the ship, and the number of cases and deaths would be written in chalk in large letters daily for the information of those on "the Duchess of Kent." Two or three days after getting into the Bay of Bengal, the cholera abated, and we were towed into Madras without any further cases. We disembarked, and took up our quarters in the Barracks in the Fort in the month of March 1860. In the month of May following, I was appointed Pay and Color-Sergeant of B. (Captain Rock's) Company, *vice* Color-Sergeant Thomas Edwards who had died in the field. My promotion was something of a surprise to me, as I was junior to four other sergeants, all of whom had been pay sergeants for some months, and whom I thus superseded. At a meeting of all the sergeants, which was held in our mess room, we decided to erect a monument to our brother sergeants of the regiment, who died during the Mutiny, each sergeant paying an equal share. This monument contains the names of all the sergeants who died during the campaign, Sergeant Smith's being the last on the list, and was erected in St. Mary's graveyard, a short distance from the gateway on the right hand side. But I am afraid that after all these years, the monument has fallen into disrepair, and the inscriptions are much obliterated. Soon after our arrival, we commenced theatricals in the Fort, and not only did the officers play, but the sergeants, corporals, and privates also. The sergeants first played the

' Brigand," followed by the "Irish Lion" in both of which I took part and we performed to crowded houses on both occasions. The overture to "Fra Diavolo which was played by the Band of the Regiment when the 'Brigand' was enacted was much appreciated by the audience. In this latter performance I took the part of FATHER NICKOLA."

The new Police Force was being raised in Madras at this period, under Mr. William Robinson who afterwards acted as Governor of Madras for a short time, and believing that I could better my prospects, I visited his office with three other brother Sergeants, and applied for a post as an Inspector of Police. Captain Carr who was Assistant to the Inspector-General of Police was directed by his chief to put us through an examination. This test was of the most elementary kind. We were provided with pens, ink, and paper, and were asked to write anything we liked for Mr. Robinson's inspection. Notwithstanding the simplicity of the examination, one of the Sergeants failed to pass. Three of us were informed that if we could procure our discharge, we should be appointed Inspectors on the day we left the Military Service.

I was color-sergeant of the guard-of-honor which received the new Governor, the Right Hon'ble H. Ward on his arrival in Madras. But his tenure of office was very brief as he shortly after succumbled to an attack of cholera, and I formed one of the funeral procession at his burial.

Even in those days, Madras was noted for its insanitary state. I recollect while returning from the Police Office which was situated on the other side of the old American Ice-house on the South Beach near St. Thomé, and on coming through Government House compound on our way to the Museum on the Pantheon Road, which we contemplated visiting, we came across an old stagnant pool of water, which for strength of odour would put one in mind of the world-renowned Gorgonzola cheese. This pool was within 250 yards of Government House gate. The stench was so overpowering that we were scarcely able to breathe and we were glad to get away from its vicinity. Times have altered, the old pool, and some ground on which stood some native shoemakers' huts, and a portion of the surrounding locality now form what is known as the Napier Park. We visited the Museum on our way back from the Police Office and after looking over the objects of interest, we visited the place where the snakes were kept. This was a small glass building, and contained snakes of all kinds. The keepers were quite fearless, and for a few annas showed us how the poison could be extracted; even from the cobras.

We had some very pleasant times in Madras for the next few months, and some of the officers and sergeants, myself included, went to two Fancy Dress Balls, one of which was held in an hotel in Black Town, and the other in the old College Hall. Some of the officers spent their money freely, especially Lieutenants Harry Gorton, O'Niell and one or two others. Lieut. Salmon went as a Red Indian, and Sergt. Craven, the Officers' Mess Sergeant, as Henry the Eighth, and in his head dress wore some valuable jewels. In a squabble that occurred during the course of a dance, his head dress was knocked off, and he lost some false or real diamonds, but whether they were false or real I am unable to say, but I know that it tookRupees 800 to square the matter. I, along with some other sergeants, went in uniform, and enjoyed the supper for which we had to pay Rs. 10 each.

The sergeants of the regiment next gave a Ball in the old regimental theatre in the Fort, which was arranged for the occasion. I was elected President of the Committee and had two other sergeants as members. The Adjutant-General, and other high military, and civil officials were present. The first named officer led off the dance with Mrs. Arbuthnot, and it was not till one o'clock in the morning that the dancers went into supper. When all were seated Major Synge of our Regiment called out to me "now Mr. President, you say grace." I must confess that I was taken aback by this request, as I was not in the habit of "saying grace." However, I soon recovered my self-possession, and gave the Shakesperian one "may good digestion wait on appetite, and health on both." This told capitally, and I received a round of applause or it. After supper, dancing went on merrily, claret cup and champagne being in great request, and these were to be had *ad-lib.* The dancing did not cease till daybreak, and some of the sergeants, if they did not keep the dance going, kept the bottle going all the following day. This little bit of pleasure cost the sergeants Rs. 1,320, the supper alone costing Rs. 400. Each one of us paid Rs. 12 out of his own pocket, the remainder coming out of the Sergeants' Mess Fund.

I applied for my discharge from the Army in the month of May, and it was not until the September following that my discharge was sanctioned. In those days, all such applications had to go to the Commander-in-Chief in India, whose head-quarters were at Simla at this period. Sir Patrick Grant being, if I remember rightly, Commander-in-Chief, and as the mail did not travel so quickly in those days, it was of course unavoidable. My principal reason for leaving the military service was that the 43rd Regiment was not expected to remain much longer in India. As a matter of fact, they went the following year to New Zealand, and lost a number of officers and men at the Gate Pah, and as I did not wish to leave the country, I should have, if I had still remained in the Army, been compelled to volunteer to another regiment, and thus have forfeited my position, and reverted to a Private again, as I did when I volunteered for the 43rd in 1854. The sergeants of the regiment offered to keep me a month free of all cost to myself if I remained and played two old men's characters in a couple of plays which they were then rehearsing. But this it was impossible for me to do, and I accordingly was discharged from the Army on the 30th September 1860, having served the Government in the Military Department, fourteen years, one month and five days.

I was appointed as an Inspector of Police in accordance with the promise made to me by the Inspector-General, and was ordered to proceed to Nellore, and three days after, *viz.*, on the 3rd October 1860, I left in a country cart for Nellore, and although there was a great deal of cholera on the road, I reached my destination on the 8th idem, and took up the duties to which I was appointed, *viz.*, as a Reserve Inspector.

CHAPER XV.

Police Duty in Nellore.

After assuming charge of my duties in Nellore, I found that I had plenty of work to do in the shape of drilling the newly-recruited police. The number of recruits was 400, and drills and parades were the order of the day. Indeed, I had more of these than when I was in the Among. Added to this, *bona fide* Police work, of which there was a plenty, and the reader will see that we were kept fully employed. Of course the Superintendent was the commanding officer of the force. There were several old pensioned Havildars from the native army who knew their drill fairly well, and who were appointed head constables and these were of material assistance to me in the drills and parades, inasmuch as they could be trusted to act as company commanders, and as guides and markers, when the force was going through battalion drill. Within three months, these recruits were not only proficient in manual and platoon exercises, but were also qualified in company drill, " street firing" *i.e.,* quelling disturbances in streets, and clearing them of mobs, and shooting generally. I was congratulated on getting the men into a state of proficiency so soon. After this they were posted to the various Taluks of the district, and had to commence police work in real earnest. I should also explain that this was not done until they had some material knowledge of their duties as Police officers, which knowledge was imparted to them during the intervals of drill and parade, when they had to attend school for the purpose, *i.e.,* about the middle of the day. Crime was rife in the district, and there were no less than twenty-six torch light robberies in 1861. For the benefit of the uninitiated, I should mention that an ordinary *dacoity* must be committed by five or more men to constitute a dacoity, but the gangs are not, as a rule, very large. The so-called " torch-light robbery " is, however, a more serious affair, and is carried out by organized gangs of from fifty to sixty men who with torches in their hands, pounce down upon a village at night, burning and torturing the inhabitants to make them disclose the hiding places of their valuables, and jewellery and then disperse as quickly and suddenly as they came.

Before the reorganization of the Police took place in 1859 crime, unless detection was followed by conviction, was often not recorded, so that it was difficult to ascertain what the actual amount of crime was in a district. Under the old system, the Collector, the Joint Magistrate, and European Assistant Magistrates were the heads of the district Police; but in fact the work was really done by the Tahsildars and Sub-Magistrates of the different taluks and towns In addition to dacoities and torch-light robberies, high-way robberies and murderers, were very frequent. The cases of grave crimes after being enquired into by the Tahsildars and Sub-Magistrates would be committed to the Sessions Court of the District where they were tried by the European Sessions Judge and two Assessors. My readers will at once observe that the initial enquiry into such cases by officials of the *calibre* of a Tahsildar or Sub-Magistrate, left the door open for bribery and corruption, which doubtless, was prevalent at the time, although it would be difficult to prove the fact. Many of the Assessors were very ignorant men, and I have often been amused by the answers they would give the Judge when called npon to do so through the Court Interpreter to declare their opinion as to the guilt, or otherwise of the accused on whose trial they were sitting. The usual reply was "your honor knows best." Of course this answer was inadmissible, and they would be cautioned by the Judge who would demand a definite answer as to whether the accused was "guilty or not guilty," and the reply invariably exposed their ignorance of the law. Often and often I have seen and heard the Judge find prisoners "guilty," even of such crimes as murder, when they were deemed innocent by the assessors, and acquit those who were found guilty by them. The trial, so far as the Assessors were concerned, was a farce and their assistance might well have been dispensed with. Bribery and corruption were prevalent among the subordinates of the Court and if the accused happened in any way to be a rich man the process of extortion went on merrily I have had reason to belive.

The assessors of the present day no doubt are much more intelligent. The "shaking of the Pagoda tree" was much more common at that time than it is now. The new Police made very little progress in the suppression of crime owing to the obstruction they met with at the hands of the committing officers, and more especially was this the case at the Sessions Court where trial after trial of prisoners accused of heinous crime, ended in an acquittal, although their guit was patent to any impartial observer, merely because the police had initiated the prosecutions.

No less than sixteen such cases were dismissed, which the police felt certain would end in conviction. Even bases committed by the Collector, and other European magistrates ended in acquittal. I should not, however, omit to state that these officers did their best to help the police in the suppression of crime. Of course this could not go on without causing much heart-burning among the police, the more so, as several letters were received from the Inspector-General calling upon the District Police officers for explanations as to the non-detection of crime This resulted in representations being made by the Superintendent and Assistant Superintendent regarding the obstacles placed in their way at the Sessions Court, and there was a change for the better. The Judge proceeded on leave, and another came to act for him, with the result that large numbers of cases worked up by the police ended in conviction. To show that the police were earnest in their desire to suppress crime, four of their own constables in the Kavali Taluk were arrested by the Superintendent for murder. The facts are as follow:—A man had been arrested on a charge of theft, and had been taken to the station-house where during the night the four policemen mentioned put him to torture in order to extort a confession from him. The torture was carried too far and the man succumbed. The constables carried the body to a tope and suspended it by the neck to the bough of a tree, so as to lead the public to believe that the man had committed suicide, and then came back to the station-house, and made an entry in the crime register that the man had been arrested for theft, but had been discharged for want of sufficient evidence. It was a moonlight night, and they had not reckoned upon the fact that thei:

actions in the tope had been witnessed by a native who promptly brought the matter to the notice of the Superintendent, who arrested the constables, investigated the matter, and sent the men to the Tahsildar for enquiry. It was sought by the defence to show that it was impossible for the witness to have observed their actions from where he was standing, but here the evidence of the Superintendent told against them. He had on two nights in succession, in order to establish the truth, posted himself where the witness had stood, sent some constables to suspend a dummy to the identical tree, and saw for himself that the native had told the absolute truth, and that the actions of the constables could be plainly discerned. The four accused were tried at the Sessions Court, found guilty, and sentenced to transportation for life. An appeal lodged on their behalf in the High Court, proved unsuccessful. In this case, had the police desired it, the matter could have been either entirely hushed up, or the case would have ended in an acquittal of the prisoners, but the crime was brought home to them although they were men of their own Force.

On the permanent Sessions Judge returning from leave, several cases were committed for trial, all of which ended in conviction, and the Police had no more cause for dissatisfaction. I have often been out in the district, and have known men who have been caught sheep-stealing sentenced to 24 hours' imprisonment in the village choultry, by the Grama Munsiff, or Village Magistrate, if the value of the sheep was not over a rupee. In England under the Penal Laws repealed in 1830, a crime of this sort was a capital offence, and many a poor fellow was hung for sheep stealing, and at the time of which I write I remember reading in the English papers of men being sentenced to forteen years' transportation for this offence.

CHAPTER XVI.

Police Work in Nellore.—*(Continued).*

The Collector of the District (James William Ballantine Dykes, Esq.) rode down to the police office one Sunday morning and directed me to go and make enquiries into a case of murder in the town, in the absence of the Superintendent who was out on duty in the district. The Collector had himself seen the bodies of a man and woman lying by the road-side, who were suspected of having been poisoned. It was the first time I had heard of the circumstance, and the Town Inspector being away, the duty of making the necessary enquiries devolved upon me, and this I at once proceeded to do, eliciting the following facts.

A man and his sister belonging to the shepherd caste were reported as having died after eating some cakes supplied to them by one Subba Reddy, the hospital peon, who was a suitor for the hand of the girl. The mother of the two deceased stated that at dusk the previous evening, Subba Reddy had brought some cakes of which both her son and daughter had partaken, and had died the same night after much suffering. But there was also another visitor at the house the same evening, a goldsmith of the name of Subbiah who wasSubbaReddy's rival in the affections of the girl. Subbiah was present when Subba Reddy brought the cakes and called his attention to the fact that he had not brought any sugar to eat the cakes with and offered to go and fetch some, and this he did, but did not return for nearly half an hour. Suspecting that the deceased had died from poisoning, I kept their evacuations and sent particulars to the Zillah Surgeon, who at once held a *post mortem* examination, and gave it as his opinion that arsenic had been administered to them from the effects of which they had died. The stomachs and their contents were sent to the Government Analyst at Madras. I had Subba Reddy's house searched and found that he was doing a good trade in medicines which he had pilfered from the hospital, and among these was found a great quantity of arsenic. I had Subbiah also arrested and his house searched as well, but discovered nothing in the shape of arsenic in it. On showing Subba Reddy the arsenic found in his house in his presence and in the presence of the two witnesses to the search, he denied all knowledge as to what it was. After some further enquiry, I placed both the suspected men together with the usual charge sheet, before the Town Sub-Magistrate, a Brahmin who investigated the case. I was not at all satisfied with the dilatory way in which this officer was conducting the enquiry, for although he made a great show of his desire in the interests of justice to bring the culprits to book, he kept postponing the case from day to day, notwithstanding that I urged him strenuously to commit both prisoners to the Sessions Court on a charge of murder. This he said he would not do in the case of the goldsmith Subbiah, as there was not sufficient evidence against him, and he was accordingly released. When the case against Subba Reddy, whom the Town Sub-Magistrate at length committed to the Sessions Court, finally came on for trial, the Judge on hearing my evidence enquired why Subbiah had not been committed for trial, for he might have been the real prisoner. I informed the Judge that the man had been released by the order of the Town Magistrate against my advice. The Judge thereupon acquitted Subba Reddy and ordered his release. Those present in Court were much surprised and I was disgusted at the turn affairs had assumed after all the trouble I had taken in working up the case, and took an early opportunity of representing the matter in my diary to the Superintendent animadverting in rather strong terms on the conduct of the Town Sub-Magistrate. I also informed the Superintendent that a Native Christian Missionary, who according to the general belief had great influence with the Judge by reason of the friendly manner in which he was received at that gentleman's house, had received presents of jewellery and other valuables from both prisoners for his services in interceding with that officer. As it happened, however, the Superintendent was also on cordial terms with the Judge and mentioned the matter to him privately, asking him in a polite way whether the Missionary had tried to exert his influence on behalf of the prisoners. The Judge admitted that he had attempted to do so, but that he had reprimanded him severely for daring to influence justice on behalf of any prisoners under trial. As for the Town Sub-Magistrate, I was quite convinced that the man was untrustworthy and totally unfit for his office, and in this opinion the Superintendent quite concurred. But he, the Town Sub-Magistrate, had come to the end of his tether, for in another case which came before him for enquiry shortly afterwards, his conduct was so unsatisfactory that the Collector ordered his dismissal from the service. With such men on the bench, cases were often decided as in England in the last century, when a great writer wrote "and rich men buy the law."

Another "cause celebre" which came on for trial before the Sessions Court about this time was a case of torture in order to extort a confession. A gang-robbery had been committed on the Streericottah Island near the Pulicat lake by a number of Yenadis. I must stop here to expl ain that these people are supposed to be the aborigines of this part of the country, and live in small beehive huts with a small hole for a door-way. The huts are scattered in groups all over the district close to the towns and villages. Both males and females are often employed by the well-to-do natives of the Nellore District, to work in their households, also as gardeners, and cultivators, and where high caste Hindus would not permit a Pariah to come near their houses they would readily aecept the services of a Yenadi; with all this, the Yenadis as a class were responsible for most of the cases of serious crime committed in the District. But to proceed with my relation of the details connected with the reputed case of torture. The Police Inspector of the Sooloorpett taluk, an intelligent Brahmin, arrested a Yenadi at Sooloorpett, in connection with the dacoity at Streericottah. The Sub-Magistrate of Sooloorpett who was at dagger's-drawn with the Inspector, on hearing of the arrest, sent word to the Inspector to bring the prisoner before his Court. This the Inspector declined to do on the ground that the dacoity was not committed in his jurisdiction, and that he would send the man for enquiry to Streericottah, which he accordingly did. It happened that Mr. Dykes, the Collector, who had been to Madras, came to Sooloorpett on his way to Nellore just at this time. The Sub-Magistrate reported the circumstances of the case to him, bringing to his notice at the same time the fact that he had been informed that the Inspector and Head Constable had tortured the Yenadi to extort a confession from him, and the Collector, on hearing this, directed that the prisoner should be sent at once from Streericottah and placed before the Sub-Magistrate of Sooloorpett, who would also enquire into the reputed case of torture. The result was such as might have beeu anticipated. The Inspector and Head Constable were committed to the Sessions on a charge of torturing a prisoner in order to extort confession, a most serious crime carrying with it a maximum sentence of seven years' imprisonment. After some delay the Inspector and Head Constable were admitted to heavy bail, while the Yenadi was sent down to Nellore and confined in the Town police station pending the trial. I was in charge of the Town police in addition to my other duties as a Reserve Inspector, and of course saw the man who was said to have been tortured. From the marks on his body it was clear to me that they were not inflicted by hands, sandals, or sticks which the man said had caused the injuries inflicted on him. On the following day, First-class Inspector Frere came from Ongole as a witness in another case of dacoity to be tried at the same Sessions, and on my relating the case of the Yenadi to him, and my opinion as to the strange marks on his body, he expressed a desire to see the man, and we both went to the Town police station. He looked at the marks carefully and asked the man how he had come by them. The Yenadi replied that they were caused by the sandals and hands of the Inspector and Head Constable who had beaten him. Inspector Frere turned to me with surprise, snd asked me if I did not know how the marks were caused. I said I did not, but that I knew for certain they were not the marks of wounds caused by either sandals or hands. "Of course not" said he "those marks have been caused by the application of the juice of the marking nut, which blisters the skin and leaves marks just such as those the man has on him." On hearing this, I wrote to the Superintendent, who was some 30 miles away in the District, telling him all Frere had said, and sent the letter by a constable whom I enjoined to proceed with all haste. The Superintendent came in the next day and wrote to the Zillah Surgeon (Dr. Adams) to come down to the Town Police Station. This Dr. Adams did, and, on hearing what Frere had to say, examined the marks on the Yenadi's body closely. The examination finished, he expressed his opinion that the marks were certainly not caused by blows either from sandals or hands, or even from sticks Both the Doctor and Inspector Frere were requested to attend the Sessions Court the next day when the trial came on. There was a large number of witnesses for the prosecution, and the Court adjourned till the following day after a prolonged sitting, the Judge refusing to allow bail for the accused, who were sent to jail for the night. The trial was continued the next day, and the remaining witnesses for the prosecution were examined, when the Judge who seemingly was convinced that the Inspector and Head Constable were guilty enquired: "Now are there any witnesses for the defence"? Inspector Frere was first called and swore distinctly that the marks were caused by the blistering of the marking nut, and that he had seen similar cases before. Dr. Adams was next called, and after being duly sworn in, stated that he was perfectly convinced the marks were not caused by sandals, hands or sticks but by the action of the juice of the marking nut. The Judge was non-plussed as he had apparently made up his mind to pass a heavy sentence on the accused, and after hearing Dr. Adam's evidence could scarcely speak for a minute. But after pondering for a a short time over what Inspector Frere and Dr. Adam's had said, remarked that the evidence of these witnessess traversed the whole of the statements made by those for the prosecution, and that he had no alternative but to acquit the accused, who were accordingly released.

It was a most fortunate thing for the prisoners that Inspector Frere had come in from Ongole in the nick of time to save them from an undeserved and disgraceful fate. Some years after, the Brahmin Inspector rose to be a Deputy Collector and a valuable servant of the British Government.

CHAPTER XVII.

Police Work in Nellore.—(*Continued*).

A Model Insprctor of Police.

The police department of the present day has doubtless its proportion of indifferent characters in its ranks, although owing to the rigid supervision exercised over the force the proportion is small compared to what it was forty years ago when the department was in its infancy and when as was to be expected, a number of "ne'er-do-wells?" had succeeded in creeping into its ranks. It is not my wish to pillory any official of the department to which I had the honor to belong for nearly seven years, but it is my earnest desire to make this narrative a truthful record of a somewhat eventful life.

With this object in view, it is necessary that I should present the seamy as well as the bright side of Police official life.

In this chapter therefore I shall deal with the exploits of one of these "ne'er do wells" who succeeded in obtaining an appointment in the police when I was at Nellore.

Mr. H—was appointed a 2nd class Inspector by the Inspector General, and posted to the Nellore District, where, owing to his having been an Inspector in the Bombay Town Police Force previously, where he was supposed to have seen a good deal of police work, he was considered by the Superintendent, Captain Aubrey James Fullerton Gordon, an acquisition to the Nellore Police, although Hindustani was the only vernacular he knew. I am afraid no special enquiries were made as to the reason of his leaving the Bombay Town Police, and as subsequent events proved, he turned out anything but the paragon he was expected by his superiors to be. Notwithstanding that he had a cast in one eye, and extremely thin lips, combined with a peculiar unpleasant smile, the Inspector's appearance on the whole was gentlemanly. He was something of a "masher" and used to swagger about the town dressed in the height of fashion, with well starched collar and cuffs and white kid gloves, etc. As Reserve Inspector I soon became acquainted with him and his peculiar idiosyncracies. His educational qualifications were indifferent, and he was unable to write his own diaries, but would obtain the assistance of outsiders to do it for him. When we became more intimate, he told me what capital places the police stations in Bombay were, as aids to the police, for, prisoners could be tortured without anyone outside knowing anything of the matter, and on one occasion he gave me an illustration of one of the methods of torture he used to employ to extort confessions from prisoners. This was to tie a man up by his wrists with a rope and draw him up by means of a pulley fixed to the roof of the lock up, and while hanging in this position, the unfortunate wretch would be rapped continuously with a ruler on the knees and elbow joints, until he confessed, while the torture inflicted could not be observed. By this means, this model Inspector said he had extorted many a confession from prisoners. To this I replied somewhat hotly that I would rather allow cases to go undetected altogether than adopt such means for obtaining a conviction. He answered me with one of his sarcastic smiles and changed the conversation.

In addition to my other duties, I was in charge of the reserve stores which were in a room adjoining the Superintendent's office, and only screened off by a partition wall built half way up to the roof, and I could over-hear anything that was said in the next room. Many an untruth have I heard him tell the Superintendent not only in regard to the cases he had enquired into, but also with regard to the name of the person who wrote his diaries. However detective ability was what was looked for in this gem of the Nellore Police and as he succeeded in obtaining a few convictions, he would probably have been promoted to the rank of a 1st Class Inspector, although possessing no education. He had been sent specially to enquire into a case of murder at a village some thirty miles from Nellore, which took him several days without his obtaining any clue whatever as to the perpetrators, and during his absence, I was deputed to enquire into the case of poisoning mentioned in the preceding chapter, which had occurred in the town. On his return to head-quarters he informed the Superintendent that during his absence another murder had been committed in the station, of which I was totally ignorant, and this was partly true, for I had only heard of the so-called murder after handing over charge to Inspector H—The Assistant Superintendent of Telegraphs, Mr. Saunders, was arrested by this worthy on a charge of having caused the death of his syce by kicking him, and after enquiry, was committed to the High Court at Madras on a charge of "culpable homicide not amounting to murder." While the enquiry was proceeding, I visited H—at his quarters and found him engaged with two or thrse little boys, witnesses in the case, whom he was putting through an examination in regard to their evidence, and whom he detained and fed in his own house to prevent their being got at by the defence. One of these little boys was the son of my cook, Rayappan, who told me that his little boy had not been home for three nights, but that he was looked after all right in the way of food. The case on being brought before the High Court at Madras caused a great sensation. Either Mr. John Bruce Norton or Mr. Mayne, also one of the leaders of the Madras Bar, was engaged for the defence, and the case for the prosecution was literally pulled to pieces, the Counsel showing that the whole evidence for the prosecution was concocted in the Inspector's house where all the witnesses were tutored. He further pointed out that the witnesses were kept in the Inspector's house and were not allowed to go home. This was fatal to the case for the prosecution, and Mr. Saunders was acquitted. Some of the Madras papers commenting very severely on the Inspector's extraordinary methods of conducting his police enquiries, the Superintendent referred the matter for the orders of the Inspector-General who directed him to consult the District Magistrate, and be guided by that Officer. Perhaps because Inspector H—was considered to have erred through excess of zeal, for I can ascribe no other reason for the matter being allowed to drop, the case was consigned to oblivion, and H—went on with his work as usual.

About 12 months after these occurrences, a French Barque, *L'Estelle et Reine* ran aground on a sandbank on the Nellore Coast, near Mypaud, about 14 miles from Nellore. H—was sent out with a number of Police to assist the

Captain and to take charge of the cargo that was being landed. Neither the Captain or crew spoke English, and as none of the police spoke a word of French, conversation could only be maintained by signs. It took some days to unload the vessel, and Inspector H—lived and messed with the commander in the same tent, while they were ashore. When the work of unloading was completed, H—was directed to march all the crew to the travellers' bungalow at Nellore, and from thence on to Madras, where he was to hand over the French sailors to the Master Attendant.

After reaching Nellore the commander of the vessel took up his residence with Mr. Simpson, an Indigo Merchant who spoke the French language fluently, and to whom he mentioned that the Inspector had stolen a lot of the ship's property, and sent it into Nellore, and also attempted to steal his silver mounted pistols. Mr. Simpson at once took the matter up, and along with the Captain went in person and made a report of the circumstances to the Acting Collector and District Magistrate, Mr. Elliot, and a telegram was sent to the Superintendent of Police at Saint Thomas' Mount for the arrest of the Inspector on his arrival at Cochrane's Basin, Madras. On the arrival of the French Captain in Nellore, Head Constable Sheik Suleiman returned with the police who were on duty with him at the wrecked vessel, and stated openly that the Inspector had sent a load of all sorts of ship's stores into Nellore by his horse-keeper, and further he mentioned to me that the Captain had accused the Inspector of stealing his pistols, which, on the Captain seizing him had dropped on the ground, from the inside of the latter's coat.

On hearing these statements from the head constable, I brought the matter to the notice ot the Superintendent who directed a guard to be placed over the house at once, allowiog no one to approach the building which had been left locked by the Inspector. There were two flights of steps leading into the house, and when he was brough back from Madras by the sergeant of police at St. Thomas' Mount, I was waiting at the bottom of them to take charge of him. He however rushed past me, lifted the venetians of his window and moved his hands about with a view to dislodge anything that might be on the window sill inside. This was obviously done with the object of making it to be believed that some one had been inside the house since he had left it. I soon stopped him at this and drew his attention to the fact that his door had still the same lock on it which he had put on, in addition to which there was one put on by order of the District Magistrate. I locked him up for the night, and early next morning had the house searched in his presence as well as those of two or three witnesses. I discovered a miscellaneous assortment of ship's stores, towels, napkins, a ship's axe, knives, forks, spoons, yards of canvas, and other heterogeneous articles, all of which bore the ship's stamp "L'Estelle et Reine." In searching the premises I found also in a tin office box, many rupees worth of native jewellery, besides Promissory Notes, so that he was evidently extremely well off for a man of his position ; but as these had nothing whatever to do with the enquiry in connection with the theft of the ship's stores, I left the valuables alone. As there was no proper accommodation for European prisoners at the police station, he was allowed to remain in his own quarters with a police guard over him, while the enquiry which took several days, was being conducted by the District Magistrate. The enquiry at length concluded, and he was committed to take his trial at the High Court at Madras. The stolen property was properly secured and tied in a large bundle, sealed in the presence of the District Magistrate, handed over to a native head constable who with a party of six men were directed to take charge of it and the prisoner, and proceed with them to Madras next day in a country cart which was provided for the prisoner's accomodation. He would have left next morning but for a circumstance which occurred during the night and temporarily upset the arrangement made. The Inspector as I have already explained was confined in his own quarters in the room in which the stolen property had been found, with a police sentry at the door, who was directed not to lose sight or him. The bundle containing the stolen goods was kept in a detached building with the rest of the Police guard to prevent any one removing or tampering with it. Access could be had to this building by two ways, the fitst by the steps from the outside, and the other by a flight of stairs leading from a small room upstairs, immediately behind the one in which he was confined, and on to a platform below. At day-break next morning one of the police on duty in the detached building came rushing to my quarters and stated that the bundle containing the stolen property had been carried away during the night. I at once proceeded to the spot and found him walking up and down in his room in a quite unconcerned manner, with the sentry at the door The men on duty at the detached building, more especially the head constable, were panic-stricken as the matter involved their being charged with gross neglect of duty. I immedietely sent word to the Superintendent and the District Magistrate as to what had happened, and commenced questioning each individual of the police guard. From the room in which the bundle was kept there was a doorway leading by a flight of steps to the garden below. The bundle it would seem was will right at 10 P M. the previous night, but the head constable apparently fell asleep after that and the duty of relieving the sentries must either have been omitted or performed in a perfunctory manner, *i e.*, without the head constable being aroused to see the reliefs carried out. One constable stated that he had seen a ghost at 12 midnight which went into the room where the bundle was kept, but that he was too terror-stricken to call out On hearing this I was convinced that the robbery was not committed by any person outside, and at once along with the head constablo and others went down the steps and into the garden to search for any traces of the thief. There was a disused well not more than thirty yards from the building close to the garden wall in which it occurred to me the bundle might probably have been thrown. I sent for the grappling irons from the police station, had the well dragged, and brought the bundle up. Meanwhile the Superintendent and District Magistrate had arrived, and the poliee guard were very pleased at having got out of a serious difficulty, inasmuch as they were only punished afterwards departmentally, for neglect of duty. It was clear that the sentry over his door must have fallen asleep and allowed him thus to make his way through the door of his back room on to the flight of steps and into the detached building, while the sentry over the property must also have been sleeping and only awakened when he saw him in his shirt and pyjamas making his way into the building, and thus conceived him to be a ghost The wet bundle was sent to the District Magistrate's Court, unpacked and the articles dried out, after which they were again packed as before and re-sealed in his presence. On the second day following these occurrences, a fresh guard proceeded with the prisoner and the stolen property in a country cart, for Madras, where on arrival he was l dged in Her Majesty's Penitentiary pending trial. Strange as it may seem to my readers, I was told before the trial commenced that he would be acquitted at the High Court. I was informed by one Mr ——who was Postmaster at Nellore and with whom he had boarded and lodged, that he heard that his brother John would form one of the jury at the trial and that he would do his best to get the prisoner off. As a matter of fact he *was* acquitted and one Mr. John——*did* form one of the jury at his trial, although the case for the prosecution was so clear that no one for a moment believed that the prisoner would be acquitted.

So much for the uncertainties of the Law. It was unwritten law that a Police Officer charged with any offence before a Magistrate of which he was found not guilty should not lose his position in Force; and with the object of getting back into the Police, he returned to Nellore and remained there about two months, using all efforts to get reinstated; but the Inspector-General and the Superintendent had had enough of him and he had to retire.

Police Work in Nellore.—(*Continued*).

Mr. John B.

Among the small circle of my acquaintances in Nellore was a Mr. John B., a Mechanical Engineer employed in the P. W. Department Workshops He hailed from Manchester and was one of those good-natured, free and easy individuals, given to over indulgence in spirituous liquors, and was no one's enemy but his own. Cholera had broken out among the convicts at Nellore and they were removed to the cholera camp about four miles from the station. Here they were employed during the day in quarrying stone, and at night were sheltered in tents. At the end of each tent was a large block stone to which chains were fastened, and in order to prevent the convicts from escaping at night, these chains were passed through each man's fetters and effectuatly secured him for the night. B. was engaged on the duty of fixing the chains to the blocks of stone, and it was while so employed that I first made his acquaintance. He was an agreeable companion and it seemed to me a pity that that an otherwise respectable man should be a slave to the drinking habit, and I remonstrated with him about it. But advice on this subject to him was merely a waste of breath. "There is the bottle" he would say "and it must be drunk." A short time after I had come to know him a convict who was found guilty of murder and sentenced to be hanged, was to be executed, but as the old gallows needed repair, he wes sent down to put it in order. Prior to this the duty of superintending the executions of condemned prisoners devolved on District Sessions Judges who were ex-officio Superintendents of district jails. Representations had been made by these officers to Government in which it was pointed out that it was scarcely fitting that a Sessions Judge who had condenmed a man to death, should not only be responsible for his safe custody while awaiting execution, but should also see him executed. As the matter was put somewhat forcibly before Government, orders were issued that executions in future should be carried out under the supervision of the District Magistrate or one of his European Assistants.

Mr. James Burn Pennington, the Assistant Magistrate, who years afterwards attained high rank in the Civil Service, and was well known in Madras, was deputed to superintend the execution, and I, as Reserve Inspector, had to attend to all details connected with the duty, and bring the prisoner from the condemned cell under a police guard to the place of execution. This was usually done in an open cart on which was a chair for the condenmed man to sit upon, while the police guard surrounded him to prevent any attempt at a rescue. On the day before the execution, Mr. Pennington requested me to see that everything was in readinees, and stated that he would be at the gallows next morning when the police arrived with the prisoner, and would give the usual signal for the bolt to be drawn when all was ready. With a view to avoid any contretemps in the arrangements, I proceeded to the gallows during the afternoon to see that every. thing was correct and in readiness. He had been engaged there all day repairing the bolt which would not work smoothly. I mounted to the trap-door by a flight of steps and to my consternation saw one of the coolies standing on it with the rope around his neck. I shouted out to him " Good God ! man, what are you doing ? " and immediately removed the rope from the coolie's neck. No sooner had I done this when the trap door was released and the man disappeared below and came down on the ground with a thud, a distance of eight feet. It was a providential thing for the cooly that I had removed the rope from his neck in the very nick of time, for he certainly would have had his neck broken and been hanged. As it was he was shakea by his fall, although not seriously injured. I was very much annoyed with B who declared that he had done the thing for a lark and that he had only drawn the bolt when he saw me take the rope off the man's neck. But it was a most cruel practical joke and would have ended seriously for him if I had not had the presence of mind to remove the rope from the coolie's neck. Next morning when Mr. Pennington arrived at the gallows everything was in readiness, and we awaited his signal to draw the bolt. But this duty was distasteful to him and at the last moment he asked me to give the signal, which of course I had no hesitation in doing. Lest some of my readers may think lightly of Mr. Pennington for this display of weakness, I should here mention that he was then only a junior officer in the service and had never undertaken a duty of the kind before, moreover there are certain natures so sensitive that they would hisitate to inflict pain on their fellow creatures even at the call of duty. I have known some military officers leave the square formed by the regiment when a man had to be flogged, rather than remain to witness his punishment.

I had seen innumerable executions during my period of military service in Central India, and had grown accustomed to the sight, so that there was nothing very praiseworthy in my not flinching from the duty.

Although it was the first time I had given the signal which sent a fellow creature to his doom, it was by no means the last, for it formed one of my duties afterwards during my service of 27 years in the Jail Department. The affair of B.'s cooly was due to a stupid practical joke; but an accident occurred at the gallows in the Madras Penitentiary facing the People's Park, when I was Keeper, that brought the former occurrence vividly to my memory again. The details of this accident I shall however reserve my narrative. The body the condemned man, when life was found to be extinct, was buried in the bed of the Pennair river which at that time of the year was dry.

One evening I had two or three friends at my house when B. came in for a chat. A dreadful thunder storm came on while we were conversing which rendered it impossible for them to think of going home, and as I had some brandy with me we proceeded to make ourselves comfortable and passed the time away in chatting and singing songs. Cholera was still prevalent in Nellore at the time and our conversation turning to the subject, "he asked me in a jocur way "Should I die will you promise to bury me with a flask of brandy and a bundle of cigars under my head in my coffin," I readily promised, not for a moment imagining that I would soon after be called upon to keep my promise, for he was one of those topers who get more hilarious with every additional glaes they imbibe. He used to tell us how when he was employed in the P. W. D. Workshop, at Madras, he removed the old gates of the Government house, and erected the new iron gates which are to be seen at the present day. Also that he had often been locked up at night for being drunk, but never in the same division, and that he had invariably been let off with a caution by every magistrate he had been brought before. When the storm gave over the party dispersed after we had spent a very agreeable evening.

Shortly after this I was sent out on duty in the district after dacoits, and on the very day I returned to Nellore intelligence was brought to me that B. had shot himself. I at once went off to his bungalow, a small house close to the anicut near the bank of the river, and found that the report was true. The poor fellow was found dead, with a bullet hole through his body. I had a Punchayet assembled and the cause of death enquired into. He had formed a temporary connection with an intelligant native woman who spoke English well, and who stated, that B. had taken his breakfast that morning, and had ordered his bullock coach which was in readiness to take him to work for the day at the Government workshop. She had, she said, put up all his food for the day in his tiffin basket (as he used always to go to work at 7 A. M. and return at 6 o'clock in the evening, and she had taken and placed the basket in the coach, near the door of which she remained standing waiting for him to come out. She had only been there a minute or two when the heard the report of a gun. She rushed in and found him lying on the floor of the house with the discharged gun by his side. The evidence of the woman left no shadow of doubt that the case was one of deliberate suicide. But the reason for the rash act was for some time a mystery. It was at first supposed that he was in pecuniary difficulties but this idea was soon dispelled when it was ascertained that he had about 800 Rupees in his cash box. The District Magistrate was most anxious to find out the cause of his committing the deed; but he was not aware that I had made private enquiries and had elicited the following facts. It would seem that B. was indulging in liquor more freely than usual, and that he had been taken to task and severely reprimanded by his District Engineer. But there was another and still graver cause which upset his mental equilibrium. He expected his wife, a Lancashire woman, out from home, and his connection with the native woman placed him in a terrible dilemma which he could see no way out of. This I believe was really the cause of his taking his own life. I gave orders for the coffin and sent word to the clergyman of the station, the Revd. Mr. Compton of the London Mission, as to what time the funeral would take place, after which, being very much fatigued, I went home to get something to eat, when the promise I had made to him on the night of the thunder-storm came back to my memory. Although the idea of placing brandy and cheroots in a dead man's coffin seemed ridiculous to me, I reflected that a promise to the dead, however absurd it might seem, should always be held sacred, and I accordingly placed a small flask of brandy containing about two drams and a bundle of cheroots under the pillow in his coffin. I followed his remains to the cemetery along with a few others, among whom was a very old Engineer Officer who had joined that very day; but the clergyman failed to put in an appearance. The duty of reading the burial service therefore devolved upon me. The Engineer Officer told me that he was very much annoyed at the clergyman's want of charity in refusing to bury him who could not have been altogether right in his head when he had shot himself.

about two drams and a bundle of cheroots under the pillow in his coffin. I followed his remains to the cemetery along with a few others, among whom was a very old Engineer officer who had joined that very day; but the clergyman failed to put in an appearance. The duty of reading the burial service therefore devolved upon me. The Engineer Officer told me that he was very much annoyed at the clergyman's want of charity in refusing to bury him who could not have been altogether right in his head when he had shot himself.

Cholera was raging in Nellore at this time and 98 prisoners out of a jail population of 500 died of the disease within 10 days. Twice a day the dead (sometime as many as five at a time) used to be conveyed in open jail carts drawn by convicts to the dry bed of the river where they were buried without ceremony. It was part of my duty as Reserve Inspector to visit the jail twice a day and see that the sentries were properly posted and the jail guard all correct. On one of these occasions Dr. Hunter Adams, the Zillah Surgeon, who was also in medical charge of the jail, after going his rounds, appeared with blanched face and harrowed looks and said to me "Good God, I don't know what to do Inspector. Besides the number of deaths, I have got 120 men in hospital which is not large enough to hold one-fourth the number." I told him of a report that I had been reading in an American paper of a similar outbreak which had occurred in an institution in the United States, and how the disease was soon stamped out by the lighting of large bon-fires all over the place. Dr. Adams accepted the suggestion and ordered huge fires to be made in every yard and ward. The result of this sensible proceeding was that the epidemic quickly abated in the jail, there being only one or two fresh cases within its walls, while the disease was prevalent in the town for two months afterwards. I myself spent some money in Dr. Jayne's remedy for cholera and distributed it among the poor Europeans and Eurasians who could not afford to purchase it for themselves, thus saving a few lives. As the reader will see from previous chapters I have had some experience of cholera outbreaks in other parts of India, but in point of severity and virulence the outbreak at Nellere exceeded anything of the kind I had ever seen before or after. It was even worse than that which decimated the left wing of the 43rd regiment on its march from Bangalore to Fort Saint George in March 1857, an account of which I have already given.

CHAPTER XIX.

NELLORE—*(continued)*.

Yenady Moonegadu and a few Dacoities.

I have in a former chapter given an account of the Yenadies and their mode of life, and I stated that alothough they did not strictly speaking belong to the criminal classes they were yet responsible at that period for most of the dacoities and other cases of serious crime which occurred in the Nellore District.

I will now proceed to describe the doings of a member of this class, who made himself notorious in Nellore for the cases of serious crime in which he was concerned.

Yenady Moonegadu lived in his beehive hut on some land belonging to Mr. Smith, the District Munsiff, and within two hundred yards of the latter's house. His occupation ostensibly was that of a gardener to Mr. Smith and as he had two wives he had built a second hut not far away for the younger of them. In appearance he was prepossessing and of good physique, and probably had an admixture of high caste Hindu or Reddy blood in his veins, as he was lighter in complexion than most of his caste. But the criminal instinct which was strong within him, he had probably inherited from his mother's side. The Reddies I should here observe were fine patriarchal looking men while their females were light in colour and generally good looking, and a Reddy most probabaly was Moonegadu's father. The Reddys belonged to the agricultural class of the district and usually occupied the offices of Grama Munsiffs and Kurnams or accountants of the various villages.

The Head Assistant Magistrate, Mr. Pennington, lived in a house, not far from Mr. Smith's and had two or three Yenadies, one of whom was his gardener, living in beehive huts immediately behind his stables.

The majority of the Yenadies were extremely poor and their social condition was only one degree removed from semi-savagery. The men would assemble from the surrounding villages at a given spot, and commit what was called a torch-light robbery by night. They were also daring burglars and notorious for their house-breakings.

In the course of my duty I had occasion to speak to Mr. Smith about Moonegadu, and was informed by that gentleman, that although Moonegadu was a useful man and performed his duties as a gardener very well, he was always absent about the period of the new moon two or three nights in succesion. At this time I was in charge of the town police as well as of the Nellore Taluk police, and my Head Constable in the station was one Ramchandra Rao, an intelligent Brahmin, who spoke English remarkably well. Ramchandra Rao came to my house one night about 12 p.m. when it was raining very hard, aroused me from my sleep, and informed me that he had had intimation of certain burglaries that were about to me committed in the town that very night, and that the house of a milk woman, who lived within a hundred yards of the police station, was to be broken into. Just before Ramchandra Rao's arrival at my house, I had had a strange dream which was shortly verified in a curious manner. I dreamt that, along with a few other police officers I was walking on the high road along the east side of the town where I observed some pools of water out of one of which an alligator crawled out and looked at me. What struck me as curious was that the alligator had Leucoderma all about its mouth. On being called out of my sleep I at once dressed, and went out with the head constable and half a dozen other constables from the police station, to the milk seller's house, to which we made our way quietly in the pouring rain. On enquiring from the woman as to the burglary, we ascertained that the information received by the head constable was quite correct, that she had only been awakened from her sleep half an hour before our arrival by the noise of some burglars trying to break into her house, and that on her calling out she had heard them moving off. The residents of the houses on both sides of hers, she said, were alarmed by the noise, and the burglars had no choice but to take to their heels. There were three or four burglaries in the town just before this, which had given me a lot of trouble, as the police could discover no trace of the perpetrators, and on this particular night also I found it would be of no use to search for the burglars about the town. Accordingly I withdrew the constables to the east side of the town close to Mr. Penningon's house, placing two constables at each of the three different outlets from the town, with orders to remain perfectly quiet as we should probably arrest some of the burglars as they were leaving the town with stolen property, while the head constable and I walked quiety to and fro on the high road not far from Mr. Pennington's house towards the church and although there were some pools of water close by of course no alligators were about, nor was it likely they would be. It was the spot however I had seen in my dream. Just before daybreak from two of the outlets the burglars were making their way out of the town with their booty consisting of large brass utensils, clothes, and other miscellaneous articles they had obtained from the night's depredations, and fortunately two of the robbers were secured, while the remainder escaped into the fields east of the town, and thus evaded arrest for a time. All of these outbreaks were traceable to Yenadies. One of the Yenadies who worked for Mr. Pennington and lived at the back of that gentleman's stables was not at home, his wife stating that he had brought another Yenady with him from a village about four miles off and had not been home since 10 o'clock the previous night. Neither could Moonegadu be found at home when his huts were searched. Both of the men arrested stated that the plot to break into the milk seller's house had been made up by Constable No. 944 who had promised to watch and see they were not disturbed and who was to receive a share of the proceeds of the robbery. His house was visited and his wife informed us that he was on guard at the police office where we next proceeded to. It was daybreak when we reached it and I called him out and told him of the charge made against him. As I felt practically certain of the truth of the accusation, I made the man a prisoner. Strange as it may seem, but here was the alligator of my dream for he had the identical disease of Leucoderma about his motuh that I had seen in my dream on the alligator's mouth. These marks I have seen amongst the natives, but I have never known them to occur on alligators. From further information elicited from the two arrested Yenadies I sent the head constable with four constables and one of the Yenadies to the village of Kankapully four miles from Nellore, where two more of the gang were arrested and a lot of stolen property recoverd. A number of brass water pots were also unearthed from a sandy bed close to Kankapully water channel where they were buried.

I had some trouble in preparing the charge sheets as there were four distinct casses of burglary, two on the night in question and two that had been committed nearly a month before. The said Police constable received two years' rigorous imprisonment, while those of the Yenadies who were proved to have been concerned in all four cases got four years each. The District Magistrate, Mr. Dykes, tried all the cases and was as much pleased as I was at the conviction of such a large number of burglars. Mr. Pennington's gardener was one of those convicted, but there was not sufficient evidence to implicate Moonegadu in these cases and he got off. It was not long after, however, before he was arrested. He was caught red-handed in a serious burglary in a village close to the seaside, tried at the Sessions Court, and sentenced to transportation for life. A few years after I had left the district I was informed that Moonegadu's first wife had been allowed to go out to the Andamans to join him. A Government resolution had been issued allowing convicts after a certain period of good be haviour, to have their wives sent out to them and it was thus that Moonegadu obtained this privilege for his first wife.

Dacoities were still rife in the district, and even close to Nellore, but nothing like a serious torch-light robbery had occurred. Several country carts on their journey from Nellore to Madras were stopped on the road and plundeied, the drivers being stripped of even the small articles of value they had with them. This was about 3 o'clock in the morning, and the robbers had been driven off by some villagers who were living close. I had just come up as the dacoits were being driven off. On the following night a similar thing occurred. About four miles from Nellore some carts had been stopped and the cartmen robbed. These occurrences were too frequent, and I was determined to outwit these daring robbers. Inspector Frere had just come in from Ongole as a witnees in a murder case to be tried at the Sessions, and on my acquainting him of my plan, offered to accompany me. I hired a common country cart with a bamboo matting tilt, and Mr. Frere and I left Nellore as two ordinary travellers. We were of course in plain clothing, but were each provided with a revolver and a loaded gun in the bandy. I had a deputy constable, strong muscular man who also was in plain clothes as the driver, and instructed him to shout out to us if any robbers came out from the low bush on the right hand side, which was the locality from which they usually emerged, and leave the rest to Inspector Frere and himself. The sun had not set and it did not strike either of us that an attack would be made so early. I had directed three other constables also in plain clothes, to proceed like ordinary travellers with bundles on sticks over their shoulders but with their swords wrapped up in clothes. I had started them in advance with instructions to go to the place where the attack had been made on the carts in the morning and to patrol about the spot all night, and that we in the bandy would not go much further, but remain there all night. We were going along slowly while the three men in undress were not more than a hundred yards from us when all at once seven robbers rushed out from the bush and attacked them believing the constable to be *bona fide* travellers, the Deputy Constable Soobiah receiving a nasty blow from a stick on his thumb. They at once drew their swords on seeing which, the robbers bolted knowing that they were not mere travellers. I was mad with rage and disappointment as I knew perfectly well that there was no chance of catching them in the bush. The Superintendent was also very much disgusted at the non-success of our attempt to capture the docoits. Had I kept the three men with me for five minutes longer I should certainly have shot one of the dacoits, if not two ; but it never for a moment struck either Inspector Frere or myself that an attack would be made when the sun was still up. I ascertained afterwards that they were a gang of Dombaravadus who had been committing three offences. They had been camping for some time in a bush about three miles from the high road. At any rate they must have received a severe fright and were probably many miles away next morning, for from that day there were no more dacoities or highway robberies on the high road near Nellore, and this itself was something gained. Not only in this respect, but torch-light robberies were reduced from twenty-eight in 1861 to two in 1866.

CHAPTER XX.

NELLORE—(*continued*).

A curious case of Theft in the District Engineer's Bungalow.

Hitherto I have in recording my experiences of Police work in Nellore confined myself to the purely official side of my duties ; but my readers must not imagine that a police official's life in the districts is one incessant round of work unrelieved by any intervals of relaxation. Of course as in other departments of the service, we had our periods of leisure, but pleasures are few in out-of-the-way places in India, and what we did have, were in a great measure due to our own resources. My chief amusement lay in shooting, and this I usually indulged in on those occasions when my duties took me out into the district. As some of my readers may be as keen sportsmen as I was in my earlier days, I purpose devoting a portion of this chapter to describing the various kinds of Shikar to be obtained in the Nellore District. But I must first enter into an account of the events connected with the case of theft with which I have headed this chapter.

Captain Smith, the District Engineer of Nellore, and (afterwards Coloned Smith, Consulting Engineer for Railways to the Government of Madras) informed me one day that his bungalow had been broken into and a lot of property stolen, among which were a box containing a new suit of Royal Engineer's uniform, and a double barrelled gun. He occupied the house in conjunction with Mr. Beauchamp, an officer of the Revenue survey, and both messed together. He pointed out a window to me from which he thought entrance to the interior of the house had been effected. On examining the premises, I could observe no evidence of the house having been broken into, but on the contrary everything tended to show that it had been broken *out of*, or as I should more correctly say, it was a " blind " on the part of one of the servants to avert suspicion from himself. I was convinced of this when from my enquiry, I elicited the fact that the two butlers, Captain Smith's and Beauchamp's were at enmity with each other. That it was done by one of the two to get the other into trouble, I felt sure. Captain Smith set great store by the lost gun and was most anxious for its recovery, as it was the weapon with which he had shot a tiger in the Woodigiri Taluk under very peculiar circumstances. He was out with his servants and camp followers in the Woodigiri jungle, when he observed a tiger on a pathway about 250 yards from where he stood, but in order to get at the animal, he had to cross a narrow valley. He marked the spot in order that he might recognize it again, the tiger meanwhile standing motionless near a small rock. He then proceeded stealthily to the spot where he had observed the brute, but on reaching it, found the tiger gone. On the following day he again saw the tiger in exactly the same place as before, and again attempted to stalk it, with precisely the same result, the beast had vanished. He therefore had the spot marked off by his lascars by means ot the little flags used in survey work, indicating the spot where he had stood and where the tiger had been seen, and gave the men instructions to signal to him if the animal should leave its position, when next he went after the brute. On the third day the tiger was at his old haunt, and Captain Smith proceeded to stalk him a third time, keeping a watch however for the signals, at the same time, but as none were given by the lascars he felt sure of his game. On reaching the spot, however, to his intense surprise he found the beast had mysteriously vanished for the third time. He turned around to look, and lo ! there was the tiger behind him and within ten paces. The tables had been completely turned—instead of his stalking the tiger, " stripes " was stalking him and was on the point of making a spring, when Captain Smith by a lucky shot planted a bullet between the brute's eyes and killed it on the spot. It was a providential thing, that Captain Smith succeeded in killing the tiger at the first shot, for had he only wounded it, the brute would probably have mauled him to death. The gun was an old fashioned double barrelled muzzle loader, carrying an ounce ball, but it had saved its owner's life, and it was no wonder that he set great store by it. I did my best to recover the stolen property, and had the house of Mr. Beauchamp's butler carefully watched, as from certain indications I felt certain he was the guilty party. Of course, on the first day I had the butler's house thoroughly searched, but had found nothing that would implicate him in the theft. There was a large well in front of this man's house, which I thought it advisable to drag with grappling irons, and this I did a few days afterwards, bringing up at my first attempt, the box containing the uniform and other things, but owing to the time they were in the water the clothes were completely spoiled. On dragging the well again I brought up the double barrelled gun which I discovered to have been nearly filed through at the breach between the two barrels so as to render the weapon useless. It was clear from this, that the theft was committed out of revenge; and not only the two butlers, but some of the other servants were dismissed. There was no evidence, however, obtainable to enable the police to take action against any of them, and the matter had to be dropped.

In different parts of the District, tigers were seen from time to time, and it was not an uncommon thing for an official to meet one suddenly in broad daylight in the course of his journeys through the jungles of the District. A Mr. Dupratt, of the Revenue Survey in the Kavali taluk, saw one in such a manner. He had finished his morning's work and had lain down under the shade of a large tree where he fell asleep. On awakening he was horrified to see a tiger lying down in a bush not far from him. He had no fire arms, and his two lascars had disappeared. Under these circumstances he thought it would be the best thing to escape himself, and this he did by cautiously making his way to the edge of the jungle, whence he made his escape into camp. In the same taluk, a Mr. Middleton also of the Revenue Survey, while riding through a jungle track on his pony, saw a tiger which passed only a few yards in front of him, and gave him a shock which rather unsettled his nerves for a time. In relating the circumstances, he told me that he was not himself again until he had got some distances away from the beast. Even Nellore town was not free from an occasional visit by beasts. A cheetah was killed in a paddy field behind the jail, not however before it had mauled a cooly who died from the effects of his wounds. The jailor and some of his subordinates turned out and succeeded in killing the animal.

Cobras and other venomous snakes were common in Nellore, as indeed they are in other districts in India, and all deaths from this cause were enquired into by the Police. A ryot who was sleeping outside his godown during the hot weather died through having been bitten on the ear by a Cobra—a strange part to be bitten on; but the snake had crawled over his head, and in throwing his hands up, the snake had turned and stung him on the part named. One of

Mr. Pennington's servants also died from the bite of a snake near the sea coast, and another native, who was bitten near the same place by a water snake in a salt water channel, also succumbed. Of course most of my readers know that there are certain kinds of water snakes that are venomous, particularly those that live in salt water. In one case a small viper called in Telugu Kuttiveedian killed a professional snake charmer. This was in Indukurpett, and I was present at the Punchayet which assembled to enquire into the cause of his death. One morning while making my way to Naidu Chuttrum from Sooloorpett, I noticed a small gathering of natives assembled near a hamlet close to the road. A police constable on his rural beat who was with the assembly on observing me came up and reported that a man who had been bitten by a snake was lying dead there. I enquired into the circumstances and found that the man had died the evening before. He was a man of good physique and was a snake catcher by profession. He had seen a field rat make its way into a hole in an ant-hill and went to catch it. He put his hand into the hole and found that there was a cobra in it as well. This aroused his professional instinct at once, and he pulled the reptile out after a little trouble. He seized the snake by the tail with his right hand holding it out at arms length so as to prevent its biting any part of his body, while he passed the left hand down the whole length of the body from the tail so as to grasp its neck and thus render it helpless. In running his left hand down the snake, it bit him on the forefinger. He took no notice of the bite but still held the reptile by the tail, and again ran his left hand down, and was again bitten. He was determined however to secure the snake, and tried again and succeeded in his third attempt. He then placed it in an earthenware pot and, fastened the mouth with a pice of cloth to prevent the snake from escaping, after which he ran off to a tank about two or three hundred yards away to obtain some herbs which these snake catchers believe are an antidote to snake poison. These obtained he returned to the spot where he had left the snake, ground the herbs into a paste and put the latter into his mouth. Soon after however he became unconscious, fell down, and was dead in half an hour. The villagers killed the snake and laid it alongside of the man's body, and when I arrived on the scene, I found them lying within six feet of each other. I must here observe that a single bite from a cobra means death within an hour, and none know this better then the professional snake catchers themselves. It shows the pluck of the poor young fellow that he held on to the reptile in spite of being bitten *twice*, when another man would have dropped it at once and ran for assistance. The unfortunate man evidently believed that the herbs were a specific for snake bite, as, in fact, many natives do even now, but no remedy that I am aware of has yet been discovered for snake venom up to the present day. While on this subject, I may say that the Revd. Clough of the American Baptist mission told me on one occasion that if he should ever have the misfortune to be bitten by a snake, he would, although a total abstainer, get all the brandy he would and drink himself into oblivion, a practice largely obtaining in the United States in cases of bites from venomous snakes, and of proved efficacy he assured me.

Whenever I had occasion to visit Naidupet I always put up with a friend of mine named Mr. Jackman of that place. He kept his poultry, pigeons, etc., in a godown in his compound ; the pigeon cote consisted of earthen chatties imbedded in the mud walls of the room when it was first built, a common practice among pigeon fanciers in India. The first night of my visit a goose had been bitten by a snake, and was found dead next morning, but no trace of the reptile could be found. The carcase of the goose was ordered to be thrown away but my servant Royapen asked for and obtained it. He cooked and ate it and said he enjoyed the flesh. The next morning another goose was found dead and a thorough search being made, a large cobra over five feet long was found coiled up in a pigeon's nest and was promptly despatched. I may say here with regard to my servant's eating a poisoned goose without injury to himself that it is an established fact that snake venom taken internally is innocuous, so long as there is no scrateh or abrasion of the skin in the mouth by which the poison could reach the blood direct.

I once had a narrow escape myself from being bitten by a Kataveedian at Sooloorpett. I had been away on my rounds in the taluk for a week and on my return to my bungalow, I looked for a certain police weekly circular among a bundle of papers lying in the corner when one of these vipers crawled over my hand out of the papers. If it had bitten me I should have known what to do; but the case of one Franklin, a keeper of the light-house on the Nellore coast, near the Streeracotta island, was a much more serious one. He caught one of these snakes and was handling it somewhat carelessly, believing it to be dead, and was in the act of showing it to his children, when it bit him. There was no Medical Officer within fifty miles, and in his ignorance of what remedies to apply, having only recently come out from home, he died within twenty four hours. So far was he from any help that even the coffin to bury him had to be taken by Mr. Jackman from Naidupett, and his body conveyed by boat to Pulicat for burial. He had not been long out from England, and left a wife and several young children to mourn his untimely end

A small headstone to his memory can still be seen close to the back wall of the Pulicat cemetery. Probably it would not be out of place to say here that in this same cemetery there are tombs of black Cuddapah stone erected to the memory of Dutch Governors and others, who lived and moved and had their being, when good Queen Bess was on the throne of England, and the inscriptions on these tombs are quite clear even at the present day.

A large volume could be written on the subject of the death from snake bite alone in India; but this is not within the province of a narrative of this kind.

While on this subject I may say that I have known even the sting of a scorpion cause death, but these cases are rare.

In the Nellore District wild fowl abound. In nearly every village are large tanks which I used to find at certain seasons of the year, teeming with wild duck, teal, mallard, and other descriptions of wild fowl. Except in the large villages where there were Tahsildar's cutcheries, neither beef, or mutton could be obtained, and I had to depend upon my gun to supply my table. Sometimes however I was either too tired, or disinclined to go out shooting. In such cases I invariably employed the village watchman who was usually a Yenady, and keen on sport, giving him my gun and eight rounds and a couple of annas " Baksheesh " to do the needful, and I never failed in getting an ample supply of wild fowl for my table the next day. In one village north of the Pulicat lake I came across a colony of pelicans, a bird which I had never before seen in India. There was a large tank near the village which was very deep, and always full of water, and was teeming with fish. These pelicans had established themselves on some high trees near the tank which was their feeding ground, and were looked upon as a " mascotte " by the villagers. The Village Munsiff entreated me not to shoot any of them as they had been their for many years, and were looked upon with superstitious reverence by the inhabitants, owing to the prosperity of the village having increased since the birds first established themselves in the tank, and said that if I shot any of them, the rest would fly away, and the well-being of the village with them.

The inhabitants of Madras are not aware that within fifty miles of then there is such a colony of pelicans, and that within 75 miles tigers, wild-pigs, and other wild animals can be found. But it is a fact nevertheless, and whoever chooses to pay a visit to the junglers of Venkatagiri will verify my statements for himself. Many a curlew have I shot, both black and white, and I have also seen flamingoes, as well as other acquatic birds, besides bustards, and floricans, the former, *i.e.*, flamingoes and water fowl abound in the Pulicat lake and large tanks; birds were seen which, when standing up, were nearly as tall as a man It was an interesting sight to witness the fllamingoes marching about like soldiers. The big Brahmani duck is in my opinion not worth powder and shot as an edible bird; but for sweetness, tenderness and daintiness give me that queen of wild fowl, the green velvety backed duck, to be found in the Sooloorpett and other tanks. I gave some of these that I had shot to the Revd. Melius of the Hanoverian Mission who was stationed at Naidupett. The reverend gentleman was charmed with them and declared in his peculiar phraseology " Dat dey ver very nice."

CHAPTER XXI.

Transfer from Nellore.

Among the many duties a Reserve Inspector has to perform, not the least important is the conveyance of treasure from the Head-quarters of his District to the Presidency Town, soon after the collection of the revenue. It fell to my lot on three different occasions to go in charge of treasure from Nollore to Madras. The amount was usually over four lakhs of rupees, and I was allowed a guard of one Head Constable, one Deputy Constable and sixteen Constables. We went by road to Krishnapatam, a distance of eighteen miles from Nellore, and thence by canal in boats, until we passed the Streeracottah island and got into the Pulicat lake which we crossed in open boats, and arrived at Pulicat where we again had to proceed by the canal to Madras *via* Ennur. Two large open boats were provided by Government for the conveyance of the treasure, half of which was placed in one of the boats under the charge of the Head Constable with a guard of eight Constables, while I took charge of the rest of the treasure and went with the remainder of the men in the other boat,

On the waste land between the canal and the sea, herds of wild or ownerless cattle can sometimes be seen grazing on the areas where grass is available. These animals were very wild and most dangerous to interfere with. How they originally came on the spot I was unable to ascertain. The Streeracottah island which we had to pass before entering the

Pulicat lake is, as is not generally known, inhabited by a diminutive race of natives, very small in stature and physique. Dr. Short, well known in Madras in connection with his researches in snake poisns, was much interested ethnologically in these people, and recorded the fact that a full grown maiden weighed only thirty-six pounds.

At certain seasons of the year when the Pulicat lake is always full of fish, the mullet during the night will jump into open boats, more especially it there are lights in them, and on the night we crossed, these fish kept jumping into the boats in numbers, a hundred and thirty-two being thus caught in the first boat, while in the one I was in eighty-two of them were captured. It was amusing to watch the constables scrambling for the fish as they jumped into the boats and alighted on the cash chests. Some of these fish were over two pounds in weight and one of the largest I caught as I was lying on my camp cot in the boat, and I had it served up for my breakfast next morning at Ennur. On arriving at Madras, the treasure was handed over to the authorities of the Madras Bank and a receipt for the amount obtained. In 1866, Major Andrew Balmer, the District Superintendent, appointed me Inspector of the Sooloorpett division, and Supervising Inspector of the Venkatagiri division which was in charge of a native Inspector, subject however to my conttol. In my capacity as Supervising Inspector, I had occasion to visit Venkatagiri frequently, and was given by the Rajah an old bungalow near the tank bank to live in during my visits. On the occasion of my first visit to the place I was amused, about an hour after my arrival, to see five or six of the Rajah's retainers headed by a venerable Mahomedan carrying a silver stick or baton of office over his shoulder coming towards me with "dhallies" or trays containing gram and other kinds of grain as presents for me from the Rajah. I asked the old man who these things were for, and was told that the gram was for my horse, and the grain for my servants. I declined of course, but the old man persisted, and said that it would give offence to the Rajah if I refused. I explained to him that I could not do otherwise under the regulations of the Government ; but there would be no objection to my accepting a little fruit or game, if the Rajah would be pleased to send it to me. Three or four days after this, I was surprised to receive a half grown wild boar which the Rajah had shot himself, for my delectation. I accepted the animal with pleasure, and after having a meal of boar the first of the kind I had ever tasted, I pickled the remainder and sent some to my friend, Mr. Jackman. I must here remark that wild boar flesh when properly cooked is very palatable.

While at Venkatagri, I received orders from Major Balmer to investigate and report on the case of a constable who had been dismissed the service on the report of the native Inspector, for shooting a tiger that had been marked down and reserved for the Rajah to shoot. I soon ascertained that there was no foundation for the charge against the constable. The facts were that a beat constable with a loaded gun used to leave Venkatagiri daily, by a pass over the hills for the Cuddapah District which joined the Nellore District at this place. This was to afford protection to native travellers going through the pass which was infested with tigers. There were always a few native travellers daily at the foot of the hills waiting until the constable came up to continue their journey under his protection into the Cuddapah District. The tiger was observed in a nullah about fifty yards from the pass and the constable shot at it, hitting it in the leg. Fortunately for him the ball in striking the bone of the animal's leg, ricochetted into a vital part of its body and killed the beast on the spot. The Superintendent, on my report, reinstated the constable and transferred him to another Taluk. Some time before this, eight carrier bullocks belongng to a party of Yerrakalas, a tribe of Nomads, were killed just above the pass. They had brought skins, tobacco, etc., into Nellore, and exchanged these goods at the sea coast for salt and salt-fish which they were taking back with them to Cuddapah. On reaching the top of the ghat, the bullocks were unloaded and allowed to graze on the hillside, while the men cooked their midday meal and afterwards had their afternoon *siesta*. On getting up to continue their journey, they could not find the eight bullocks for some time, but eventually discovered the animals lying dead some distance away, killed by a tiger or tigers. On one occasion, when I was at Venkatagiri, I camped half way between that place and the ghat at a small artificial tank, with the object of shooting any wild beasts that might come to drink water at the tank during the night. I took up my position under a bush close to the margin, together with two constables and my cook. It was foolish of me to do this, for the tank was surrounded by bushes and there was not the slightest chance of my hitting any animal from the position I occupied, but of course I did not discover this fact till the next morning, after having passed a dreary night. On our way back, we came across some pig, but could not get a shot at them, as the animals were too far away. The Rajah's army consisted of about 300 troops, dressed in the most fantastic style, many in cast off unifroms of the old Company's sepoys, and he used to have a grand review of them once a year. The men were a sight to look at, for I had not seen anything so outrageous as the show these men made on parade, as regards their dress. The Rajah had also some very good elephants on view. He invited me on two occasions to his palace to see him but after reflection I politely declined. There was a controversy between the Rajah of Venkatagiri and the Kalastri Rajah, I believe, over a small piece of land which was practically valueless, except as a shooting ground. The case was tried by the Sessions Judge at Nellore, and there were a great number of witnesses on both sides, including the beat constable and the European Police Inspector at Kalastri. Mr. John Dawson Mayne, Barrister-at-Law of Madras, was the chief counsel for the Rajah of Venkatagiri. A large number of influential people of both districts were interested in the case, and the excitement over it was great. Mr. Mayne travelled in a palkee to Venkatagiri, a mode of conveyance with which he was not accustomed. On his leaving the palace the Rajah's servants brought him I was told large quantities of oranges and other fruit which they kept putting into the palkee at one door as it was going along, while Mr. Mayne who perhaps did not wish to be "crowded" kept throwing the fruit out at the other.

The Station House Officer of the Venkatagiri Police Station came to me one morning, and reported that a woman had drowned herself in a small tank close by, and as the native Inspector was not in Venkatagiri at the time, the duty of making the usual enquiry devolved on me. The woman's body was dragged from the tank which was a few yards from the hut in which she lived, and was that of a young and good looking woman about 22 years of age From the enquiry it was clear that she committed suicide by throwing herself into the tank ; but I was considerably surprised when, on asking who she was, I was told that her husband was in England. This, however, was really the case. The man was cook to ———, an individual who was touring England on behalf of the natives of India, and caused some sensation by his speeches on the subject of the oppression and illtreatment of the natives by the Europeans in India. This man had I belive been head clerk of the Sessions Court at Nellore and had acquired a knowledge of law, besides which he was naturally intelligent and a fluent speaker. I had read some of his speeches in the English papers, and I little dreamt of being brought into contact with him officially and of taking a closer interest in him than he liked. I instituted enquiries and elicited the fact that not only had he been visiting the Venkatagiri Rajah, but the Kalastri and other Rajahs, and natives of influence in the Madras Presidency in an attempt to stir up sedition and revolt against the Government in Southern India, while the sepoy rebellion was going on in Bengal. I also learnt that a craft containing a number of sedition-mongers on board had appeared off the Nellore Coast probably with the object of raising the standard of rebellion in Venkatagiri and other places. Had these Rajahs given way, the consequences to the Madras Presidency, denuded as it was of British troops would probably have led to something serious. I wrote a full account of the man's doings in my diary, and as the matter was one of importance, the Superintendent reported the case in full to the Inspector General who in turn probably brought the circumstance to the notice of Government.

What action was taken on my report I am unable to say, but some three years afterwards when I was keeper of H. M.'s Penitentiary in Madras, the Head Constable of the Jail guard brought me a sealed cover from the Chief Secretary to Government, on opening which I found a warrant for the detention of ——the very man about whose proceedings I had written some years before in Venkatagiri in my police diaries. Of course I had him locked up as he was a State prisoner. When the ship he was coming out in, reached Madras, a Police Officer was in readiness to receive him, instead of the enthusiastic crowds of his countrymen, whom he probably expected would meet him on landing. He was kept but a short time in the Penitentiary, for orders were received from Government for his transfer to the Central Jail at Trichinopoly where he died not long after.

CHAPTER XXII.

Nellore, (*continued*).

My appointment to the Central Jail at Salem.

Those who are interested in the breeding of cattle for agricultural and dairy purposes are aware that the magnificent bulls and milch cows of the Nellore District are not to be surpassed by any of their kind in India at the present day. To none other than Mr. Dykes who was the Collector of the District in 1860, and who took the greatest pains to improve the breed of cattle, is the present excellence of the breed due. This gentleman took apractical interest in the subjcet and organized two large cattle shows during the periodof my service in the district, at which a large sum of money in prizes was sanctioned by Government on his recommendation. I was fortunate enough to obtain a prize at one of these cattle shows for a she-goat which I exhibited, while a friend or mine secured one for the best pony; but nearly all the rest of the prizes were carried off by Reddies. The shows were an unqualified success, and some of the bulls and cows exhibited could scarcely be surpassed by any animals exhibited at agricultural shows in England Mr Dykes did not confine himself to improving the breed of cattle alone, but introduced an improved method of farming among the ryots. For this purpose he obtained the sanction of Government for the purchase of a large number of agricultural implements in England. These were obtained from the firm of Ransome and Sims, Ipswich, and consisted of ploughs and harrows, sowing and drilling machines, etc. With a view to initiating the ryots into the uses of these implements, two of the firm's employes were also brought out at the same time for the purpose of giving the necessary instructions to the cultivators The Chief Secretary to Government, Mr. Sim, who was a friend of Mr. Dykes was much interested in the project, and paid a visit to Nellore for the purpose of seeing what was being done.

Mr. Dykes was a high-souled, kindly-hearted gentleman, who took an interest in the well-being of even the poorest of those whom he ruled in the Nellore District. At Christmas time, there were sports for the Police, as well as for the general public of the town, at which large sums of money were given by him in prizes out of his private purse. and the festivities included a grand dinner to which he invited all the officials of the place, both high and low, not omitting the poor Europeans and Eurasians of the town. The dinner was the most sumptuous ever given in the station, and one to be remembered, especially by the poorer class of the guests whose staple food was mainly rice. Mr. Dykes also dabbled a little in literature, and his work "Salem—a Collectorate" if still in print, will be found worth reading, if any of my readers are fortunate enough in obtaining a copy of the book. I was always reminded of the legend Mahaluxmi," or "The lotus covered tanks" which occurs in the book, whenever I was present at a punchayet held over the body of any unfortunate woman found drowned in any of the tanks in which the lotus grows.

Mr. Dykes had in his Assistant, Mr. Pennington, a most hard-working, and energetic lieutenant, and I am indebted to this Officer for many valuable hints as to the evidence required to ensure conviction in cases which were brought before him for trial, and which would probably have broken down, were it not for his timely advice. Among my immediate superiors, those whom I admired and respected most, not only for their zeal and ablity as police officers, but for the interest they took in the welfare of their subordinates, were Captain Gordon, who left the police for the Jail department, and subsequently died at the Cape; Major Balmer who succeeded him, and afterwards rose to be Acting Commissioner of Police for the town of Madras; Lieut. Highmore who subsequently was Assistant to the Inspector General of Police; and Lieut. Kilgour, afterwards Colonel Kilgour, Deputy Inspector General of Police. Of these last named I was sorry to hear that Lieut. Highmore, who was one of the handsomest men of his time, died in Madras a few years afterwards. Among my own comrades in the Police, those who were much thought of by their superiors were Inspector Frere, who obtained a Deputy Collectorship for his services, and Mr. Snugg; while among the native Inspectors who had distinguished themselves by their good services in the Department, none stands out more clearly in my memory than the Head-quarter's Inspector Appiah, an intelligent and well-educated Brahmin, as also Doraswamy Moodaliar, who afterwards rose to be a Deputy Collector. I should also mention here a friend of mine, Mr. A. Beeson, who on the break-up of the Irrigation Company lost his appointment in that Company, and was on my solicitation appointed to a fifth-class inspectorship by Major Balmer.

Mr. Beeson was originally in the First King's Dragoon Guard from which regiment he had taken his discharge. He was very intelligent, wrote excellent diaries,-and having an aptitude for languages quickly learnt to read and write Telugu and Hindustani. It was not surprising therefore that he was promoted to a fourth-class inspectorship soon after. I left him on my appointment to the Gentral Jail at Salem in 1866 and I heard some years afterwards that he had joined the Jail Department which he subsequently left on obtaining a more lucrative past in the Salt and Abkari Department from which he eventually retired on pension. Mr. Beeson's name is well known to the Madras Public in connection with the Eurasian and Anglo-Indian Assocation of which he was one of the moving spirits and his public speeches advocating the cause of the poor whites and Eurasians were aways interesting and sound I was very sorry to hear of his death about two years ago, for I had only heard from him a short time before he died.

We used sometimes in order to pass away the time, have revolver-shooting competitions amongst overselves, and I always succeeded in acquitting myself creditably at these. I had been a fair shot while in the Army, not only with the old flintlock, but with percussion musket as well, but I should most likely have taken "a back seat" with the long range rifles of the present day. The colts revolver was in use by the Police Officers at Nellore, and I made some very good practice with this weapon. I could break bottles at twenty yards without any difficulty whatever, and on one occasion on a bright moonlight night I shot a pariah dog which was fully sixty yards away from me. The dog had come into my tent and made free with the food in my tiffin basket, and was sixty yards off when I got a shot at him. Although I took deliberate aim at the animal, I think, considering the distance he was from me, there must have been an element of luck in the shot. On another occasion in the day-time, I shot a pariah dog when he was twenty-five yards away. There was nothing remarkable in the shot itself, but the strange part of it was that the animal fell on his knees with his nose to the ground and never moved or struggled in the least from that position. The ball had gone through his brain, and death must have been instantaneous. Lest my readers should think me cruel in needlessly taking the lives of these animals, I should inform them that these village pariah dogs are perfect pests and daring thieves, and in the hot season are a source of danger to the public, for many of them get rabid at this time of the year. For this reason a staff of dog killers is employed in most towns, by the authorities for the destruction of stray and ownerless dogs.

Mr. Smith, the District Munsiff, asked me to sleep at his house one night as he wanted me to shoot a pariah dog which was giving him trouble by running through the house at night. I slept in a room occupied by Mr. Dupratt and another friend, my bed being near the door, while the cot on which Mr. Dupratt and his friend slept, a large double one, was only a yard off. I kept awake for some time watching for the animal which at last came in at the door and was underneath my bed before I could get a shot at him. I fired just as I saw the brute make his way under Mr. Dupratt's bed, and I shall never forget the fright I gave him. He jumped up speechless with terror, with his hair standing on end, until I explained the cause of the explosion and allayed his fears. Mr. Smith I am glad to say was never more troubled with this dog after that. One of my most curious shots however was when I was out in camp after docoits. I had twenty men with me whom I formed into three parties to patrol the different villages during the night, returning in the morning, Captain Gordon had given me the use of his own tent, a commodious double poled one, and besides myself, my Police Orderly, a tall Mussalman, and my cook, Royapen, slept in it. My bed was between the two poles, my head being close to the back wall of the tent, and, as was always my practice I had my revolver under my pillow. The orderly and the cook slept near each other with their legs across the doorway. Something aroused me during night, and on raising myself I saw a dog going in the direction of the tent door from my ration basket. I had received eight loaves of bread from Nellore that day, and jumped up to see if they were all right in the ration basket. I found that the dog had made a hole in the canvas bag in which the loaves were kept, and had completely spoiled three loaves. This filled up the cup of my wrath, and I lay down, drew out my revolver, and waited for the animal to make his appearance again, which I knew he would do when all was quiet and so he did after a little while. It was a bright moonlight night, and I distinctly saw the brute come in at the door and stand with his forefeet between the orderly and cook, looking in my direction to see if I were awake. I slowly raised the pistol, took deliberate aim, and fired. The brute fell down stone dead. It might seem at first a risky thing for me to have done, for I might possibly have hit one of the men had I missed the dog. But the brute was so close that none but a man who had never handled fire-arms in his life could have missed him. The sound of the shot had not awakened either the orderly or cook who slept calmly and peacefully on, for of all sound sleepers the low caste native of India is the champion. Nothing on earth I believe will arouse him once he closes his eyes in slumber, except perhaps a pot of cold water, or a sharp prod with a stick. On getting up in the morning, I saw the dog lying where he fell, across their legs. The orderly's pants and the cook's cloth were saturated with blood. When I aroused them, they were thunder-struck on seeing the state they were in. In 1864, I along with other police officers, and Government servants appeared for the Law and Departmental Examination, which was held that year in the Sessions Court house, and was conducted by Mr. Pennington. The test included a number of subjects, *viz.*, the Penal and Criminal Procedure Codes, the Law of Evidence, the Police Act and Departmental subjects, etc., and each examination paper contained twelve questions. Out of eight-seven inspectors and other candidates who went up for examination in the whole Presidency, I was second in

Law and eleventh in departmental subjects. As to the Penal Code, knowing it as I did almost by heart, I thought I should be able to make a good show in it. But "the best laid plans of mice and men gang aft agley," and to my surprise and disappointment I found that I was below the majority of the candidates who appeared in this subject. I was nevertheless passed by the examiners well to the front.

In August 1866, Captain Gordon who had meanwhile joined the Jail Department, and was Superintendent of the Central Jail at Salem, offered me the post of Jailor under him, stating that although I would at first get Rs. 50 less than I was receiving, the pay of the Jailor, he believed, would be shortly raised, that I would have free quarters near the Jail, and I would also get ten per cent. of net profits on all manufactures turned out in the Jail. I wrote and thanked him for the offer which I accepted. Major Balmer, Captain Gordon's successor expressed his regret at my leaving the Police, but at the same time to prevent a break in my service gave me leave of absence to enable me to join. I had made many friends in Nellore, with whom I was loth to part, but "needs must, etc." I leave my readers to finish the proverb—and so I bade adieu to them and with my family went on towards Madras in a couple of covered bandies. On reaching Naidupett, I stayed with my friend Mr. Jackman, who was at this time a man of some property, and held the lease of some land, part of which was rented to him by the Rajah of Venkatagiri. On his pointing out to me that I would save four days if I journeyed by water across the Pulicat Lake instead of by road through Sooloorpett, I decided to follow his advice, particularly as he said he would arrange to have a boat in readiness for me at the station west of the lake. Accordingly at 2 o'clock in the afternoon, after paying the two bandymen, I got into the boat, alone with my wife and two children, and our baggage, and proceeded to make things as comfortable as I could for them. The boat was a large open one with a tarpaulin awning at the stern to protect us from the weather. We had hardly been an hour on the lake when a thunderstorm burst and the rain came down in torrents. The thunder roared, and the lightning flashed continuosly during the day and up to midnight and was something startling. The boatmen tried to make us as comfortable as they could under the circumstances, but very little could be done in such a storm, and it was 12 o'clock at night when we get into the canal at Pulicat. The storm was then as violent as ever and not only were we drenched, but the clothing in our chest of drawers and trunks was saturated. The storm had passed at daybreak and the sun came out when we arrived at Ennore. We arrived in Madras at 3 o'clock the same afternoon, hired a conveyance, and went on towards the outskirts of Perambore, where Mr. Jackman had two houses, one of which was unocoupied, and which he placed at our disposal. We remained here two days getting our clothes dried, and then took the train for Salem. Nothing particular occurred in the train until we neared our destination, when my son Fred, put his head out of the window, and had a new hat I bought him at Madras, blown off. He roared out to have the train stopped, so that he might get back his new hat. The little fellow knew no better and did not understand why a train could not be stopped like a bandy. On the following day I reported myself to Captain Gordon and assumed charge of my duties as Jailor under him. In concluding my reminiciences of Nellore, I may mention an incident that occurred when visiting the treasury guard one Sunday about mid-day. I picked up about 20 letters close to the Nellore Post Office and the Collector's cutcherry, and on looking up I saw some of the letters between the venetians of the windows of the Collector's office and others were found at the treasury windows, some of the letters should have been despatched up country a month before. Evidently some intrigue was being carried on to get the European Postmaster into disgrace. The Police Superintendent could not understand, how the letters came there and the Superintendent of Post Offices, was in a quandary regarding the matter, but even he could not fix the guilt on the perpetrator. Letters often go astray but the wholesale making away with letters like the above, to get an officer into trouble is seldom met with. This could only have been done by the native subordinates in the Post Office as the Postmaster was the only European there.

CHAPTER XXIII.

Jail Duties at Salem.

When an official is transferred from one department to another, where the routine of duties is different altogether from that with which he was hitherto been accustomed, a certain period must always elapse before he can be accustomed to his new work. Such was my case, but not for any lengthened period, for although never a Jailor before, I had studied the Jail Manual and knew exactly what would be required of me. It was not long therefore before I became thoroughly acquainted with my duties. The Jailor I had relieved was a man without any education whatever and owing chiefly to his deficiency in this respect he did not give satisfaction. Captain Gordon remarked to me that his inability to read and write, and to carry on his duties satisfactorily was more his misfortune than his fault, for otherwise, he was a very good man. For this same reason the old Deputy Jailor's services were dispensed with and a new man, who had been an Inspcetor in the Police Department engaged in the place.

Just before I had joined, the Jail Department was the step child of Government, and languished in the cold shade of official neglect, but a happier era had come, and Government took a warmer interest than it did in the department. As a result, there was a marked improvement in the *personnel*, and much more was expected from the officials than before.

It was for this reason therefore that Captain Gordon wrote and offered me the Jailorship under him. There was no separate Jail for female convicts at Salem at this time, and a building was at once commenced by the Public Works

Department. The building of new quarters was also under taken for the Superintendent, the Jailor, and Deputy Jailor and plans and estimates were in addition made out for the construction of a new hospital for sick prisoners. The out-door convict gangs were in consequence kept very busy making and burning bricks and afterwards carting the material to the sites of the proposed buildings.

The Salem Jail was a second class Central Jail containing 600 prisoners and as it was not an easy matter to find remunerative employment for such a number, I did everything that lay in my power to help the Superintendent in introducing new industries into the Jail. The weaving of various kinds of cloth, iron work, carpentry, and other industries were introduced. Captain Gordon sent me to Bangalore to obtain an insight into carpet weaving, and to engage a maistry and a few hands who understood the work. The Jailor at Bangalore one Mr. Cress, a pensioned Sergeant Major was an old friend of mine and gave me every aid in his power.

He told me of an execution that had just then taken place in the Bangalore Jail, of two men convicted of murder. One of the condemned men who was rather well-to-do asked that he might be hanged with a silken rope for which he was willing to pay. This was of course granted and the condemned man "took silk" for the first time in his life. Mr. Cress kept the silk rope as a curio. On my return to Salem, some of the more intelligent of the convicts were trained, and carpet-weaving was undertaken in real earnest in the Jail. In a few months, several drawing-room carpets were turned out, six of which were sent by Mrs. Gordon to some friends of hers at the Cape, and found a ready sale at a good price. Mr. Longley, the Collector of the District, paid a visit to the jail on one occasion, and purchased some bed-ticking, which he converted into suits for himself. The cloth was stout and strong and made very good working clothes and Mr. Longley was an official who worked as a Briton should work. Colonel John Wilson, the Inspector-General of Jails, a Scotchman by birth also bought a piece of very fine check made of English spun cotton. On my telling him that the price was eight annas a yard, he remarked drily that it was "Vera gude, Mr. Tyrrell, but verra dear." With the advent of all these new industries, the profits on the manufactures as a matter of course rose, which meant an increase to my emoluments. There was a large piece of ground attached to the jail which was used for gardening purposes, and in this also there was a noticeable improvement. In addition to this, two empty plots of ground inside the jail at the back of two of the blocks were sewn with English vegetable seeds, and excellent cabbages, cauliflowers, knol-khol, radishes, etc., were raised in the cold weather.

Salem, like many other places in India, was infested with snakes. Cobras were numerous, and two or three as well as a few scorpions were always discovered and killed in the shed in which the sun-dried bricks were stacked preparatory to their being conveyed to the brick kilns. These reptiles could not be got at until the bottom row of bricks was removed. It is not generally known that the whip snake, called in Hindustani, the *Dhaman*, is believed by the natives to be the female of the cobra, and that its weapon of offence and defence is its tail which it sues by grasping any fixed object by its mouth and swinging the tail about. It is impossible to convince the natives of the absurdity of these notions, for once a native gets an idea of the kind into his head, it becomes with him an article of faith, and wild horses will not be able to drag it from him. Lieut. Irvine, a friend of mine, once came across a quantity of cobra's eggs in an old "*payal*" close to his house. On destroying them he found in each egg a young cobra, hood and all complete. All these could not have been males for every brood must contain its proportion of the sexes, and this goes to prove that there is no difference in the appearance of the male and female cobras. I once found a snake's egg on the road in front of my house. It was soft to the touch, and I knew it could be nothing else than a snake's egg. I size it was not much bigger than a bantam fowl's egg, but a different shape. On opening it with my penknife, out jumped a little snake about seven inches long, and stood erect in a moment, with its tongue darting out and ready to strike. Of course, I am aware that a large snake can coil itself within a comparatively small compass, but it seemed wonderful that one of seven inches in length, and of proportionate thickness, could find room within so minute a space as the egg which it came out of. Moreover, when one considers that it takes years for the higher animals to develope their powers of thought and activity, and that here was a little reptile ready for action and able to take care of itself from the moment of its birth, the mystery of the thing is puzzling. Salem, at this time, was known as a "hanging" district owing to the number of murders committed in it, and a paid hangman was maintained to carry out the executions. This Official I dispensed with, and employed and old native shoemaker who was in for seven years, to do the work. He was paid Rs. 2 for each execution, which sum was placed to this credit and paid him on his discharge. The rope used was of common cotton, and as at Nellore the condemned men were conveyed in an old jail cart drawn by convicts, to the place of execution. There were no local Billingtons and Calcrafts to show how an execution should be carried out scientifically, neither were there Sheriffs and other officers as in England to impress the beholders with the Majesty of the Law, with a captial L. nor was there a Chaplain to administer spiritual consolation to the condemned; but the executions were nevertheless as expeditious and humane as any that could be performed to in the British Isles. The total cost of an execution to Government in the Salem Central Jail was Rs. 2 for the hangman, besides the value of the rope, and a piece of jail wove cloth made into a cap to cover the condemned man's face. At one of the executions, the condemned man who had murdered two people, evidently recognized some one in the crowd who had assembled to see him carried to his execution, and caused some amusement by calling out to his friend to tell (mentioning a man's name) that he would haunt him that night, and seeing others also in the crowd whom he had known, kept shouting out to them the whole way, that he would frighten the life out of some of them that night, until the gallows was reached and his tongue was stilled for ever. Whether his "spook" haunted those he had threatened that morning, I am unable to say. The Jails at this period were guarded by the police, who also furnished the guards for the out-door convict gangs, as well as the escorts which were usually under a police sergeant, for prisoners condemned to death, when the latter were conveyed to the place of execution.

I was much interested when I found, in an old almirah, containing jail records, a bundle of old warrants, many of them of years gone by, when there was a Muhammadan Law officer attached to the Sessions Court of each district, who would deliver his "Futwa" or judgment of the case according as it appeared from the point of view of a Muhammadan Law officer, that is, so far as the Muhammadan Law had a bearing on the case, and the punishment inflicted under that Law, *e.g.*, the loss of an arm would be the equivalent of five or seven years' imprisnment, and so on. The translations of these "Futwas" were not in very good English, but they were interesting as being relics of the earlier days of "John Company Bahadur." The simplicity and directness of the language in some of these "Futwas" was refreshing, but all of them finished up with the formula "but Gcd knows best."

Captain Foord, District Engineer of Salem, and son of Colonel Foord, the Chief Engineer to Government, met with his death about this time under very tragic circumstances. He had been out shooting and was attacked by a bear which was mauling him when he called out to his servant to shoot. The man in his perplexity and excitement fired missing the bear and hitting his master. Before he died poor Captain Foord wrote the circumstances of his death on a small slip of paper exonerating the servant.

Captain Gordon and Lieut. Edgecombe, both since dead and Lieut. Campbell Walker, of the Forest Department, who rose to be the head of his department many years afterwards, had a chat one evening at the brick-kilns near the jail, chiefly regarding the appoaching annual races at Salem, and the preparations that were to be made for the event. This Lieut Campbell Walker, was a great horseman, and lover of the noble sport, and maintained his reputation as such until quite lately, when he was Inspector-General of Forests, Mysore, affer retiring on pension from H. M.'s service. He rode at the Salem races on this occasion, as also did Veterinary Surgeon Shaw who kept a stud of race horses, and was a noted gentleman jockey. Captain Fitzgerald of the 1st King's Dragoon Guards from Bangalore brought down his celebrated horse " Woodman " which won two or three of the principal races, and he would have won the blue ribbon of the meeting also, if the animal had not grown restive and bolted " just before the start was made " with its rider to Siramangalam station, three miles away from the course. I had a pony myself in one of the races which I named " Shut-em-up " and I got a young Eurasian boy to ride for me, and I am glad to say he came out winner. Captain Fitzgerald brought with him to Salem his Soldier-servant, or batman, who had a particularly fine looking bull dog whom he called " Bulger." I took a particular fancy to his animal and induced the owner to part with it to me for Rs. 55, but I will reserve an account of poor Bulger for the next chapter.

CHAPTER XXIV.

JAIL DUTIES AT SALEM—(*Continued*).

Being always a lover of dogs, I took a great delight and interest in my new possession " Bulger " who was a Bull. Mastiff, and turned out as good an animal as I expected. He was admired by all who knew him, not only for his fine looks but also for his good temper and playful disposition. Before he was twelve months old, he had tackled and severely punished a hyæna that used to prowl around my premises. The struggle must have been a severe one, for Bulger received two or three nasty bites from his opponent. I heard the noise of the struggle and went out with my gun. I saw the hyæna which was within range, but owing to some cows I had, being within the line of fire, I was unable to shoot the beast. A month after this, the brute paid my house another visit during the middle of the night, and there was another battle royal between it and "Bulger" who however suffered severely this time, the skin of his left cheek being torn off in the struggle. The wound was a troublesome one to heal, and it took some time before Bulger was himself again. Mr. Irving, the Assistant Magistrate, was anxious to obtain a pup from him, and for this purpose left his bitch "Venus" with me, when going out on "Jummabundi." One of the Railway Officers also left a large handsome bitch with me for the same purpose. Mr. Irving's bitch was a large handsome bull-terrier, with more of the bull than the terrier in its breed, and used to be for hours together hunting for frogs in a pool of water close to my house. So desperately in earnest was she in this chase, that she would actually froth at the mouth after killing the frogs. Not long after this, I saw her hanging on to my horse's head by the animal's nose which she had seized and would not let go, notwithstanding that the horse reared and plunged and tried to shake her off. A week after this, the horse got rabid and commenced biting at his own legs and tearing out pieces of skin from them, until I brought a pistol from inside house and terminated the poor animal's sufferings. I got seriously alarmed after this, and had the bitch chained up, the the more so as I was informed that she had bitten a well bred mare, which also died from the effects of her bite belonging to a Mr. MacFarlane, a gentleman of private means, whose house was close to the jail. Besides this the brute had bitten the bitch the Railway Officer had left with me. I might have shot the animal there and then, but I was unwilling to take this step as its owner, Mr. Irving, was very much attached to it, and the animal, moreover, looking so harmless, and would allow my little daughter a child of ten years, to play with and pull it about, without attempting in the least to do harm. I thought I had chained the brute up securely when a report was made to me while I was busy in the Jail office, that the animal had broken loose, and bitten the conviet maistry who was in charge of the convicts, whose duty it was to bring water to my house in the jail water cart, and had also at tacked my cow and buffalo, I sent the convict maistry to the hospital where his wound was promptly washed and cauterized. It had before this twice bitten Bulger and went for him again but Bulger who was at other times the pluckiest of animals, had evidently a premonition of what would happen to him, and did not wait to make a closer acquaintance with the bitch. I saw him run helter skelter for his very life from the mad beast. My little daughter again laid hold of it and chained it to the leg of my dining table. I now began to be seriously troubled about the brute, and should have locked it up in a godown, but for the fact that it was occupied by the bitch belonging to the Rai!way Officer. Moreover, the animal did not appear to be mad, and made no attempt to bite my daughter, that I decided to let it remain until the return of Mr. Irving who was expected in Salem the following day. I was again at work in the Jail office at five o'clook that evening, when the European Head Sergeant of the guard came in, in hot haste, to tell me that the bitch had come rushing into his house, had jumped on to the bed where his wife was lying ill and had bitten her on the breast. I at once requested the Hospital Dresser to see the woman without delay and then asked the Head Sergrant for particulars. He told me that he had at first mistaken the bitch for Bulger who was always a favorite with him and his wife, but discovered his mistake when it was too late. Directly it had bitten the Head Sergeant's wife, it bolted out of the house, and made its way to the town of Salem nearly two miles away. I ran to my quarters, seized my gun, and went in pursuit. Going into the large compound in which the Collector's Kutcherry and other buildings are located, I ascertained that the beast first run into a Mr. Leonard's house but finding no one in made, for the bungalow occupied by a Mr. DeSouza, a brother of the Consul-General for Portugal at Calcutta. Two cows were standing in front of the house in the act of being milked, and one of these animals it seized by the nose, and bit severely, and then made a dart for the inside of the house. There were some members of the family and visitors in the drawing room when the alarm was given that a mad dog had bitten one of the cows. There was an immediate stampede of the party, while some ran into an inner room for shelter, others clambered on the tables, chairs, etc., and to be out of reach of the animal, which after it had relinquished its hold of the cow came into the drawing room, ran all round, and then went out, and seized the other cow. But it was its last bite, for Mr. DeSouza's servants who had meanwhile armed themeselves with long bamboos, promptly dispatched it. When I arrived on the scene the animal was lying dead close to the front door of the house. The bitch belonging to the Railway officer was taken away before these events occurred. On the recommendation of a friend, I rubbed the wounds Bulger had received with vinegar and salt twice a day, and administerd Cockle's pills to him along with his food. The wounds of the cow and buffalo, I also treated in the same manner with vinegar and salt, and I am glad to say that none of the three animals developed symytoms of rabies. Nether did the convict maistry and the Head Sergeant's wife. The Railway officer's bitch, however, which was one of the first to be bitten, got rabid a few days after, and had to be destroyed. As to the vinegar and salt which I applied to my animals, I am unable to say whether they had any effect in neutralizing the poison in the wounds, but if they did no good at any rate they did no harm. I have often thought over this subject during the thirty four years that have passed since these events happened but have never been able to arrive at any definite conclusion. The facts however afford food for reflection. The first three animals bitten, *viz.*, Mr. MacFarlane's mare, my horse, and the Railway officer's bitch all got rabid and died. Next followed Bulger, then the convict maistry, and the Head Sergeant's wife, and lastly Mr. DeSouza's cows, and not one of these showed any symptoms of hydrophobia. Mr. DeSouza's cows I should observe received no treatment whatever. The obvious conclusion is that a bite from a rabid dog is more dangerous when it is first developing symptoms of rabies and not when it is actually rabid. But this is a subject too deep for the non-professional mind, and can only be treated satisfactorily by the Medical profession to whom I leave it. Some months after these occurrences, I gave Bulger away to a friend of mine, an Inspector in the Madras Town Police, who being pressed for cash, sent the dog to the Madras Stable Company for sale where it was sold for Rs. 80.

The owner of "Venus," Mr. Irving, some years afterwards became Collcetor of Vizagapatam, where he died from wounds inflicted by a cheetah which was killed near the Town, and which he had shot, but had not wounded mortally. About this period, Deputy Surgeon-General Short was Superintendent of Vaccination in the Madras Presidency, and was engaged in his researches in connection with the attempt to discover an antidote for snake poison, as the Rajah of Travancore had offered a large reward to any person who could cure snake bite. Dr. Short always had a large stock of cobras and other snakes with him, which he used to handle fearlessly. His practice was to get pariah dogs bitten by snakes, and then experiment with the remedies brought to him by those persons who professed to have discovered an antidote for snake poison. The results of these experiments he used to have published in the "Madras Mail." I worte to him on two or three ocoasions and sent him some roots which the natives positively assured me were certain cures for snake bite, although I had no faith in them myself. I also sent him two bottles of Perry Davis's "Pain Killer" which I knew to be a sure remedy for scorpion stings, etc., and which I had tried on a Eurasian employed at the stone quarries at Nellore, who had been bitten on one of his fingers by a Kattiveedian (a small viper). I had made him rub the wound continuously with the stuff, and administered a dose or two of it internally as well—and as he had recovered I thought it might prove of some use to Dr. Short, if I sent some to him. Shortly afterwards a letter from him appeared in the "Madras Mail" stating the several experiments he had made and the remedies he had used, none of which however proved of any avail as the dogs had died within an hour or so—(mentioning the actual time in each case)—of being bitten. He concluded by saying, that he had tried the remedy I had sent him from Salem, and as it was getting late and the dog was still alive he had had it tied to a tree for the night, with a view to making a fresh experiment the next day.

A few days after this a further letter from Dr. Short appeared in the "Mail" stating that the dog referred to had escaped during the night, but that he had experimented with the remedy on two other dogs, and that both had died, one within two and the other within three hours. The remedy employed was "Perry Davis's Pain Killer," applied both externally and internally. Although it was shown to be of no use in the case of cobra poison, the remedy I firmly believe could be successfully employed in the case of bites of the smaller varieties of venomous snakes. Even the American notion of swallowing large doses of spirits, which the Revd. Clough told me of at Nellore would, I think, be of benefit in such cases. Had Mr. Franklin the Light House keeper on the Nellore Coast, of whom I have made mention in a former chapter, as having been bitten through the careless handling of a Kattiveedian, had used either of these remedies, a tomb to his memory would not now be standing in the Pulicat Churchyard inasmuch as death from the bites of such snakes does not take place till the lapse of 24 hours or more.

I shall conclude this chapter by remarking that although no direct remedy for cobra poison was discovered, Dr. Short proved it very clearly that potash neutralized snake poison of all kinds, for example, he would inject a solution of the poison and the potash combined into a chicken or fowl, and would find that the poison had no effect whatever on the bird, whereas a minute dose of the poison alone would kill it in a few minutes. The great obstacle however he found in administering the antidote was the rapidity with which the poison took effect, and the difficulty of injecting the potash into the system quick enough to neutraliz the poison. Even if this difficulty could have been surmounted, the discovery would have been of no practical benefit to the millions in India, for only in large towns where Medical aid is easily procurable, can such remedies be administered in time to save life.

CHAPTER XXV.

Jail Duties at Salem—(*Continued.*)

By this time I had become thoroughly initiated into all the duties connected with the administration of a jail in India. The life of a jail official, however, I found somewhat hum-drum, compared with what it was in the Police Department, otherwise there was nothing to complain of in the change.

Sometimes, though very rarely, escapes of prisoners would occur which would cause a little stir and excitement among the jail officials, but beyond this the life was uneventful. Some prisoners escaped one evening under rather peculiar circumstances and were the means of getting the guard whose duty it was to watch them into trouble. I have explained in a preceding chapter that the jail guard was furnished by the Police whose duty it was also to guard the convict gangs employed on extra-mural labour. There was some difficulty in obtaining water for the prisoners, more especially for bathing purposes, and for this reason the convicts used to be marched under Police guards morning and evening, to a small stream that ran about a quarter of a mile to the east of the jail. As however all the prisoners, in accordance with the practice then in vogue were heavily fettered, there was not much chance of their escaping, although some three or four hundred convicts would be taken out at one time. There was however another gang of convicts called the "scavenger gang" whose duty it was to remove the night-soil from the jail and bury it in pits near the jungle which was about three-quarters of a mile from the jail building, in the direction of the Shevaroy Hills. There was a narrow jungle track with thick bush on each side, leading from the stream to the locality where the nigh-soil was buried. The scavenger gang consisted of thirty-six low caste convicts, and a good many of them were Yerrakalus, a jungle tribe, who were mostly in for long periods. The night-soil was removed both in large urinals, or tubs with handles to them, through which would be run a long bamboo and the urinal lifted thus on the shoulders of the men, two being allotted to each urinal, and in earthenware chatties carried on the head and shoulders of each man with a "cumbly" hood to protect him from being soiled. It usually took several trips each day before the whole of the previous night's accumulations could be removed.

The Police guard whose duty it was to accompany these thirty-six men, consisted of one Deputy Head Constable, and six constables posted as follows :—one constable at the head of the gang, one or two on either flank, and the remainder in the rear. Each constable had his musket loaded with ball, and his bayonet fixed, ready for any emergency. One Sunday when no officials were about to notice any breach of rules or neglect of duty, the Deputy Head Constable who was in command of the guard which accompained the scavenger gang to the night-soil pits and back, thought there would be no harm, if he took it easy for a while and accordingly rested himself under the shade of a tree on the way, while the party went on. His example was immediately followed by all the other constables except the one at the head of the gang, the party, however, returning each time corrrectly to the jail, with the convicts and guard in their respective places. This went on for three or four trips without any incident. The neglect of the deputy head constable and his men had however given the Yerrakalus the idea of effecting their escape, and they seized the opportunity when the last trip was made, that is towards the evening. Seeing that the only constable with the party as they neared the pits was the one at the head of the gang, one of the convicts roughly snatched the constable's musket from him, while another poured the contents of his chatty over the unfortunate man's head, thus addding insult to injury. Eight of the convicts, all of them Yerrakalus, then made their escape into the jungle, throwing the musket away after they had proceeded a short distance. The other twenty-eight remained passive and made no attempt at escape. The alarm of course was given, and the deputy head constable and his five satellites who were taking their case a quarter of a mile off came hurrying up. But it was too late, for the birds had already flown, and it was hopeless to think of tracing them in the jungle after darkness had set in. So they returned back crest-fallen with the remainder of the gang to the jail. I was in the office, which was at the entrance of the jail, when the party came up, and the Deputy Head Constable duly reported the escape of the eight Yerrakalus. The constable who had his musket snatched from him was in a pitiable state owing to his unnatural *douche*, and loudly proclaimed his innocence. It was clear he was in no way to blame for the escape. Next morning the District Superintendent of Police came to the jail, along with the Suprintendent of the Jail, and a full enquiry was made into the matter. Each constabe of the guard, as well as some of the convicts in the scavenger gang, was examined separately, and their evidence taken, after which the District Superintendent of Police made the whole of the scavenger guard prisoners, except the constable who was in front of a the gang, and who was declared to be free from all blame. This individual to prove his innocence the more clearly appeared in the same suit he wore when he had received his involuntary baptism of filth, the previous evening. As his presence introduced a new and disagreeable element into the atmosphere which was not there before, the unfortunate man was told to keep at a distance, and I could not help smiling at Captain Gordon's saying to him "get out of the way, there is no doubt *you* were present." The deputy constable and the five constables, through whose neglect the eight convicts had effected their escape were tried by the European Magistrate and were sentenced, the first to six months, and the others to four months' rigorous imprisonment each. Information of the escape, with descriptions of the men, having been sent to all the surrounding Police stations, seven of the eight Yerrakalus were recaptured within a few days, while the eighth man was caught about three months afterwards.

Captain Gordon about this time had contracted a bad cold which settled on his lungs and seriously affected them. He was therefore compelled, on the advice of the Medical Officer to take twelve month's leave on medical certificate to the Cape which was before the opening of the Suez Canal and the days of quick passages between India and Europe, the recuperating ground for invalid officers from India. Captain Liardet, a friend of Captain Gordon's, acted as Superintendent of the Jail on the latter's departure, and I recall the fact with much satisfaction that I received the greatest kindness and consideration at this officer's hands. He was frequently engaged in carving the heads of walking canes of which he always had a selection on hand, and these when completed he would present to his friends. I was the recipient of one or two of these canes myself. He was very fond of Salem mangoes which are noted all over the Madras Presidency, and in some parts of the Bombay Presidency also, for their excellent quality and flavour. He retired from the service many years ago with the rank of Colonel, and is now residing at Ootacamund where I am glad to hear he is still hale and hearty and likely to live to a green old age. I have seen his name appear several times in the *Madras Mail* in connection with sporting events at Ooty.

I had been in Salem for two years and three months, and I saw no prospect of the increase of pay which Captain Gordon believed I would receive when he first offered me the post. This was no fault on the port of Captain Gordon, for he fully believed what he said when he wrote to me at Nellore. Before he left, however, he told me in a friendly way, that I should never get, in the Salem Jail, the salary I had received in the Police Department, and he offered to give me a letter to his cousin, Mr. James Gordon, who was on the staff of His Excellency the Viceroy at Calcutta, who, he was sure, would do something for me. After giving full consideration to what Captain Gordon had said and the kind offer he had made I decided to act upon his advice, and proceed to Calcutta where I thought I would do better than anywhere else, and I accordingly sent in my resignation. On reaching Madras I saw Major Tennant whom I knew as Deputy Inspector-General of Police, and who was at this time Acting Commissioner of Police, for the Town of Madras. This gentleman advised me not to go on to Calcutta, but to take up a post in the Town Police, which was then vacant and which he kindly offered me. On the principle of going father and faring worse I accepted the offer, although I had no reason to doubt that Mr. James Gordon, afterwards Sir James Gordon and Resident in Mysore, would have done something for me for the sake of his cousin. Sometime after Captain Gordon's departure, Mrs. Gordon wrote to me a very kind letter from the Cape giving particulars of her husband's death. He was thought to be improving, and his lungs were getting stronger, when he went out one day on a shooting excursion. Shortly after his return home, however he broke a blood vessel and died within an hour or two. Mrs. Gordon, who was a sister of Colonel Cloete, Inspector-General of Police, Madras, and of Colonel Josiah Cloete of the Revenue Survey, about two years afterwards married a General officer. Another sister married Mr. Elliot who died in harness as Civil and Sessions Judge of Salem. This Mr. Elliot was a son of the well known head of the Madras City Police, who, as was then the practice, exercised the powers of a Judge in civil cases in addition to his police duties.

To return however to Mr. Elliot junior, I felt very sorry when I heard of his death, as I had known him both when he was acting Collector and afterwards Sessions Judge of Vellore and latterly as Civil and Sessions Judge of Salem. I weighed him in the jail office not long before he died and he weighed exactly fifteen stone, although he was not more then 5 feet 6 inches in height. He was of a ruddy complexion and was the picture of health, and I little thought to hear of his dying so soon. But a European of his weight runs great risk in a hot place like Salem, for he went off very suddenly. Before closing this account of my experiences of jail life in Salem, I should like to say a few words about the place and some of its residents. Mr. Dykes in his work "Salem—a Collectorate" makes mention of the "Fisher" family. The first Mr. Fisher owned a large tract of land in the district, and was, as a matter of fact, known as the Salem Zemindar, and his method of management of his property is very highly commended in Mr. Dykes' book. Some of Mrs. Fisher's descendants are, I believe, in Salem at the present day, a daughter having married the Revd. Foulkes of the Madras establishment. The mangoes from this lady's garden were so highly esteemed for their excellence, that fruit merchants from Bombay would send for them for the Bombay market. There are many ways of eating mangoes, but I could not help smiling at what Captain Gordon declared to be the best way of enjoying the fruit. This was, he said to get into a bath tub full of water, have a quantity of mongoes in the tub with you, and *there* you were as happy as possible. Very good hunting knives and spear heads for pig sticking used to be made in Salem, chiefly by Arnachellum, whose staff was patronized by all gentlemen Shikarees, and who did a very good business in his time.

During my stay there, Salem had an evil reputation for its outbreaks of cholera which made sad havoc on two occasions among the jail population.

As to shooting, tigers, bears, hyænas and other wild animals are numerous in the Shevaroy Hills which should, I think, afford good sport for those who prefer big game shooting. The sides of these hills are dotted with coffee plantations, and there used to be frequent visitors to the hills from Madras. Oranges and pears are plentiful but of indefferent quality. There was residing in the Shevaroy Hills at this period an old Missionary, who was styled a Bishop, and who was said to have Swedenborgian veiws, for, although his children would be dying of fever, he would never administer any medicines to them, but believed only in prayer and the laying on of hands. Unfortunately for him, this did not prevent deaths in his family from fever.

CHAPTER XXVI.

Police Duties in the City of Madras.

After entering the Madras City Police, I was appointed to the Chintadripetta Division, *vice* Inspector Burghall who had been granted three months' leave. Major Tennant informed me that the work of the Division was in a backward state and asked me to use my best efforts to bring it into better order.

On taking over charge, I found it even worse then I expected, but during the three months of my tenure of office, I succeeded in evolving order out of the chaos that existed in the Division, particularly in the clerical portions of the work. Inspector Burghall, like two or three other Inspectors, used to employ a writer on small pay to do the clerical work and as a result, the registers, etc., were not maintained properly, and some undetected cases were omitted. I soon rectified all this and succeeded also in detecting a few burglaries, and other crimes that had been committed in the Division. On relinquishing charge of the Chintadrapetta Division, I was appointed to B. Division in the room of Inspector Taylor who had got into trouble. This Inspector Taylor was a well known character in Madras at the time, and was nicknamed "Tiger Taylor" owing to his masquerading as a "Tiger" during the Mohurram festival, in his youthful days. He was very strong athletic man and had a thorough acquaintance with the Vernaculars, especially with Hindustani. This, combined with natural detective ability, enabled him in the guise of a Mussulman, to detect and bring home some rather intricate cases of crime. Mr. T. G Clarke was the Senior Magistrate in the Town, and had for his colleague, Mr. Richard Powney Campbell. My duties brought me into contact frequently with both these officers, with whom I am glad to say I was on excellent terms. Mr. James Ansell was Deputy Commissioner of Police, and although very good to his subordinates, his knowledge of law was inadequate for an officer of his position. It was my duty to place all prisoners and charge sheets before him at his office, which was then located on the bottom floor of the Magistrate's Court, and as I had been in the Mofussil Police, he assumed that I possessed very little knowledge as to how police wrok was conducted in Madras. I was very busy one morning, and in addition to other work, I made out three charge sheets appertaining to three different prisoners. He read them over attentively, and then remarked to me that I had charged the prisoners under wrong sections of the Code, directing me to alter the sections to others which he named. I accordingly made out fresh charge sheets in accordance with his instructions, although I knew perfectly well he was in error ; but on placing the prisoners and the fresh charge sheets before Mr. Clarke, he remarked to me, after reading the charges "I thought you knew the law but here you have charged the prisoners under wrong sections of the Code." He then directed me to charge them under the very sections I had previously done. I explained to him how I had already done this, but was over-ruled by the Deputy Commissioner of Police, who directed me to make out the charge sheets in the manner I had placed them before the Court. Mr. Clarke smiled at this and said he would alter the sheets, which he immediately did, convicting all the prisoners.

While in charge of the B. Division, the Editor of the *Madras Mail* Mr. (afterwards Sir Charles) Lawson sent for me and reported that a peon of his had absconded with Rs. 500 which sum he had been entrusted with to deliver to Messrs. Binny and Co. The peon it appears was sent with the money some hours before, and as he had not returned, Mr. Lawson's suspicions were aroused, and he sent word to Messrs. Binny and Co. to enquire from them as to whether they had received the amount. On their replying that they had neither seen the man, or the money, Mr. Lawson sent for me. I at once set to work to trace the missing man, and with the assistance of two or three constables found him sleeping, or pretending to do so, in the verandah of a house close to Partharasarthy, the Liquor Seller's Shop, which was situated midway between the *Mail* Office and Messrs. Binny and Co.'s premises. He pretended to have been drugged, and we had to shake him up a little before he could be made to answer any questions. He then stated that he had met a man whom he thought he knew, who had given him some sweetmeats, after eating which he was suddenly attacked with giddiness, and had laid down where the police had found him. This story was so palpably false that I made him a prisoner and locked him up in the B. Division Police Station which was then situated on the Beach. On making enquiries, I discovered that the peon on receiving the money instead of proceeding straight to Messrs. Binny's made for his house, a small one situated in Rayapurm, where he had buried the amount in a hole near the back of his compound. He had been seen by some persons near his hut during that afternoon, and I accordingly searched his premises, and unearthed the money from the place in which it was buried. The bag containing it was intact, and I was thus able to restore the full amount to Mr. Lawson, without the loss of a single rupee. For this little escapade the peon got a term of either six or nine months' imprisonment.

About this time one of my most unpleasant duties was to go my rounds at night, owing to the vile smells emitted by the drains. If one place was worse then the rest, it was the locality known as Munnady, where the atmosphere was so thick with all kinds of abominations, that, a Yankee chief constable of my division once remaked to me, if one were to put his stick up it would stick in it. It was even wrose when the main sewer north of the Fort, known as "Kelly's folly" was opened for the purpose of being flushed, for the chief character of the atmosphere then was *filth*. I always respect a strong smell, for it possesses a subtle power which commands one's immediate attention, and the stronger it is the more I respect it, so much so that I always keep a respectable distance from it if I can. On these occasions, therefore, when this drain was opened, I always took good care to keep windward of it until it was again closed. I heard of two or three Commissioned Officers residing in the Fort speaking about the matter to the first Bishop Fennelly, when the latter chaffingly replied that he did not think there was any harm in the smell, but that on the whole he rather enjoyed it. During my nightly rounds many a best constable came to grief through being found asleep coiled up in some verandah. The Commissioner always dismissed these men when they were brought before him. He was glad when such offiences were brought to light, as it kept the police on the alert, and such reports were rare before.

Madras of the times I am writing, was not what it is now. It was a wretched looking place for a Presidency Town, and did not contain, scarcely, a single building worthy of mention.

Just before leaving the Police a second time to join the Jail Department, I was standing one Sunday morning at the entrance to Popham's Broadway, when a Corporal of Artillery came up and asked me if I were the Inspector of Police, and on my answering him in the affirmative he stated that a murder had just been committed in the old Artillery bomb proo barracks in the Fort. I at once called for a coach, and telling him to jump in, proceeded to the scene of the murder, where I made the necessary enquiries and took down the depositions of those who had witnessed the deed. A man, by the name of Rogers, had been stabbed to death by a comrade, named Gimson, with whom he had had a quarrel the previous day at a cricket match on the island. There was another altercation at breakfast on the morning of the murder, and Gimson had made use of an offensive epithet to Rogers which the latter resented by reaching over across the table to where Gimson was seated opposite, and slapping him with his open hand. Gimson then rushed savagely at Rogers with his knife, and they were locked together for a few seconds in a deadly struggle, when Rogers fell stabbed to the heart. I called for the knife which some one said had been taken away by the Medical Officer, and this gentleman coming into the barrack room while I was speaking, handed it to me. Ascertaining that Gimson was a prisoner in the guard room, I went to the sergeant of the guard and took the prisoner into my custody. My coach was standing outside the railings close by, and while I was taking him acrcss from the guard room, the prisoner shouted out to a number of his comrades who had assembled in the verandah of the barrack room to see him taken away "I have just put an end to him, and I would do it again if I had the chance." This was very worst thing he could have said to prejudice his case. I locked him up in the old Justice's Jail in the rear of the old Madras Market. He spoke not a word on the way, but just before he was locked up he broke out again with "I am glad I killed him. I would do it again if I had the chance." He was sullen and inclined to give trouble, not liking to be locked up, but as I had two or three Police Constables behind me he had no alternative but to submit. I sent a report of the case at once to Major Drever the Commissioner of Police, who had just returned from Eng-

and. The following morning, Gimson, together with other prisoners, was marched to B Division Police Station, where I made out a charge sheet against him, charging him with murder. The case was investigated by Mr. Compbell who, after a somewhat lengthened enquiry, committed the prisoner to the High Court on two separate charges, viz., "culpable homicide amounting to murder" and "culpable homicide not amounting to murder." The prisoner was lodged in the Penitentiary pending his trial. On the day of Gimson's arrest I had his victim's body conveyed to the "Mortuary" in the General Hospital where a "post mortem" examination over it was held in the evening. Before sending the body away, I saw no less than three stabs on it, all of which had penetrated the flesh, while I counted on it less then four other rents, or seven in all, in his flannel shirt through which the knife had gone without touching the body. The evidence of the Medical Officer who performed the "post morten," when the case was being enquired into by Mr. Campbell, was to the effect, that death was due to one of the stabs of the knife going through the murdered man's heart. My evidence was of great length as I was obliged to mention every particular that had come under my notice. A few days after these occurrences, I was appointed Keeper of Her Majesty's Penitentiary when Mr. Willie Grant who was then only a Solicitor, paid a visit to the Jail with the view of obtaining permission to see the prisoner, on behelf of Mr. Miller, Barrister-at-Law who had taken up the case for the defence. I directed a warder to take Mr. Grant to Gimson with whom he was closeted for about three-quarters of an hour, arranging the line of defence. I was just outside the front gate when Mr. Grant came out and I expressed a hope that he had received all instructions from the prisoner. He replied "yes ! but the case is a very bad one. However we'll get him off the capital charge. The worst part of it is the evidence of the Police Inspector who arrested the prisoner, but I think Miller will pull him to pieces at the High Court." I was tickled at this and remarked to him "Look here Mr. Grant, I am the Police Inspector you mention, I have spoken the truth and I can speak it again, no matter who examines me." He was taken aback at this and answered "Good God, I didn't know it was you, or I should, not have opened my mouth. I shall take care to leave you alone." I could have made it worse for the prisoner, for, although in my evidence I mentioned the words he had used to his comrades when being taken from the guard room to my coach, I remained silent as to his vindictive outburst when I was locking him up in the old Justice's Jail. Chief Justice Sir Colley Scotland was the presiding Judge, and at the trial I was let down very lightly by Mr. Miller who had evidently had his cue from Mr. Grant, and forebore asking me many questions. In addressing the jury, however, he reminded them of what the Inspector had said, and how they all knew that the Police would do their utmost to obtain a conviction. But this was mere bluster, and I doubt if it convinced either judge or jury, for if there was anything wrong at all in the evidence for the prosecution, it was the duty of the Counsel for the defence to probe it, and this, Mr. Miller had failed to do when I was being examined. Gimson after a lengthy trial was found guilty of culpable homicide not amounting to murder, and sentenced to 10 years' penal servitude, a punishment which every one said he richly deserved, but my readers will hear something more of Gimson before his long sentence expired for he was a man of a very bad temper.

CHAPTER XXVII.

Jail Duties in the Madras Penitentiary.

There are certain days in every man's life, which stand out from others in that they mark the opening of a new and possibly a more promising chapter in his career. Such was the day I assumed charge of my new duties as keeper of Her Majesty's Penitentiary, for I thus obtained the first step to higher and more lucrative posts in the Jail Department. I took charge of my new office in October 1869, but my appointment caused a great deal of jealousy among the Inspectors in the Madras Town Police, as the pay and perquisites of my new appointment were higher then those of a First-class Inspector, viz., Pay Rs. 200 with Rs. 15 horse allowance, ten per cent. of the net profits on Jail manufactures, and free quarters. There was great soreness also when I was first appointed an Inspector in the Town Police, as myself and Inspector S. Simpson also from the Mofussil Police were the only two European Inspectors who had passed the Examination in Law and the Police Test. But I had my work cut out for me, for the Jail was in a fearful state of corruption and irregularity. Major Tennant, who was at the time Acting Commissioner of Police, and *Ex-officio* Superintendent of the Jail, had informed Major Drever, when handing over charge to the latter officer, that unless the then keeper was compelled to resign it would be a hopeless task to get the Jail in order. As a matter of fact, this individual had had no claim on the Government when he was appointed, for he had no previous service under the State. Major Drever after consulting Lord Napier of Murchiston, the Governor of Madras, sent word to me to wait on him at the Madras Club, where he was staying. On seeing him, he told me that owing to the very high account that Major Tennant had given of me he had decided to appoint me keeper of the Penitentiary, and accordingly issued the necessary orders. The old keeper was granted seven days' leave, on the expiry of which he sent in his resignation, and the Penitentiary knew him no more.

Meanwhile I was directed to take charge at once, and make out a complete inventory of all stock, manufactures, etc., in the Jail, as no stock-book had been previously maintained. Major Tennant, who had after giving over charge to Major Drever, joined his substantive appointment, viz., Deputy Inspector-General of Police, Northern Range, wrote to me sometime afterwards from Vizagapatam, saying, that my appointment as keeper was a benefit to the State.

My new office was by no means a bed of roses, for even all my European subordinates with one honorable exception were working against me. Plotting was rife not only among my subordinates but amongst the prisoners, to undermine my authority, for they all knew that the "good old times" had gone, never to return. Saturday afternoon was the time on which those prisoners who were entitled to the privilege were allowed to see their friends, and even in this matter irregularities had crept in. Male prisoners would be allowed to see their wives in store rooms and other out-of-the way places. But I soon put a stop to this. There was no suitable room with a grating, behind which the convict could be kept during the period of his friend's visit, so I had, on these occasions, the convicts formed into one line, and their visitors into another about six yards off with a police guard between to check any irregularities. At this period, the Contractor's Store-room was inside the Jail and he and his servants were allowed to go in and out at will. Nothing could have been worse than this for the maintenance of discipline, for it opened the way to the smuggling of all kinds of contraband articles into the Jail, and I put the matter before Major Drever, who after some trouble had the Contractor's Store-room built outside the Jail enclosure. There were also three paid men for weighing rations, etc., who were "hand-in-glove" with the Contractor, and whom the Commissioner on my suggestion discharged, as it was only a waste of public money keeping them on for all the good they were. This went a great way towards checking irregularities. There was, moreover, a paid Hospital servant who did some business in smuggling forbidden articles into the Jail. This individual, I was informed, had been engaged some years before, for the purpose of bringing such bazaar medicines as were found necessary by the Medical Officer for the treatment of sick convicts. I found some difficulty in getting rid of this man, as the Senior Apothecary in subordinate charge of the Jail Hospital always sided with the man whom he said he always found to be useful and reliable. One

Sunday, however, the Apothecary's confidence in his paragon was fated to be considerably shaken. The man was sent out to the bazaar to purchase some native medicines, and on his return, knowing it was a Sunday when he would not be likely to be disturbed, he swallowed some tincture of opium and became insensible. The Senior Apothecary got alarmed when affer repeated trials he could not bring the man round, and sent for his son, who was a Medical Officer on the Madras Establishment and who was on a visit to his father. Their joint efforts, however, also failed to restore the man to consciousness, and the son left shortly after. I was present during their operations, and seeing that their efforts were futile, and the case was getting serious, I sent for Dr. MacCrae who was then in Medical charge of the Jail. The Senior Apothecary meanwhile kept muttering to himself "*I thought* this man could be trusted, but he has abused my confidence, and I have lost faith in him" or something to that effect. As soon as Dr. MacCrae arrived, I told him what had happened and what steps had been taken to restore the man to consciousness. , He set to work at once, but found the task much more difficult than he expected. At length he asked me to bring him a "cat-o-nine" tails which he commenced to use pretty freely on the unconscious man's body. After a further interval of about an hour, the man recovered consciousness, and was declared all right. I then asked the Doctor whether the man was in a fit state to be sent out, and on his replying in the affirmative, I took the man to the gateway of the Jail where I sent him adrift never more to return. As a matter of fact, the man's services were not at all required in the Hospital which could get along very well without him, and although his dismissal effected a small saving to Government, it was a decided advantage to the Jail, as a disciplinary measure, for it put a stop at once to some of the traffic in illicit articles inside the jail precincts. It was the usual practice for the Commissioner of Police in his capacity as Superintendent of the Jail, to visit the Penitentiary every Monday morning, inspect the prisoners, punish defaulters, and make enquiries into all matters that were brought before him. On his next visit, therefore, I mentioned all the circumstances connected with the discharge of the paid Hospital orderly, and he expressed his pleasure at my having got rid of the man. Monday was the only day when the Superintendent visited the Jail which for the remainder of the week remained under my control, except in any serious matter when I would have to take his order. It was probably on account of the onerous nature of the duties that the pay of the keeper of the Penitentiary was higher then any other Jail in the Presidency. I found Dr. MacCrae an excellent officer to work under, for not only did he help me in maintaining discipline in the Jail, but kept an eye on the Contractor who was a most untrustworthy character, and required to be carefully watched. Dr. MacCrae died a few years afterwards, and no one could have regretted his death more than I did.

It should be remembered that the Penitentiary of the year 1869 is not the institution it is the present day. There was no Jail either for female convicts or juvenile offenders, no close prison, neither were there any cells worthy of the name. There were no under-trial wards, and the Government printing work was done in an old long building within the walls. This was a great drawback, as some of the pressmen were paid workmen who frequently went in and out of the Jail from their work, and I knew for a fact that one or two of their number were not above smuggling illicit articles into the Jail. Only recently (in 1901), I paid a visit to the Penitentiary and the additions and alterations as well as the excellent condition in which the institution is maintained now, were a revelation to me. There is accommodatian in it now for every class of prisoners, and the excellent state of the place will well repay a visit from any one interested in Jail matters. Mr. MacCready, the present Superintendent, is a very hard-working officer, and his worth is appreciated by Government, for by his exertions not only has he saved the State a very large amount of money in printing work, but has also increased the Jail receipts by the large out-turn in Jail manufactures. I may say here that the appointment of Superintendent of Prisons for the Town of Madras was offered to me more than eight years ago by Colonel MacDonald Smith, the then Inspector General of Jails. I was at the time Superintendent of the Central Jail at Cannanore, and at the earnest request of Mr. MacCready, I waived my claim in his fovour, and I must say I have had no reason to regret my decision, for I feel sure that I should never have got the Manufactory Department into such a flourishing condition as it is in now.

It may seem out of place for me to speak in praise of the present condition of an Institution with which I have been myself connected. But when such high officials as Lords Connemara, Wenlock, Sir Arthur Havelock, and the persent Governor Lord Ampthill, have all written of it in terms of high commendation it appers to me but just and proper that one, who knew the Jail in its worst days, should say a word in praise of those who have brought it its to present high state of efficiency.

CHAPTER XXVIII.

Jail Duties in the Madras Penitentiary—(*Continued*).

At the time of my appointment to it in 1869, the Penitentiary was a rectangular building about 200 yards long by 120 wide, surrounded by double walls, the outer wall being much higher than the inner one, the intervening space between the two walls being patrolled by guards who went around eight times every hour. The several buildings for the accommodation of the prisoners were on the North side, or that nearest to the persent People's Park, at that time a native burning ground. The entrance gate faced the sea on the East, and the Southern side of the Jail rested on the banks of the "Silvery Cooum." A road ran along the whole of the Northern wall and was used by the public day and night. The yards of the several blocks were well known to many of those who had relatives confined within the Jail, and this led to parcels containing tobacco, snuff, betel, ganja, and other commodities being thrown over the wall to the prisoners. So accurate was the knowledge possessed by the friends of the prisoners that these packages would drop into the very yards they were intended for. It was next to impossible therefore to put an entire stop to the smuggling of illicit articles into the Jail. A big packet containing some of these articles fell at my very feet once when I was taking an early morning walk round, between the walls. Such articles when discovered were promptly destroyed. The site of the road I have just referred to is now occupied by the South Indian Railway track. On the West of the Jail enclosure was an old Mahomedan grave yard which had not been used for years, while the Cooum side of the institution was utilized by the inhabitants of Chintardripetta as a public latrine during the night and early morning. One Monday morning after Major Drever's inspection, he told me to come along with him to this last named spot and we went along the wall by the side of the Cooum. There was an open sewer running along the western wall which emptied itself in the Cooum, and the stench from this, as well as from the surrounding filth was so great that we were almost overpowered. Major Drever told me he could not stand the smell any longer, and we therefore made a run for it back to the Jail. On getting inside, Major Drever said he was nearly choked, and asked me if I had any brandy to give him a glass. This I readily did, and after he had drank it, he commenced taking up the cases of misconduct, breaches of discipline, etc., on the part of the convicts that I had entered in my journal during the previous week ; it did not take very long to go through a number of cases of this sort and award punishment, which was usually in the form of cells, conjee, or bread-and-water diet, and in graver cases, whipping. Monday was generally a black day for some of the convicts, and some 20 or 30 of them usually got a test of the Cat," which was then the instrument with which whipping was inflicted. In very serious cases as many as 150 lashes were administered, while in minor ones, from 20 to 50 would be the number inflicted. On the occasion of one of Major Drever's inspections, a convict maistry of the name of Chinnasawmy, run up to him to make a complaint without first obtaining permission from me. I felt there was some underhand work going on, and that the maistry had been set to make the complaint. But Major Drever cut the matter very short. The man was reduced from his position as maistry to that of an ordinary convict for the abrupt and disrespecful way he addressed the Superintendent in making his complaint, and was then asked to state his case. He made some complaint about my preventing him from going into the Deputy Jailor's Store-room. He was at once ordered 50 lashes for this and got them promptly. The Deputy Jailor who had to count the number of lashes was upset at the turn things had taken, and lost his head completely. He would certainly have made a mistake in the number of lashes to be administered if I had not stopped him. The Major observing this remarked to him sternly "By God. If that man had got one extra lash I would have flogged you." The Deputy Keeper's predecessor was also an old soldier, and had been dismissed his appointment in the jail for getting a lot of household furniture made in the carpenter's shop, without authority and without paying for it. At the time of which I am writing he was a Bailiff in the High Court. Major Drever was thus acquainted with all the villainy and underhanded tricks that were being carried on. Conspiracies against me were still going on, and happily I was enabled to bring one of these to light, and put a stop at least to some of the plotting. I had occasion to go to the press room, and while looking through the English Letter Book by way of search, I came across a letter purporting to have been written by my daughter to a European prisoner in the jail, of the name of Thornton. The letter book was kept by a Eurasian Convict Maistry, named Yelsmore, who on being asked for an expla.

nation as to how the letter came there, said that it had been handed to him to keep by Thornton. I reported the whole matter at once to Major Drever, for although my quarters were inside the Jail, I was perfectly sure that my daughter, who was a mere child at the time, was not sufficiently advanced in her studies to have written such a letter. Major Drever came to the Jail next morning, and made a searching investigation into the affair. He sent for my daughter and quickly satisfied himself that she could not possibly have written such a letter, and moreover had no knowledge whatever as to who the man Thornton was. Yelsmore still maintained the statement that he knew nothing of the affair beyond the fact that the letter was given him to keep by Thornton, and the latter declared that the letter was thrown to him by my daughter from my quarters. Major Drever was in a terrible passion at this dastardly attempt to get at me through my child. He directed Yelsmore to be reduced from his Maistryship to the position of an ordinary convict, dismissed from the press-room and set to breaking cocoanut husks ; while Thornton was ordered to receive 50 lashes with the "Cat." This Thornton was a character in his way. He had received a long term of imprisonment for having when at Ootacamund entered a ball room and stolen some articles of wearing apparel belonging to some of the ladies. Among other things he had abstracted a cloak belonging to Miss Gorton, a daughter of the Archdeacon of Madras. Thornton afterwards confessed that the matter of the letter was a made-up affair with the object of bringing me into disgrace. One would have thought that the discovery of some of these plots would have put a stop to further attempts against me. Not a bit of it ! Major Drever came to the Jail in great haste one morning, and gave me an anonymous letter to read, asking me at the same time if I knew who the writer was. I told him I did, and could swear to the man. The letter contained a tissue of lies, and Major Drever was told in it, he would get into trouble, as a copy of it had been sent to the Government of Madras. I mentioned the name of the author, who was an official in the High Court, and a connection by marriage of the Deputy Keeper. Major Drever had ascertained where the letter was posted from, but this did not help much in discovering the name of the writer. On hearing what I said he directed the Manager of his office to write to the man I had named, asking him for certain information regarding a case connected with the Sessions Court. This was done with the object of obtaining a specimen of the man's handwriting for comparison with that in the anonymous letter. On his next visit, Major Drever looked hard at me and said that I was right and that there was no doubt that the man whose name I had mentioned, had written the letter. I said I was certain of it, because the man came on a visit to the Deputy Jailor, with the view of finding out results, and had on seeing me concealed himself behind a pillar in front of the Deputy Keeper's door. This in itself was suspicious, as he at other times would always wish me a courteous "Good Morning." With all these annoyances, it will be seen the Jail was becoming a veritable purgatory to me, instead of the haven of rest which I at first expected, and I often exclaimed to myself with much bitterness "I am weary of this watch-dog life of mine." Most of these attempts to ruin me were due to the machinations of the Deputy Keeper, who, doubtless felt grieved that he was not appointed Keeper. He was a pensioned Sergeant-Major and was a man of no educational qualifications whatever, for although he had over 40 years' service in the country he was not qualified in the least for such a post. The plots against me were so carefully and secretly laid, that it was practically impossible to bring them home to the author and as the man could not be discharged on mere suspicion, I had to make the best I could of an invidious position. Had any of them succeeded I should have been ruined for life.

About ten years afterwards (*i.e.* in 1879) when I was Superintendent of the Palghat Fort Jail, I heard that the then Superintendent of the Penitentiary, had forced the Deputy

Keeper to retire on a gratuity of Rs. 800, the equivalent of a month's pay for each of the ten years of his service in the Department.

Shortly after these occurrences, Major Drever was compelled through ill-health to proceed on furlough to Europe and Lieut.-Col. George Bligh Bowen was appointed to act as Commissioner of Police. Colonel Bowen had known me when I was in the Nellore Police, he being Deputy Inspector-General at the time, and on his appointment to the Commissionership, used his best efforts with the Governor, Lord Napier, to get the Jail into a satisfactory condition. Estimates were sanctioned for separate prisons for female convicts, and juvenile offenders, and cubicles for the latter. A Carpenter's shop, and press room were constructed outside the jail, and the motive power to work the machinery in these, was supplied by the tread-mill and crank. All this work was quickly pushed on, and nearly all of it was done by prison labour. Colonel Bowen took the greatest interest in the work, and used to be down at the Jail every day to inspect it. He also obtained the sanction of Government to the purchase of the site of the old disused Mahomedan cemetery I have spoken of, which he soon converted into a decent garden, and iron railings with masonry foundations were run along from the end of the Jail by the road up to the Chintadripettah bridge. There was a large mound opposite the General Hospital and East of the site of the present Madras Railway Central Station, which was an unsightly excrescence, and which Colonel Bowen used to call "Mount Blanc." This he obtained permission to remove, and large gangs of convicts were daily employed in digging and carting away the earth. This increased the width of the strip of ground on the Cooum side of the Jail which was used as a latrine by the people of Chintadripettah, to three times what it was before. Thus the Penitentiary had for the first time since its foundation, something like a garden of its own. The place where the mound was is now occupied by the small garden opposite the General

Hospital wall known as "Adam's Park." The mound in question must have been there for centuries, for in carting it away we came across some strata of the most beautiful white sand I ever saw. For years after this, the Jail grew its own vegetables, and in one year sold no less then 600 Rs. worth of Nepaul chillies. Lord Napier visited the garden one morning, and was greatly pleased with all he saw. Great quantities of country greens were grown such as "Dhall greens," "Arrkeeray," "Moolekeeray" or garden greens, country radishes, etc., for the use of the convicts, beside English vegetables in the shape of knol-khol, cabbages, and vegetable marrow, which found ready sale. I told His Lordship that I had myself eaten the country greens and found them nearly as good as cabbages in health preserving qualities. He asked me to send a small basket of them to Government House for trial. I made a selection of the green and sent them by a European Warder to His Lordship who very kindly gave the Warder a present of five rupees. On his next visit Lord Napier told me that he had had some of the greens cooked and found them excellent. Three Warders' quarters were built on land now belonging to the South Indian Railway, and His Lordship sent a number of orange and other fruit trees to be planted in the compounds, and this was done. He had also other trees planted in the Jail grounds. On one of his visits, Lord Napier was accompanied by Sir F. P. Haines, the Commander-in-Chief. He asked for a pruning knife with which he commenced pruning the trees about him, and gave me this excellent piece of advice. "Plant as many trees as you can for they'll be growing when we are dead and gone." Lord Napier took a great interest in the Jail and its garden, and he often used to pay it a visit unaccompanied by any of his staff. Indeed I have known him to visit the Jail no less than three times in one week without even an Aide-de-Camp with him, or without any previous intimation being sent to the Commissioner of Police. He was also very keen as to the cleanliness of the

Jail latrines, and in the drinking water filters being kept in proper working order.

CHAPTER XXIX.

JAIL DUTIES IN THE MADRAS PENITENTIARY—(*Continued.*)

Besides the old disused Mahomedan Cemetery referred to in the preceding chapter, Colonel Bowen with the sanction of Government purchased the triangular piece of ground running from the General Hospital Bridge, along the Poonamallee road, to the West end of the Penitentiary wall, also from the General Hospital Bridge along the road running South towards the bridge leading to Saint Mary's Cemetery. This tract which was waste ground was also converted into a Jail garden, and was watered from a tank which existed in the middle of the ground. The three new quarters for the Warders were built on this land, which, at the same time was planted with fruit trees supplied by His Excellency Lord Napier. The garden has long since disappeared, and the fruit trees which were at one time His Excellency's pride were cut down to make way for the South Indian Railway track and Park Railway Station, along side the Penitentiary wall. The Accacia trees also which were planted by His Lordship's orders in the new female prison yard, cut down and used for firewood. A number of new buildings, notably Rajah Sir Ramaswamy Moodeliar's Choultry, have sprung up within the last ten years on the side of the Penitentiary wall next to the Poonamallee road, and have completely altered the aspect of the locality as I knew it thirty years ago. The new blocks for juvenile offenders and female convicts were soon constructed, and these prisoners were thus provided with separate accommodation. Three large rooms immediately below the cubicles of the juvenile prisoners were utilized as store-rooms for the Printing Press, but the printing machines themselves together with the carpenters' shop were, as I have said before, removed to the buildings erected for the purpose outside the Jail gate. So that with the exception of cocoanut husk breaking, coir-picking, rope making, and cloth weaving, all labour was performed outside the Jail walls in the shops I have named. This was a decided advantage in the way of preventing the smuggling of forbidden articles into the Jail The Printing Press was visited daily by Mr. Morgan, the Superintendent of Government Printing, who was responsible to the State for the amount of work turned out, and a great saving was effected by utilizing convict labour for the type setting and the purely mechanical part of the work. This was clearly shown in the annual statement drawn up by Mr. Morgan for the information of Government, indicating the total out-turn and actual cost, and comparing the figures with those of private Printing Establishments for similar work. If the tread-mill was disliked by the convicts, the crank was hated by the prisoners whose lot it was to be employed on it, for it was the most laborious of the occupations in the Jail. No shirking was, however, possible as the prisoners on this duty were all locked in, with a European Warder, with two or three convict maistries to watch that they did their duty properly. Among the European prisoners was a life convict of the name of Baker, who had before the period of which I am writing been transferred to the Madras Penitentiary from the Ootacamund Jail on account of ill-health. Baker was a gunner in one of the batteries stationed at St. Thomas' Mount, and was sentenced to be hanged (the sentence afterwards being commuted to a penal servitude for life) for the murder of a Police Sergeant of the name of Kelly, a pensioned Bombardier of Artillery. Baker had been creating a disturbance in a toddy tope near the Cantonment for which he was "wanted" by the Police. When leaving the barracks for the tope he had taken his carbine and some rounds of ball cartridge with him. He was followed up and brought to bay, but threatened to shoot any one who approached him, and kept pointing his carbine at every one who attempted to get near him. As a matter of fact he had fired off some rounds from his carbine at long range without, however, doing any damage. Kelly, however, was not to be daunted. Remonstrating with the man on his folly, and advising him for his own sake to give himself up he approached him, when Baker deliberately levelled his carbine and fired, killing poor Kelly on the spot. Lord Napier had just then entered on his duties as Governor of the Presidency, and was presented with a petition for mercy on behalf of the prisoner signed by a number of influential ladies and others. His Lordship commuted the death penalty to penal servitude for life, a well meaining but mistaken act of clemency, for the murderer richly deserved hanging, and this was the opintion of the general public of Madras. He was sent to the Ootacamund Jail where he gave some trouble and was punished. This engendered a spirit of revenge in him, and his vengeance was chiefly directed against the keeper, Mr. Bailey. One day while the latter was visiting the defferent cells, Baker seized him, and would have put an end to him if the noise of the scuffle had not brought a European Warder, who was close by, to the keeper's assistance. As it was, the injuries received by the latter were of so severe a character, that he was incapacitated for a long time from performing his duties. For this offence, Baker was sentenced to receive 150 lashes, and one can readily believe that the Warders who had the administering of the punishment felt very little pity for the prisoner. Baker's constitution broke down after this, and his lungs got affected for which reason he was sent down to Madras, as being a warmer place. On his arrival at the Penitentiary, he was kept in Hospital where I visited him two or three times daily, and where he received the best of Medical attendance and diet with extras in the from of custards and rice puddings, etc. He died in the Hospital one Sunday morning, and I reported he death to the Commissioner of Police who ordered a coffin to be made for him in the Jail. The body was given Christian burial in St. Mary's Cemetery to which place it was carried by a few short-term European and Eurasian convicts, while I and two European Warders followed the coffin to the grave side. Lord Napier, when speaking of this man, several times declared that he regretted only one action during his tenure of office as Governor and that was his commutation of Baker's sentence, who he said richly deserved hanging.

There was another prisoner by the name of Shaw who about this time brought himself prominently to notice by his evil ways. He had been a Sergeant of Artillery in Burmah, and had been tried and sentenced to a long term of imprisonment for some serious offences. He was received into the Penitentiary preparatory to being sent on to work out his sentence in the Ootacamund Jail, and Major Drever told me to be careful of the man and sent him off at once with a strong escort, as he was a desperate character. I should explain that the police guard at the Jail were all under the orders of the Commissioner of Police, and directly under my control. I accordingly sent the prisoner away under the charge of a European Warder, a Head Constable, and two Constables all of them strong men and of good physique. About two years after, Shaw was sent back to the Penitentiary like a bad shilling. The reason assigned for this step was that he had a week chest and Ootacamund was too cold for him, but I really believe they had had enough of him up at Ooty, and were glad to get rid of him, for he was certainly one of the greatest scoundrels it has been my misfortune to come in contact with. Shortly after his arrival, he succeeded in getting admitted into Hospital, and was in it several times, leading an idle life, with no work to do, and much better diet than that of his fellow convicts. He was a confirmed opioum eater, and his passion for the drug was so strong that he would not stick at trifles to procure it. I may here say that I have known instances of opium being smuggled into the Jail by prisoners on their first entrance, concealed in certain unmentionable parts of their bodies. Whenever I had a suspicion that a new prisoner had opium about him which I myself could not discover, I informed the Medical Officer who generally succeeded in finding it stowed away as I have stated.

Not being considered strong enough by the Medical Officer to do a full day's work, he was put to light labour. He was several times sentenced to undergo solitary cells, low diet, etc., for misconduct, but this had not the least effect in curing him of his bad habits, for he was always engaged in some plot or other, not only with the European convicts, but with the natives as well. On one occasion he asked to be taken before the Superintendent (then Captain Wyndham Hughes Hallett) as he wanted to make a request. I did this of course, but because Captain Hallett refused his request, he threw his cap at that officer, using some very strong expressions against him, and that in the presence of a number of other convicts who were at work close by. I had him removed to a cell at once and locked up, and on the following day brought him before Capt. Hallett who directed him to be given fifty lashes. The Jail Doctor however gave it as his opinion that the man was not strong enough to bear flogging, and he was accordingly sentenced to seven days' solitary cells. While in the Penitentiary a letter was received to his address written by a friend in Burmah. In it the writer spoke of their joint exploits in the past, how they used to drug persons, and rob them and indulge in other crimes of a similar nature. If anything further was needed to show the Superintendent what thorough paced rascals he and his friend were, this letter supplied it. Such letters were in accordance with the rules withheld from the prisoners. He was sentenced in Burmah to ten years' penal servitude; but owing to his continued misconduct, he had earned very little remission, nor was there much in the way of a gratuity to his credit, in consequence of the small amount of labour he had performed. Each day, he was entitled to scarcely anything at all under the remission rules. At length his time for release arrived, and in accordance with the Superintendent's orders, I got two complete suits of clothing made for him in the Jail, including socks, boots, and hat, and before he was released I placed eight rupees in his hand to enable him to subsist a few days, before proceeding to

England in a sailing vessel. I then took him to the Jail gate and set him free. He did not leave, however, without threatening the Superintendent and me with all kinds of dire penalties. He said he would even go to the Governor-General and "play the devil" with us. He was going on in this maniacal way for sometime until I had the gate shut against him. About 12 o'clock the same night he was found lying unconscious on the roadway over the Chinadripettah bridge behind the Penitentiary. He was conveyed by the police to the General Hospital, but nothing could be done to restore him, and he died the same night. There was a Coroner for the town at this period, and at the Inquest held the next morning I was sent for, and asked if I recognized the man. I immediately stated who he was, and stated that he had been released from the Jail at 5 o'clock the previous evening. Also, that I had heard of his being seen after his release in the Goojelly (or Evening) Bazaar near an arrack shop, with one Jeremiah formerly a pleader, but at this time an old Jail bird and one who was often found at night lying in the gutters drunk and incapable. Lest this man be confounded with another person of the same name I must here say that there was another Jeremiah, a brother of this man who was also a pleader, but a very worthy respectable man, and who may still be alive. Jeremiah was sent for and made a long statement. He recognized the body as that of the ex-convict Shaw, and said that he had himself only been released from the Jail about three days before and had promised Shaw to arrange for a "jutka" to be present near the Jail on the day of the latter's release. This he did, and when Shaw came out, both of them drove to an arrack shop near the Evening Bazaar, where they drank a bottle of country spirit between them. After this Shaw asked for and was shown into a shop where he could procure opium, and purchased enough of the drug to poison a dozen men. They then went back to the arrack shop, and had some more arrack. By this time, it was growing dark, and Shaw who had not been about the town before asked to be driven to the house of a young man named Colquhoun who resided in Chintadripettah, and whose father was then doing time in the Penitentiary. Shaw had swallowed two large doses of opium on the way, and with the spirit in him began to get troublesome, so much so that the jutka driver was anxious to get rid of him. When they got to Colquhoun's house this young man on seeing Shaw's condition declined to take him in. After this, Shaw became more troublesome and getting insensible as well, and unable to get out of the jutka, he (Jeremiah) not wishing to be embroiled, thought it prudent to take his leave. What happened afterwards, and how Shaw came to be found lying on the Chintadripettah bridge, Jeremiah said he did not know, nor could he say what the number of the jutka was in order that the driver might be traced. Probably the driver seeing Shaw's muddled condition had pulled him out of the jutka, left him on the road and had driven off ; but as the man could not be found, no further light was thrown on the affair. Shaw had been an opium eater for years before this, and it was clear from the post mortem examination held, that he had swallowed a very large quantity of opium, the previous evening.

The Coroner's jury, therefore, found that he had died from the effects of an overdose of the drug. He had been boasting to the prisoners before he left Jail what he intended doing when he got out ; it was his intention he said to rid the Penitentiary of Captain Hallett and myself and he further promised the prisoners that they should have cause to thank him for what he would do on their behalf. Not only, said he, would he visit the Editors of all the Madras papers to enlighten them as to our doings, but he would also proceed to Calcutta, and obtain redress for all the prisoners at the hands of His Excellency the Viceroy. Poor wretch, little did he think at the time how near he was to his end.

CHAPTER XXX.

Jail Duties in the Madras Penitentiary—(*Continued*).

In 1872 the old order of things under which the Commissioner of Police was *Ex. Officio* Superintendent of the Penitentiary was abolished, and a new appointment, viz., that of Superintendent of Prisons for the Town of Madras, created, the Penitentiary being thus removed from the supervision of the Commissioner of Police. Captain Wyndham Hughes Hallett, an officer of the Royal Artillery, who had been Superintendent of the Central Jail at Salem, was appointed to the new post. Colonel Bowen, before leaving the Jail Department, had introduced considerable improvements in the weaving-industry carried on in the Jail, which now was on a much large scale than formerly. In addition to the old hand-looms, there were now in use the latest English looms worked by steam-power, and a Mechanical Engineer was employed on Rs. 200 a month to look after the machinery which worked these. Two additional European Warders were also entertained to relieve the extra labour which thus devolved on the jail staff. As was to be expected, the usual difficulties which attend every innovation were encountered, but after a time things began to work more smoothly, and the project achieved a certain measure of success.

Captain Hallett, being no professional Engingeer himself, brought two gentlemen with him one morning, who were thoroughly qualified in this line of business, to inspect and report on the working of the weaving machinery in the Jail. The opinion expressed by these gentleman, as to the manner in which the work was carried out, made Captain Hallett somewhat dissatisfied with the Jail Engineer, and I could not help smiling when he remarked to me that these gentlemen talked from a different platfrom from what our Mechanical Engineer did. Of course I understood Captain Hallett's allusion, and replied that our Engineer only got Rs. 200 a month, a sum which was hardly sufficient to procure a first-class man. The long buildings, however, in the Penitentiary, in which the work was being carried out, were found to be really unsuitable for the work, and after a trial of twelve months, the whole of the weaving plant was transferred to the Central Jail at Coimbatore, while Colonel Bowen was at the same time, appointed by G.O. to officiate as Superintendent of that Jail, *vice* Mr. Henry Grimes granted furlough to Europe. It was a relief to me when these operations were removed from the Penitentiary, for I was held responsible that there was proper amount of work done in this branch, also of the Jail industries, one of which I had no professional knowledge to enable me to exercise a proper supervision. As for the Mechanical Engineer, if I remember rightly, he was sent to the Central jail at Coimbatore to assist Colonel Bowen in erecting a suitable building, and fitting up the machinery, which, I believe, is carrying on its weaving operations up to the present day. There was an increase in expenditure in the Coimbatore Jail owing to the introduction and fitting up of the new plant, and I heard that there was a paper war between Colonel Bowen and Mr. Grimes on the latter's return from furlough. But "all's well that ends well" for nothing serious came of it. One of the new European Warders entertained was a man of the name of Phelan, a pensioned Sergeant-Major of the Battery of Artillery, in which Captain Hallett served when a Subaltern. Phelan was a tall man and of good physique, but I quickly discovered that there was very little of the angel in his temperament, whatever, he might have been in years gone by, and I told Captain Hallett this, and he eventually dismissed him for bringing arrack into the Jail premises. The other man, whose name was Smith, and who acted as Clerk and Storekeeper in the Weaving Establishment, was caught with a bottle full of the spirit, while inside the Jail and, when asked what it was, declared it was medicine he was taking. His appearance, however, showed that he had imbibed rather too freely of his "medicine," and he was also discharged. One of the most unpleasant part of my duties was to look after the Warders, who gave me a great deal of trouble, and I found it was very difficult to cheek their irregularities. One man a Mr. M. who had been a Musician in His Excellency the Governor's Band, was recommended for the post of a Warder, to Captain Hallett by Colonel Sylvester who was then occupying a high office (Military Secretary I believe, if my memory does not fail me) under the Government of Madras. Although I informed Captain Hallett that the man had two years before this been in Jail for two months for striking a Corporal in the Band, yet owing to the fact that it was only a Military offence and not an offence against the Criminal Law, as well as owing to the weight Colonel Sylvester's recommendation carried with it, this man was duly appointed, and was for a long time a thorn in my side, through the trouble he occasioned me by his irregular ways.

He was thoroughly acquainted with Tamil and Hindustani and this helped him considerably in establishing a clandestine correspondence between the prisoners and their friends outside, of which he was the medium. I had reason to believe that he was in the habit of visiting the relatives and friends of prisoners who were confined inside the Jail, and it can be easily imagined that it was through no charitable motives to either, that he ran the risk of getting himself into trouble, for conveying messages to and from the prisoners as such proceeding is subversive of all discipline, and renders the individual guilty of it liable to immediate dismissal or even imprisonment. The business, though risky, was highly remunerative, and he was too astute a bird to be easily caught. Indeed it would have required a detective to be at his heels to do this. He was also often seen following prisoners on their release from Jail and when questioned about it, he would say that it was simply to give them good advice not to come back to the Jail again. However I was able to get rid of him shortly after, without bringing him before the Superintendent on any of the counts I have named. He was anxious he told me once to get an apppointment, as a Sergeant in the Madras Police, and I recommended him to apply for the post as it would suit him much better than the Jail. He did so and how he succeeded I will presently show.

At this time, Mr. Beeson whom I had known in the Nellore Police, and who had since left it begged me to get him a post as a Warder in the Penitentiary as he was without employment. I was on duty at the High Court Sessions, and was standing at the doorway below during the afternoon, when I saw Major Balmer, who had on Colonel Drever's return from England, relinquished his acting appointment as Commissioner of Police driving past in a carriage. On observing me, however, he stopped his carriage, and called out to me to come up to him. In the carriage were also Colonel Drever, and Colonel Cunliffe, the Superintendent of Police at St. Thomas' Mount. On my coming up, Major Balmer asked me about the man (M) who applied for a Police Sergeant's post. I told him that I was anxious to get red of him as the Jail would be better off without him. I also said that if he took him into the Police, it would make an opening for Mr. Beeson whom Major Balmer knew, and whom I was anxious to serve. Colonel Drever on hearing this, laughed aloud, and said it was very good of me to foist a man I did not want, on to the Police, and gave them the benefit of his cleverness. " Yes!" I said " for I know in the Police you will soon be able to run him to earth, and I haven't either the time or the means of watching him." The three gentlemen then drove on. On the following day (M) was appointed a Sergeant in the Town Police. But he held the appointment for a short time only, for he soon committed himself and was discharged.

Of course difficulties of this sort will arise in connection with the Warders, even in the best regulated Jails, for human nature is the same all the world over, and I do not suppose that the European Jail Warders in India are as a class any worse than their brethren in English Jails. In this connection I may say that there was an outcry in the newspapers some years ago regarding the carrying on of a clandestine correspondence in one of the principal London Jails between the prisoners and their friends outside, through the medium of the Jail officials who were handsomely remunerated for their trouble. This was accidentally brought to light, and caused some commotion at the time. Let us hope, however, that there is nothing of this sort in the London Jails now, even if there still exist a few black sheep among the Jail officials in India. One of the worst cases of this kind that came under my notice was one which occurred some years afterwards in connection with a European Pensioner of the name of Montgomery who was a Warder at the time in the Penitentiary, while Mr. Symonds was Superintendent of Prisons for the Town of Madras. There had been appearing in one of the Madras papers a number of scurrilous letters regarding the administration of the Penitentiary, which I was certain were written by prisoners inside, and which Montgomery was suspected of conveying outside and getting published. I had just finished reading one of these effusions one day, when Montgomery entered the Jail and proceeded to the European yard to relieve the Warder on duty there. I followed him closely without being perceived by him. He went up the staircase to the upper storey, and when I went up after him, I found him inside a cell engaged with two prisoners to whom he had given the paper to read, and who were in great glee at seeing their atrocious letter in print. One of the prisoners was named Reeves who had got into serious trouble, although a man of good family and connections, for he had a brother, a Major in the Royal Engineers. I at once took Montgomery and put him outside the Jail and directed him to attend the Superintendent's Office at 12 o'clock the same day. At the time appointed, when the Superintendent was in his office, I gave him the newspaper to read, and then handed him my journal which contained a report of the case. Montgomery was sent for, and asked what he had to say for himself. He could urge nothing in his defence, and was promptly dismissed. Here was a man receiving Rs. 50 a month with free quarters, which together with his military pension ought to have sufficed to keep him and his family in comparative ease and comfort—and yet, for a trifling gratuity, he preferred to run the risk of losing his good name, to bring his family to the verge of ruin, and to forfeit all chance of obtaining a decent livelihood afterwards. But this is not a solitary instance. I could quote many cases of stupidity and short-sightedness on the part of European and Native pensioners who have similarly lost an assured living and a decent pension from the Jail also, when they were too old to work, through their own folly.

Some two or three years after this, I was appointed by His Grace the Duke of Buckingham and Chandos, Superintendent of the Palghat Fort Jail, which had then been newly established on account of the great influx of prisoners into the Jails in the Presidency owing to the famine, and here learnt the end of poor Montgomery. There were only five or six graves in the little cemetery close to the Church. All of these had head-stones to them except one which had nothing over it to show who was lying there—but I used always to see a bunch of flowers, put there by some pitying soul, and this led me to make enquiries about the grave from my friend Mr. Elsworthy, the Principal of the Palghat College. He told me that a European Pensioner of the name of Montgomery was buried there—that he was returning from Calicut where he had been to look for employment, and that while on his way back he was found dead in the train at Palghat Station. He was buried by the European residents of the Station, although his name was not found out till afterwards, and it was some kindly hearted, pitying lady in the station who brought a bunch of roses to the Church every Sunday and placed it over the poor fellow's grave.

CHAPTER XXXI.

Madras Penitentiary—(*Continued*).

I shall confine myself in this Chapter to chronicling the doings of an ardent devotee of the dramatic art, and one whose name is well remembered in Madras for his talents as an amateur actor, Captain Hughes Hallett, the Superintendent of Prisons for the Town of Madrs, who understood the dramatic profession as if he were " to the manner born." Not only was he a talented performer himself, but every entertainment that had the benefit of his experience, was sure to meet with success. Indeed I have heard it mentioned that he was far superior to many professionals in this respect, and this was the opinion of the general public of Madras. No entertainment in the days I am speaking of could be given without Captain Hallett having a large share in the management. He was therefore an acquisition to the Madras Dramatic Society the success of whose performances was mainly due to Captain Hallett's histrionic talent and experience.

The Society usually gave its entertainments in the Old College Hall, and the Madras public had often the pleasure of witnessing such plays as Sheridan's "School for Scandal" (played at the Banqueting Hall) and others by leading dramatic authors, performed by amateurs who in point of ability were equal to the best professionals. Many of the lady actresses I should also say seemed to be adepts in the art. Although it would not be in my province to make any invidious distinctions between individual performers, yet I should like to mention the names of some of those who through their striking personality and clever performances are fresh in my memory. Colonel Hunt, Superintendent of Army Clothing, was known for his admirable personations of old men's characters, Mr. Chisholm, the Government Architect, for his talents as an amateur actor and vocalist, while Captain Simpson, commanding H. E. the Governor's Body Guard, and other officers will be remembered for the way in which they threw themselves into their respective parts, and kept the interest of their audience alive. In addition to the public entertainments, there were private theatricals as well, one such being given at the residence of Mr. Cunningham, the Administrator-General and Government Prosecutor, and afterwards a Judge of the High Court at Calcutta. This entertainment was got up by Captain Hallett and Major Kenny Herbert who was as well known and as popular among the residents of Madras as Captain Hallett. What Anglo-

Indian housewife is there who has not reason to bless Major Kenny Herbert for his admirable work on Cookery. But to return—His Grace the Duke of Buckingham and Staff, and the leading residents of Madras were present at the performance, which, so far as performances go, was a gem in its way. The programme consisted of "The Bounding Brothers" an exquisite burlesque in which Captain Hallett and Major Kenny Herbert took the leading roles, and a one-act play in which the two characters were taken by Captain Hallett and Mrs. Kenny Herbert. "Bounding Brothers" was a kind of provincial show, Captain Hallett taking the part of *showman*, while Major Kenny Herbert was the *strong man* and *acrobat*, and how they deceived the audinence, I, who at Captain Hallett's request, assisted in the stage management, alone knew, besides themselves. The "Strong Man's" part was to swing two 56 lb. weights over his head, as well as to lift a dozen of them at a time, and the facility with which Major Kenny Herbert performed these marvellous feats of strength won him rounds of applause from the audience who were surprised to find him a man of such strong muscular power. But the weights were a hollow sham for it was I who had got them made in the workshop of the Penitentiary out of stiff card board, and painted and lettered them to represent 56 lbs. weights. The balancing feat was also a marvel of skill. In this Major Kenny Herbert balanced a long pole on his chin with great dextery, but the pole had a small hook at the top, invisible to the audience which fitted nicely into a ring fixed to the roof of the stage to keep it steady. The cleverest feat of all, however, was his perforemance on the tight rope on which he walked across the stage with an infant in his arms, a dressed doll being used instead of a baby. This brought down the house, and Major Kenny Herbert was cheered over and over again. In this also the audience were deceived. I had brought a very thick coir rope form the Penitentiary and fastened it to uprights inside the wings. Touching the rope and running parallel with it, but hidden from the view of the spectators in front, was a plank resting on strong pillars also screened from the view of the audience. It was on this plank that Major Kenny Herbert exhibited his dexterity which, to the spectators, seemed marvellous for a non-professional performer. Captain Hallett was, however, by no means idle all this while, for his amusing comments as the showman on each of these feats were received with roars of laughter. These being over, Captain Hallett promised the audience a treat in the shape of what he called his *Stattees.* A number of wooden drums were made in the Penitentiary on which were painted the names of the "Stattees" that were to occupy them, *viz.*, "The Emperor of China," "Sir Walter Raleigh," "Henry the Eighth," "Mary Queen of Scots," "Queen Boadicea" and other prominent characters in history, altogether about ten. These drums were arranged around the stage, while the curtain was down, and the various characters took up their positions. Major Bloomfield's wife, a lady of great personal attractions, represented Mary Queen of Scots and Miss Carmichael, daughter of the Chief Secretary to Government, took the part of Queen Boadicca. Colonel Hunt was "Sir Walter Raleigh," while other ladies and gentlemen, whose names I have now forgotten filled up the other parts. The scene was a very pretty one when the curtain rose, for Captain Hallett had thoroughly drilled his "Stattees." He first commenced with the "Emperor of China" whose manifold virtues and great qualities, he extolled to the skies, whereat the "Son of Heaven" graciously bowed his head. He then went on to "Henry the Eighth" whose amiable disposition won his warmest praises especially the habit which "Bluff King Hal" had of cutting off his wives' heads. After the life and adventures of "Sir Walter Raleigh" were gone into, Captain Hallett went on to describe the other personages in his racy and humorous style. "Queen Boadicea" was a magnificent, upright figure with a wealth of flaxen hair, while 'Mary Queen of Scots" was represented kneeling and in a prayerful attitude. The "Stattees" were naturally an unqualified success and received a well deserved and enthusiastic *encore*. The entertainment was brought to a close by a play in one-act in which the male character was taken by Captain Hallett, and the female by Mrs. Kenny Herbert. I have forgotten the name of the play, but it was cleverly acted and purported to show what a husband should be according to the view of his wife, and what the latter should be from the stand-point of the husband. The dialogue was brisk and lively, and I remember to this day, Captain Hallett's "aside." "*She had me there*" whenever Mrs. Kenny Herbert made use of a telling argument from the woman's point of view. Another of these private entertainments was given at the house of Mr. Carmichael, the Chief Secretary to Government, and chiefly consisted of vocal and instrumental music and the best of its kind in Madras. Two or three ladies, one of whom was Mrs. Drever, wife of Colonel Drever, Commissioner of Police, played selections on the piano, while Dr. Macleane (Mus. Doctor) afterwards Collector of Nellore, also took a prominent part. A number of the leading Native gentlemen were invited and commenced talking while Dr. Macleane was playing, a circumstance which so annoyed the worthy Doctor, that he broke off in the middle of the piece and immediately left the stage. It took some time to soothe the Doctor's ruffled feelings, and coax him on the stage again. The entertainment wound up with the "trial scene" in "The Merchant of Venice," and in this Captain Hallett made a great hit in the character of "Shylock the Jew." I forget who took the part of Portia, but whoever it was, did the part thorough justice for the acting in some parts was sublime. Indeed the whole cast of the piece showed very careful selection, and was filled up by experienced lady and gentlemen amateurs. The whole entertainment was a success. Many of the present generation of playgoers in Madras may not have heard of Captain Hallett and the leading amateurs of thirty years ago, but they must have read his letters regarding theatricals in India, which have appeared in the *Madras Mail* during the past three years, as well as his letters on the subject of the London stage, which appear from time to time in the same journal under the initials "W. H. H." Last year he wrote at some length on the subject of the Passion Play enacted at Ommerabergau on the Continent which he had been to see, and of which he gave a detailed account, even to mentioning the exact dimensions of the stage. One of the female characters he likened to "a daughter of the gods, divinely tall and most divinely fair."

One of the most amusing performances it has been my good fortune to see in Madras was Gilbert and Sullivan's Opera "Trial by Jury" which was held in the Old College Hall, Captain and Mrs. Simpson taking the leading parts. The Jury was something to remember as it consisted of some very high officials of the Government, and was the most intelligent body of twelve men ever got together for the trial of a breach of promise case. Dr. Cornish, Surgeon-General with the Government of Madras, was one of the free and "Enlightened Twelve," while the gentleman who caused the most amusement was a Clergyman who entered the Jury box with an umbrella under his arm looking the picture of guilelessness. This was the first of Gilbert and Sullivan's Operas I had seen, and I was greatly pleased with it.

While I am on this subject, I may say that I took part on several occasions in the theatrical entertainments, even at the Banqueting Hall, and other public buildings, given in aid of local charities, such as the Friend-in-Need Society; the Roman Catholic Orphanages, and others. On such occasions I usually recited, and once when reciting "the Soldier's return" a pathetic piece, I had learned at Lahore in 1851, an old Parsee gentleman who was seated only a short distance behind H. E. the Governor gave a tremendous sneeze just as I was warming to the work and had got to a pathetic part. The sneeze was such an awful one that it electrified the house, broke the spell of silence which reigned in the room, and brought me to a standstill. I was so startled and thrown off my balance, that I could not proceed for some seconds. These entertainments which were got up by me and my friends were of course not to be placed on a level with those given by Captain Hallett and other well known amateurs, but they were as I have stated enacted for charitable purposes, and answered their purpose very well, as we generally collected a respectable sum of money on these occasions, for amateur theatricals were much better patronized and appreciated then than they are now.

CHAPTER XXXII.

Madras Penitentiary—(*Continued*).

Prisoners I Have Known.

I purpose in this and a few following Chapters to give an account of some of the convicts in the Penitentiary in my time, who by their peculiar idiosyncracies brought themselves somewhat prominently under the notice of the Jail officers. Of these one was *Cumbum*, who in 1870 was undergoing a sentence of eight years penal servitude in Her Majesty's Penitentiary. He had been convicted eight times on charges of house-breaking, theft, and other serious crimes, for which as I have said he was undergoing a long term of penal servitude. In a former chapter, I mentioned how a dream I had was realized in a somewhat strange manner. My nightly dreams while I was in the Penitentiary were usually of cobras and other poisonous snakes, but one morning I dreamt that a toad had fastened itself tightly on my right cheek, and in my efforts to pull the brute off I awoke. The Americans say "ware snakes." However that may be, the generally accepted belief is that such dreams are the results of an impaired digestion, or an overworked brain. While agreeing in the main with this view, my own experiences convince me that it cannot be accepted in all cases, and probably many of my readers are of the same opinion. But this is a question for the Psychical Research Society rather than one for a practical man, and so I will proceed with my narrative. Cumbum was undergoing seven days' solitary cells for a Jail offence, and on the morning of my dream, when the European warder on duty visited his cell according to rule, Cumbum reported sick and was at once conveyed to the Hospital for the Medical Officer's inspection. On being questioned by the Doctor as to the nature of his ailment, he pulled off some rags which were tied round his arm and exibited the marks of three very serious cuts which he said were inflicted by me. He declared that I had entered his cell the previous night, and had given him three blows with my walking stick. The Medical Officer after examining the wounds told the man he was lying, for the wounds were at least three days old and were moreover inflicted by a sharp instrument. Of course his arm was in a very bad state. I was sent for and informed of the complaint made against me by the man. I had his cell thoroughly searched and found on the ledge of the upper ventilator of the cell two pieces of glass evidently broken from the bottom of an old beer bottle. These I took to the Doctor who declared that they were most probably the instruments which caused the wounds, which he was certain were not due to any blows from a walking stick. It may not be generally known that natives in general, but prisoners in particular, use such bits of broken glass to remove superfluous hair from their persons and these bits of glass are probably picked up when the convicts are employed on extra-mural labour, and secreted in their clothing. For this little bit of fiction, Cumbum was awarded an additonal seven days' cell. He was, I believe, the toad of my dream, for his face was like that of a toad in lineament and expression, and his reasoning faculties were not much higher, for had he possessed the least particle of common sense he would have known that reports of this kind are utterly futile, and can only redound to his own discomfiture and possibly of those who had made him their catspaw. I should here make it clear that neither the keeper nor any other Jail official can enter the cell of any prisoner during the night as every prison key is locked up at night in a box, the key of which is in the custody of the Head Constable of the Guard. From the indulgence shown to the prisoners by certain members of the Jail staff the Jail was considered rather a desirable place than otherwise to be in, and a not unnatural spirit of revolt was engendered by the measures taken to keep the old offenders in order. In regard to this, I may say not only were certain of the paid officials helping the prisoners in every possible way which could be done without detection, but were actually joining in their plots against the Keeper and the Superintendent. Such being the case it was not long before Cumbum made another false complant, *viz*,—that the keeper had entered his cell at night and attempted to cut his throat. Search was made in his cell, and the piece of glass which he had used to cut his throat with was found in the gravel just in front of his cell with blood stains on it. Cumbum was tried magisterially for making this false accusation and received an additional three months' rigorous imprisonment. This punishment had no deterrent effcet on him for he rather liked Jail life, but did not approve of the innovation which had been introduced, and which placed greater restriction on him and his comrades in jail. Urged by his backers it was not long before he brought another charge against the Keeper. He with several others, all hardened criminals, were locked up at night for better security in separate cells in the lower storey of the European block, which was not required for the European prisoners at the time. Cumbum one night gave a blood curdling yell which aroused half the inmates of a prison, and brought the Police and had European Warder on night duty at once to his cell, when he complained to them that the Keeper with Warder Mansell had entered his cell, and that the Keeper had struck him on his arms several times with a stick. He was found to be bleeding from severe wounds. I must here observe that Warder Mansell was detested by the old offenders, merely because he was a strict man, and did his duty conscientiously. Cumbum must have had incorrect information, or he would have waited for another night before putting his plot into execution, for Warder Mansell on the night in question was not on duty, but in bed at his house in Vepery. Thus the complaint on the face of it was a lie, in addition to which a large piece of glass with blood stains on it was found in the gravel in front of his cell door, and Cumbum was awarded fifty lashes by the Superintendent. The flogging evidently had a wholesome effect for he made no more false charges after this. I afterwards heard that on his release he emigrated to Mauritius as a cooly, and is now probably leading a virtuous life. Whether this be so or not the City of Madras can well spare him and many of his stamp.

The next case of prisoners I have known is probably a record- one and will interest Criminologists. Moung Hyat was a life prisoner, and was received with a hundred other convicts from Burmah. He was sentenced to death for dacoity with murder, but this sentence was commuted to one of transportation for life. While in the Rangoon Jail he murdered a fellew convict for which he was a second time sentenced to death, but this time also the death penalty was commuted to transportation for life. So that when he was received in H. M 's Penitentiary in Madras, it was clear enough that he had been sentenced to death twice and that he was then undergoing *two life sentences*, and that he was anything but an acquisition to the Penitentiary. He was punished two or three times for giving trouble, and one morning he was determined to " murder " Warder Mansell, who as I remarked, was hated for his strictness. Mansell was walking along the foot-path towards the inner gate of the Jail, when Moung Hyat who was working in the shed, rushed after him with a very heavy bamboo. One of the convicts, who had seen Moung Hyat out of the shed, shouted out a caution to Warder Mansell who without turning around put up his arm just as the bamboo descended. The blow fell, and fractured Mansell's arm in two places, and the poor fellow was ill for two months; although many of the more hardened wretches would have been glad if he had been killed outright, some of the convicts rushed up and seized Moung Hyat whom I at once locked up. For this offence he was awarded 150 lashes with the "Cat," but the man was case hardened, and took the punishment without flinching. As there had been a good many cases in the Presidency of life prisoners assaulting Jail officials, and as prosecution before a Magistrate could at the period I am writing of, have only been attended with a further term of imprisonment, recourse was had to flogging which was found to be a much more effective deterrent, and this was the course adopted for a time.

But a representation was made to the Government, and two fresh sections were added to the Penal Code, which made offences of the kind *capital* ones in the case of life prisoners. Moung Hyat got on well after this for about twelve months, and being a fairly good carpenter, I employed him in the Carpenters' Shop outside the Jail. One morning on being checked for idling by a Chinese Maistry, a life convict, he became irritated, and struck the latter on the head with a hammer. He was at once seized by some of the other prisoners. On hearing of the occurrence, I immediately visited the Carpenters' Shop, sent him under a proper guard into the Jail, and had him locked up. The Chinaman, I sent to Hospital where he remained under treatment for twenty-three days. Were it not for his pig tail which was coiled around the top of his head, and which Chinese prisoners are allowed to wear, he would have been killed outright. The case was enquired into magisterially, and the prisoner was committed to the High Court. Among the witness for the prosecution were Captain Hallett and myself, and the two warrants showing that the prisoner had been twice sentenced to death in Burmah, and that in each case the sentence had been commuted to transportat on for life, were produced. The evidence was conclusive, and the prisoner was found guilty, and sentenced to death—the first one who came under the operation of the new sections of the Indian Penal Code. This is probably a "record" case for after committing two murders in which the sentences were commuted, he was executed for no murder at all. After his sentence, Moung Hyat complained bittterly stating that he would willingly have suffered death for either of the two murders he had committed in Burmah, but he could not comprehend the justice of a sentence which sent him to the gallows for a mere assault on a Chinaman which inflicted but a trifling injury. Mr. Rowlandson, the Registrar of the Diocese, came with Captain Hallett to witness the execution. Another convict who was sentenced to death for murder was hanged the same morning, their graves being dug the previous day by the side of the gallows. In a few minutes the bodies were cut down, laid in the graves with the ropes around their necks, and their Jail clothing on. The graves were quickly filled up, turfed over with turf that had been cut and kept ready the previous day, and watered. All this took only about twenty minutes, and the two murderers were lying in peace in their graves by the " Silvery Cooum."

Years afterwards a New Jail Code appeared, according to the provisions of which the bodies of convicts executed cannot be cut down until the lapse of an hour, although life was probably extinct within a few seconds after they had been hanged. I myself have had to watch many a malefactor hang for a full hour ascertaining the time by my watch after which in accordance with the rules, I would ask the Medical Officer in the usual form "Tell me if life is extinct" to which he would invariably reply " Of course it is." I would then ask him to make sure and satisfy himself. I would then direct the body to be cut down and removed to the Jail burying ground for interment.

CHAPTER XXXIII.

MADRAS PENITENTIARY— *Continued*).

PRISONERS I HAVE KNOWN.

It may not be generally known that Thuggee still exists in India Although by the exertions of the Department for the suppression of Thuggee and Dacoity in India, the real

Thugs that is the "Phansigars" or stranglers have long since been suppressed, there is still a form of Thuggee extant known as "Thuggee" by the administration of poisonous drugs.

Nagoji was a well known character as a Madras convict. He had had five previous convictions, and had just finished a seven years' term of imprisonment in the Rajahmundry Central Jail to which he had been transferred from the Penitentiary, for theft of jewellery from a child to whom he had administered poisoned sweetmeats. I should here make it clear that under the remission rules, a well behaved convict can earn a substantial reduction of his sentence. Thus a man doing a term of seven years can, if he behaves himself, go off with less than six, and this was the case with Nagoji. But the trail of the Serpent was on the man, and the old criminal instinct in him asserted itself, and he was tried at the High Court for a fresh crime. When brought before the presiding judge, Justice Holloway, His Lordship looked keenly at the man and remarked to me "Was not this man tried by me some years ago for theft by means of administering poisonous drugs"! "Yes, my Lord I replied"—"Ah!" said the Justice "I remember his face," and Nagoji got a stiff term of imprisonment as the result. He was by trade a carpenter, and as he was a good one, I put him to work in the carpenter's shop. Nagoji had had a fairly good time of it in the Rajahmundry Jail, and found the new and severer discipline in the Madras Penitentiary most galling to his spirit, and he chafed under it. One morning while going my usual round of inspection in the carpenter's shop, Nagoji followed me nearly to the end of the shop with a "half wrought" in his hand, that is, a roughly hewn piece of wood used for making the leg of a table or a chair, and struck me a blow on my back. Luckily for me, the blow fell just on the muscular part of my right shoulder, for had it fallen on my spine, the consequences might have been serious. As it was, the blow staggered me, although I didn't fall. On turning around I saw Nagoji in the act of raising his bludgeon again to make another blow, but as I was armed with a good stick myself, I smiled at his efforts to to get at me. Observing this he threw the piece of wood at me. He was seized from behind by two or three European and Eurasian prisoners. Captain Hallett investigated the case, and sentenced the man to receive a hundred lashes. Before receiving his sentence, he was asked whether the Keeper had any prejudice against him, and whether there was any feeling of enmity between him and the keeper. He said "No." He merely committed the deed, he declared, to get transferred from the Penitentiary, as he wanted to get back to the Rajahmundry Jail. The men who had rushed up and seized Nagoji were rewarded by Government with remissions of portions of their sentences. One man got a reduction of eight months, one of six and two of four months each. In the abstract, the measure was a good one as it showed prisoners that they would be rewarded if they prevented assaults on Jail officials, but in the case of these men, the reward was unmerited, for every prisoner in the shop saw Nagoji stalking me without raising a cry of warning to me. On another occasion, when Colonel Bowen was Superintendent of the Jail, and about two or three years before this occurrence, I was inspecting the mat-making and coir workshop inside the Jail, were some of the worst characters were at work, when a number of the convicts made a rush at me with mat-makers' knives and other weapons. I might have fared badly had it not been for fourteen European Sailors employed in the same shop, who came to my rescue and disarmed my would be assailants, a number of whom were sentenced to receive a hundred lashes each for this outbreak. These Sailors had been sentenced to six months' rigorous imprisonment for persistent refusal of duty on board their ship, and had only recently been sent into Jail. Their plea was that the Captain of their vessel not only had detained their clothing, but had kept back their wages, but of course this was no excuse for their persistent refusal of duty. Colonel Bowen had each man's statement taken down, and forwarded to the Chief Judge of the small Cause Court, and obtained premission for them to sue the master of the ship in *forma pauperis*, as the vessel was about to leave port. I took the Sailors on two successive days to the Court where their case was thoroughly gone into. The Captain who had been summoned was duly examined with his witnesses, and Jack got full redress. Not only was all their property and clothing ordered to be made over to them, but all arrears of pay due to them were directed to be paid into the Court. Poor Jack was very grateful to Colonel Bowen, and loud in his praise of that gentleman for interesting himself on their behalf, for had the vessel left the harbour they would have never received their money or property.

It was a part of my duty to attend at all sittings of the Criminal Sessions Court held at the High Court, every quarter and a most irksome duty I found it, for the sittings would be prolonged until each trial was completed. Sir Colley Scotland was the Chief Justice and Sir Adam Biddlestone the Puisne Judge at the time. On several occasions, trials were not finished before nine and ten o'clock at night and once I was not back at the Penitentiary with my prisoner until midnight. The Judges probably suspected that the Jury would be got at if the cases were adjourned and adopted this means to prevent anything of the kind. It is many years since the High Court was lighted up so late at night while criminal trials were going on but this happened recently at the sensational trial of the two planters McGowan and Bailey *for culpable homicide amounting to murder, culpable homicide not amounting to murder and causing grevious hurt, etc.*, when the trial which lasted for 8 days was concluded at 7-30 p.m. on the last day of the trial when a verdict was brought in of causing grevious hurt and the present Chief Justice, Sir Arnold White, who was the presiding Judge agreeing with the verdict of the Jury sentenced Bailey to receive 4 years' and McGowan to 3 years' imprisonment.

I have mentioned in a previous Chapter how on my first appointment to the Madras Town Police in 1869, I had acted for Inspector Burghall, when he went on three months' leave. The several Commissioners of Police were not at all satisfied with this Inspector. There had been several cases of house-breaking at night in some of the gentlemen's houses, and from one, *viz.*, that of a Colonel, on staff employ, a lot of Jewellery was stolen, and Inspector Burghall was believed to be very active in endeavouring to arrest the perpetrators. He actually did arrest one old offender from whom he received some of the stolen jewellery, and instead of reporting the matter and prosecuting the man, he let the thief go and appropriated the jewels himself. He made a present of some of the jewels to a Mrs. Fuller, a woman well known to him, and who was at the time living in a house close to the "Thousand Lights" on the Mount Road. The fact leaked out some time after, Burghall and Fuller were arrested, and the jewels recovered. The case was enquired into magisterially, and Burghall and Mrs. Fuller were committed to the High Court for trial. I have explained in a former chapter that there were no separate blocks in the Penitentiary for under-trial prisoners, both male and female, at the period I am writing of, and as a consequence, Burghall, who was as wily as a fox, succeeded in communicating with his fellow prisoner. After a prolonged trial, the prisoners were acquitted by the Jury to the surprise of every body, for the evidence against them was most conclusive, and the case was as plain as a pike-staff. Colonel Drever who was Commissioner of Police and Superintendent of the Jail at the time was nearly mad with disappointment at the verdict. When seeing the two accused leave the dock free, he remarked to me in somewhat bitter terms "Burghall has been tried by a Jnry of his own country-men and they have acquitted him. What more need be said in the matter." Burghall did not altogether get off without puhishment, for he was dismissed the Madras Town Police, and died some years afterwards at Secunderabad. This

Burghall was the author of a book which was published some years ago, and was written for him by a friend who had some literary talent, giving his reminiscences of detective work in Madras. He possessed a good deal of low cunning, but his talents as a detective were *nil*, and such a thing as honesty never entered his breast.

CHAPTER XXXIV.

Madras Penitentiary—(*Continued*).

Prisoners I Have Known.

It is rather difficult to know where to commence, when one has so many events to narrate, disconnected from each other, and possibly trivial in themselves, yet which to me loomed large as I came upon them at the time of which I am writing. I have mentioned before about the stench from the "Silvery Cooum," but I did not think it would ever approach the effluvia the river emitted twenty-five years ago. In the year 1870, the exhalations were so powerful that even inside the Penitentiary with its high walls to protect one, the stench was unbearable. This led to some agitation on the part of the Madras public, and the Government directed the Department of Public Works to take measures to remedy the evil. An opening was cut near the upper end of the Government House compound, and water was let in from the sea in order to flush the river. More than three hundred convicts were employed on this work for a considerable time, and the result was not altogether unsuccessful for there really *was* a subsidence of the dreadful odours which we in the jail more than others experienced. I had read from time to time complaints in the local papers of the insanitary condition of the Cooum, but I can assure my readers that it is never anything near what it was in 1870. But I promised my readers in the last chapter some further accounts of prisoners I have known, and I must not digress.

Adam Colquhoun had been a Sub-Engineer in the Department of Public Works, and was found guilty, and sentenced by the Tinnevelly Sessions Court on two separate charges of Criminal Breach of Trust as public servant, for each of which he received five years' rigorous imprisonment and ten thousand rupees fine. He was transferred from Tinnevelly to H. M.'s Penitentiary at Madras to undergo his sentence. Being by profession an Engineer, Colonel Bowen who was in charge of the Jail at the time, employed him in connection with the erection of the new buildings which were being put up, *viz.*, the Printing Press, Carpenters' Shop, etc., where as he thoroughly understood his work, he was found most useful. Before his trial and conviction at Tinnevelly, Colquhoun had been in jail previously for a period of eight months on a charge of having committed adultery with Mrs. Coleman, the wife of the Hon'ble Mr. George Coleman. As he was a man of some means his lines in the jail at this period had fallen in pleasant places. He succeeded in getting into the Hospital where he had nothing to do, and where both his wife and Mrs. Coleman were admitted to see him. The latter I should here remark was constant to him till she died. He was thus practically a man with two wives. As an instance of the easy times Colquhoun had during his previous incarceration, I should observe that Inspector MacNamara, one of the oldest Inspectors of the Madras Town Police, gave me his most solemn word that he had seen Colquhoun driving out one night along with the then keeper in the latter's carriage. The crime of adultery of course was then, as it is now, regarded by the world, with indulgent eyes, except perhaps by those infortunates whose happiness it has blighted, and Colquhoun did not suffer professionally. On looking throughout the old records, I discovered that Colquhoun had made many friends in jail, and his memorial to Government praying for immediate release on the ground that further confinement would result in his death was, to say the least of it, amusing, but the authorities were not to be caught with chaff of this kind, and very wisely declined to interfere. The keeper had been a Sergeant in the Town Police, and was apparently "Squared" by

Colquhoun and his friends. He quickly realized the fact on his new sentence that there was another keeper who " Knew not Joseph and his brethren" and that he (Colquhoun) would have to mind his "P's and Q's." Thus he had not such a lordly time of it as before. After the lapse of a certain period after their first confinement, convicts are allowed to see their friends, and this Colquhoun, in common with others was allowed to do. I remember the application made by his wife one Saturday evening to be permitted to see him. She came with her children, and a Mrs. Lloyd who she said was his aunt. Mrs. Lloyd was a good looking woman and seemed to me rather young to be Colquhoun's aunt; but I allowed the visit. A few days afterwards I discovered that this " Mrs. Lloyd" was really his old flame, Mrs. Coleman. She was really a prepossessing woman, and might have turned the brain of many a better principled man than Colquhoun whose moral fibre was of the coarsest. But she never came on a second visit.

The old gallows that was formerely erected opposite the People's Park was removed by reason of the crowds that used to gather to witness executions, and who could with difficulty be kept back by the Police from the vicinity of the gallows. The entrance to the trap was by means of a doorway in the wall through which the condemned man would make his way on to the wooden platform outside by means of a ladder, together with the hangman who adjusted the rope. The first execution that I superintended at this place was that of a man who had murdered his wife in the Parcherry near the Egmore Police Court, and then thrown the knife on the roof of the house. This was the only Native I have known to " exhibit fear" at the last moment and gave trouble. He tried his best to prevent his cell from being opened, but he was overpowered, pinioned, and carried to the gallows. Here the Brahmin Head Constable of the guard gave him a few words of admonition, advising him to pray to the gods, and not to fear. This little exhortation had a quieting effect on the condemned man who became calmer after it. I was most anxious that everything should go off without a hitch, as I and the keeper were at that time really responsible that executions were properly conducted. The Deputy Keeper was outside and was to await a signal from me before he ordered the bolt to be drawn. Myself, the hangman, and two Head Constables had barely cleared the platfrom, when the bolt was drawn and the drop fell. It was by the luckiest chance we escaped being precipitated on to the masonry floor some ten feet below and seriously injured. I found that the two paid hangmen, two chucklers by caste, were nearly useless as hangmen, and they did not even know how to adjust the knot. They had been for years the public executioners in Madras, and their fee for each execntion was four pagodas, or Rupees sixteen ; but this was the last occasion on which they were allowed to officiate, for I got rid of their services, and employed instead an old convict who was thoroughly instructed and received rupees two for each execution. Some years before this, all executions were carried out in the presence of the Sheriff who was responsible that everything was done in proper order. If not conducted exactly with a fanfare of trumpets, there was always a great deal of show about each execution when this official was present.

One of the executions prior to the one I have just related was that of a sailor, named MacNamara, who had been sentenced to death in 1869 by Sir Colley Scotland for the murder of the Master of his vessel, Captain Page. MacNamara and another man, named Thornton, had been sent to jail for mutinous conduct while on board, and had only been released on the morning of the murder. They proceeded to the beach where they saw their Captain and asked for an advance of money which he refused point blank. This exploded MacNamara's ire, and he went for the Captain with his jack-knife, stabbing the latter as he was about to return to the ship. The wounds proved fatal, and poor Captain Page died in the General Hospital to which he was taken, although not at the time in the Jail Department, I was present at the trial. MacNamara suffered the extreme penalty of the law, and his corpse was buried in quick-lime inside the jail. The bodies of native convicts had for years been interred outside the jail on the banks of the Cooum. Here the new gallows was erected, and Colquhoun was employed on the work. Captain Hallett was at the time the Superintendent, and one afternoon instead of coming directly inside the Penitentiary as was his custom, he got out of his carriage and walked round to the place where the new gallows was being constructed. Here he observed Colquhoun signalling to some one across the river. He watched the latter for some time without being himself seen, and then came inside the jail. On going into the office he directed Colquhoun to be sent for and placed before him. Capt. Hallett had made an entry in the Punishment Book of what he had seen Colquhoun doing, and called upon the latter to answer the charge. Colquhoun could not deny it, and was reduced from his possition as Maistry to that of a convict. Captain Hallett also wrote an order in his journal that he, Colquhoun, should never be employed on any work outside the jail walls again. Of course Colquhoun was signalling to his wife and Mrs. Coleman who were living in a house in Chintadripetta opposite the gallows on the other side of the river. Strange to say I had had a dream that morning in which Colquhoun was mixed up. I dreamt that a large white mullet had come out of the Cooum and made its way into the trench which was being dug to lay the foundation for the new gallows, and Colquhoun was in great glee over the capture he had made. When I awoke I felt sure something would happen before the day was over, and the result was as I have stated from this day no work could be got out of Colquhoun, for he got admitted into hospital and there he remained. He did his utmost towards demoralizing the other prisoners, and I must confess that he was very nearly successful in this.

CHAPTER XXXV.

Madras Penitentiary—(*Continued.*)

Prisoners I Have Known.

If one looks at it in the proper way, there is a humourous side to nearly every incident of our lives, but it all depends, I think, on a man himself whether he possesses enough of the "Elixir of life," by which I mean a sense of humour, combined with a cheerful disposition, and a desire to look on the brighter side of things, to make his existence tolerable. Nothing I believe ages a man so quickly as constantly looking on the darker side of things. Although constitutionally a man of cheerful dispoition, I found my jail life most depressing. There is no fun in having to look upon every one you come in contact within your daily routine of duties as a potential enemy, and this was my case, and is the case of every Jail Officer who does his duty conscientiously, for I could have counted the number of those who were well disposed towards me on the fingers of my hands. But to proceed. In digging the foundations for the new gallows we came across the skeletons of three criminals who had been executed some years before for the murder of a wealthy native boy who was wearing a quantity of gold jewellery on his person at the time. They had inveigled him by the offer of sweetmeats into an old disused temple near St. Thome, where they had murdered him and buried his body. The case caused some sensation in Madras at the time.

Executions on the new gallows were much more private than in the old place, as none but those whose duty it was to be present could get near the place, and the Cooum river prevented access to the spot outside the Jail, so that the public could only witness the executions from the Chintadripetta road beyond the river. A few natives hardier than the rest, and with a more morbid taste would however wade half way into the stream to get a nearer view ; but these I am glad to say were disappointed, for the drop was into a pit into which the individual who was to be executed would fall through the trap, so that all the public could see was the rope alone. I used every endeavour to make the executions as humane as possible, and for this purpose I had the ropes thoroughly stretched and greased beforehand, so as to prevent them stretching after the drop fell. Inspector Sam Simpson, afterwards Deputy Commissioner of Police, Madras, whose death a year or two ago after retirement was recorded in the papers, and who was a friend of mine, used to visit the Jail the evening previous to an execution, and assist me in making the necessary preparations. After the rope was properly greased and placed in position on the scaffold, we would have three 56 lb. weights carried to the gallows, fastened to the halter and let them remain on the trap while we got down and drew the bolt. The tremendous jerk when the weights fell which were allowed to hang for a while would effectually stretch the rope. The object of all these precautions was to render death instantaneous, and relieve the condemned persons of any unnecessary suffering, and I am glad to say it had the desired effect, for some of them died without a muscle quivering. This is a gruesome subject to dwell upon, and I only describe it for the information of those of my readers who desire to know how executions were carried out in the Penitentiary.

I have said before that Colquhoun having money at his command had "squared" some of the Jail officials. He did this with the Apothecary as well, and "lived in clover" in the Hospital. The native orderlies who desired to curry favour with the Apothecary, were at his beck and call, and he was able to get a number of little comforts which no other convict enjoyed. In regard to the latter he had as a matter of course to adopt more precautions when there were other European prisoners in the same ward with him. I should here state that when he was brought from Tinnevelly Jail to the Penitentiary, his appeal to the High Court against his conviction was in course of preparation, and that a Vakil who had assisted him in his defence had also come with him to

Madras to aid him in his appeal, and was allowed by Colonel Bowen to visit his client at stated times. One morning the Vakil got chatting with me about the case, and mentioned how when Colquhoun was awaiting trial in the Palamcotta Jail, his wife and Mrs Coleman who was disguised as a Vakil, would accompany him into the Jail when he visited his client. Doubtless he was speaking the truth, but it was at the same time a broad hint to me. As however I entirely ignored the hint he became less familiar to me in talking of Colquhoun's affairs. The appeal was of course a long affair, but it ended in the High Court confirming the sentences. After this he asked for and obtained permission to memorialize Government, and this also took a considerable time to prepare. The document was a lengthy one and every point which told in Colquhoun's favour was set forth eloquently, for at this time there were probaby only a few lawyers who could draw up an appeal better than Colquhoun; but the memorial had no better success than his appeal to the High Court. I should here mention that Colquhoun while in hospital succeeded in getting a number of letters smuggled outside the jail to his friends, which were all written in his ward at night on the fly-leaves of the Hospital Bibles. A few of these letters fell into my hands from time to time, and on reading them I could scarcely credit the fact that they were merely written with the stump of a pencil on the torn fly-leaf of a Bible. One of these, a most interesting one, directed his wife and Mrs. Coleman to be on the General Hospital Bridge at a stated hour, and that he would signal to them from the verandah of his ward in the upper storey of the hospital. This was quite feasible as I found on testing it for myself, for the bridge mentioned was plainly visible from the place where he had intended to signal. Another letter also written on the fly-leaf of a Bible directed Mrs. Coleman to go to the jail, and buy towels, napkins, and other little things from the Deputy Keeper who was entrusted with the sale of such articles of Jail manufacture, and that she could at the same ime obtain any information she required from that individual about him (Colquhoun). The supply of Bibles was limited, and once the fly-leaves were exhausted, Colquhoun would, I thought, be without paper. Not he! his ingenuity was too great to be baffled so easily. On the recommendation of the Apothecary, the Medical Officer wrote in his journal a request that the European prisoners might be furnished with paper for necessary purposes, a thing never heard of before, and the Superintendent ordered me to supply some very thin paper, as the request seemed a reasonable one. This was all Colquhoun wanted, henceforth the paper difficulty was solved, and many an ingenious production written on this paper, and even letters to the public Press found their way out of the jail. As time went to some astonishing effusions appeared anonymously in one of the local newspapers in which the Jail management, mostly that with which Captain Hallett and the keeper were concerned, was condemned in no measured terms. One of these headed " The Whited Sepulchre " caused a great sensation amongst the Madras public who being ignorant of the interior economy of the Jail put implicit faith in the statements, and this gave Captain Hallett a great deal of annoyance. The public were asked to believe that the Superintendent and the keeper, who as a matter of fact were doing their best to serve the interests of the State, were perfect demons, while those of the Jail officials who were lax in their discipline and joined the prisoners in their intrigues, were held up as angels of light. The Revd. DuBois, once well known in Madras, and with whom I was also slightly acquainted, obtained the Superintendent's permission to visit the jail, and on his arrival I showed him around. We got talking about the letters that had appeared in one of the papers, and I told him I knew who the writer was. After bantering me a little on the subject he said " yes, you are right," and then told me he had been in the Editor's office several times, where he had seen the Editor and a certain Solicitor, afterwards a well known Barrister of Madras, laugh heartily over these villainous productions, which they thought the finest of jokes. Both were friends of Colquhoun's and became prominent members of the Madras community before their deaths, while the newspaper I should not omit to state has long since ceased to exist. I remarked to Rev. DuBois that although such letters might appear delightfully funny to those who read them, it was scarcely so to us who were so grossly maligned. We were however soon righted in the public estimation for Mr. Pereira, the Editor of the *Madras Standard*, a rival paper, who was actuated by a sense of justice, asked for permission to see and report on the working of the Penitentiary. Captain Hallett consented, and Mr. Pereira made a long visit and went into everything closely. The result was a long and interesting account signed by himself of what he had seen, which duly appeared in the *Madras Standard* and not only directly traversed all the libellous statements that had appeared in his contemporary, but was highly appreciative of the management of Captain Hallett and the keeper. This had the desired effect on the public mind. Colquhoun who was detected writing some letters was sentenced to receive thirty lashes, but as the Medical Officer would not pass him for punishment, he continued his intrigues as before. Although sentenced to seven days' cells the Medical Officer would not permit any reduction of diet, and the punishment had not much of a deterrent effect. He was confined in one of four cells in the upper storey of the European block set apart for that purpose, and a fine airy place. After he had done five days in this cell, I removed him from it to the next, and then thoroughly examined it, and found three letters in the upper ventilator of the cell. These letters I showed to the Superintendent who found them most interesting reading. One was to his wife and was partly in cypher, which Capt. Hallett managed to get deciphered by a friend at the Club. In it Colquhoun made mention of his letter regarding "the Whited Sepulchre" which he thought would create a sensation and lead to an enquiry by Government, and directed his wife to proceed at once with another memorial to Lord Napier who he thought would probably order his release. A second letter was to a Mr. Gordon who had come out from England only a short time before, and whose father was at the head of some association at home which concerned itself with redressing the so-called wrongs of Indians and Englishmen in India. This Mr. Gordon had some connection with the Press, and used to visit the same house occupied by Mesdames Colquhoun and Coleman. The third letter was to the Editor of the Newspaper of which Colquhoun was so frequent a contributor. For writing these letters, Colquhoun got seven days' cells, as the Medical Officer, as before, would not pass him for corporal punishment. There were in the jail at this time two Native Christain convicts, brothers of the name of David and Thomas who had been officer's servants, and had been sentenced to long terms of imprisonment for house-breaking and theft. These men were employed in the hospital as cooks, and were brought before the Superintendent for attempting to smuggle forbidden articles to Colquhoun. As the case was a bad one Thomas who was the more guilty one of the two was ordered to get fifty lashes, and David to seven days' cells. Before the sentence on Thomas was carried out, it had come to my knowledge that the Apothecary had promised him that although he could not help but pass him for corporal punishment, if he (Thomas) would only scream out loud enough up to the sixth lash, and then pretend to faint dead away, he (the Apothecary) would step the flogging. I reported this ingenious little plot to Captain Hallett, and when matters actually did turn out as I had reported, and Thomas got off with nine lashes only, the Superintendent was greatly annoyed, and removed the two men from Hospital duty and ordered them to be put to hard labour at cocoanut-husk breaking. Both the men had been helping Colquhoun throughout in the hospital, and there was not the shadow of a doubt that the little farce by which Thomas escaped the full amount of his flogging was worked out by Colquhoun in conjunction with the Apothecary.

CHAPTER XXXVI.

MADRAS PENITENTIARY—(*Continued*)

PRISONERS I HAVE KNOWN.

When a man writes a narrative of his own life, it is best for him I think to take his readers into his confidence, and let them know his inmost thoughts and feelings, and why he adopted a particular line of conduct under certain circumstances. This I have striven to do in the previous portions of my history. I have stated that a Jail officer's life is by no means a bed of roses, and every circumstance of my career in the Department confirmed the fact. The iron had entered into my soul. But a man must do his duty in whatever walk of life he may be in, and however distasteful it may be to him. When I took charge of the Penitentiary, there was a wealthy convict in it, a Mussulman of the name of Abdul Kadir, who had been doing a long sentence of imprisonment for forgery, and as he was a man of some substance it was stated that he spent a lot of money to make his life in the jail as easy as possible. His sentence had nearly expired when I was appointed keeper, and he found the jail under me quite a different sort of place from what it was under my predecessors. He said to some of the prisoners whom he had made friends with, and who had before they were sent to jail, held respectable positions—" What does this new man want to trouble, and search me for. I was never searched before. I gave the last man a thousand rupees, and I am prepared to give him the same sum, if he would only let me alone." I was exceedingly glad when he was released for such men give a great deal more trouble to Jail officers than the poorer class of prisoners. Another prisoner of the name of Saiban Kutti, a wealthy man who had been sentenced at Tellicherry to five years' rigorous imprisonment for forgery, and who had been transferred to the Penitentiary, has been living in clover before my appointment, for he had succeeded in smuggling into the jail some large sums of money. Such men have always a number of hangers on amongst the prisoners, and also, I regret to say, amongst some of the Jail officials. He had obtained leave from Colonel Drever to get a Koran for his use in order as he declared to have the consolations of his own religion during his period of affliction. I had some doubts of this man's religious bent, and had him narrowly watched by one or two prisoners in whom I could put some trust. I received intimation that he had received a large sum of money into the jail a part of which he had distributed amongst those of the prisoners and Jail officials who had specially befriended him, and a part of which he had in the shape of bank notes concealed in his Koran. I walked into the yard in which he was confined, took the Koran from him, examined it and found two hundred rupee notes concealed under a paper cover with which the book was neatly covered to keep it from becoming soiled. He got seven days' cells for this offence, and the money was confiscated to Grvernment. It is next to impossible to get such men to do any work at all, for their tasks are performed by other prisoners who are in their pay. When he found that with me he had to do his share of labour, he conveyed a message to me by another prisoner, to the effect that he would as he had done before, be willing give me two thousand rupees if I would only let him alone. But I was not to be bought, and seeing this he succeeded in getting into hospital where he was able to get more comforts than he could obtain in any other part of the jail. It is well known to any Officer with Jail experience, that there is more plotting and more smuggling of contraband articles into a Jail Hospital with perhaps only thirty or forty sick prisoners in it than there is in the rest of the jail with several hundred convicts. As a matter of fact the Hospital is the only weak point in the administration of a jail, and there is more scheming and underhand work carried on in it in one day, than there is in the rest of the jail for a whole year. Indeed it is almost impossible to know what plots are being hatched amongst the sick prisoners, for a sick man knows he has always some one of the subordinates at his back to support him. However, from time to time, I got some valuable information from the jail convict servants, and one morning a maistry came running to me to say that Saiban Kutti had got a lot of gold coins with him. I made as much haste as I could but the patients had taken the alarm, and were lying on their cots as harmless as doves, and as oblivious of my presence as if there were no keeper in existence at all. They had not time however to conceal the whole of the coin, for I found some five franc gold pieces concealed in a broom placed in a corner of the room, others hidden in a chatty containing dry earth, and some concealed in Saiban Kutti's mattress. The total value of all these gold pieces was Rupees 135 and the whole sum was of course confiscated to the State. For this offence Saiban Kutti would have been assuredly flogged, but as he was physically unfit to stand corporal punishment, he received the usual seven days' cells. The little circumstance alarmed the Hospital servants and orderlies and there was quiet for a while, but only for a short time, for they were soon up to their old tricks again, and I had to keep a very watchful eye on them. In addition to this haul of money, I managed to unearth a number of small sums which were secreted in different parts of the several yards and I also discovered a sum of nine rupees concealed in a belt worn by convict block warder Moonean, who had been doing a sentence of fourteen years' penal servitude for the murder of a brother horsekeeper in Waller's Stables. Of course all the prisoners concerned in the concealment of money received their due meed of punishment. There had been a small manuscript book maintained for years containing entries of all sums of money found on the persons of convicts and the total amount if I remember rightly was only rupees seven and some odd annas. In the course of a year or two I had discoved over four hundred rupees which goes to show the carelsss way in which the jail was managed formerly. On Moonean's offence being brought to light, the convict block warders who had been making money in a small way for years, grew alarmed, and began to mend their ways. Two of them reported cases of misconduct in their blocks, and in return were set upon and severely injured by a number of the old offenders, some of whom had been in jail sixteen times. I had the ringleaders quickly locked up and entered the whole case in my journal for the Superintendent's information. Capt. Hallett was determined to uphold the authority of the convict block warders, and prevent them from being terrorized, and sentenced ten of the guilty men to a hundred and fifty lashes each. The last of the ten when it came to his turn to be tied up made a bolt for it and jumped into a big well in the middle of the yard where the punishment was being carried out. He was soon got out, and made to go through his punishment. There were about four hundred of these old offenders in the Penitentiary, and many of them had been in jail from time to time from an early age. If the jail became overcowded, large gangs would be transferred to other Central Jails which had accommodation for them. The Superintendents of these institutions used, I regret to say, always complain bitterly about the worthless characters we sent them, and said that these men were demoralizing their Mofussil brethren. Colonel MacDonald Smith (afterwards Inspector-General of Jails) who was acting as Commissioner of Police for the town of Madras, visited the jail one Monday morning while the weekly inspection of the jail was being carried out by the Superintendent. Mr. Symonds was then Superintendent of Prisons for the town of Madras, and Colonel Smith who had previous to his appointment to the charge of the Madras Police, been Superintendent of the Central Jail at Rajahmundry, remarked to me "Look here Mr. Tyrrell, a batch of convicts you sent to me at Rajahmundry some years ago were the biggest blackguards you could have selected, for they completely demoralized the other prisoners in the Rajahmundry Jail." I told him he was mistaken as we had far worse men than he had ever received at Rajahmundry. He then went around the yards inspecting the men in the different blocks, and when he saw a face he recognized as having been in the Rajahmundry Jail, he called out to me " there is one blackguard " and " here is another " and " there another scoundrel " and so on. In one of the yards he pointed to a convict named Kadirvelu who was doing his eighth term of imprisonment and said " here's another scoundrel "—" No more a scoundrel than you are " blurted out Kadirvelu in very plain English. The Colonel was taken aback, but went on with his inspection. I saw Mr. Symonds turn away his face with a grin on it, and although I could not help smiling myself, I shouted to the man as sternly as I could to " Silence." I dare say if the Colonel had known the convict would have understood him, he would not have spoken as he did. After leaving the yard, Mr Symonds, and I had a hearty laugh over the matter, and as for the convict, it was out of the question to punish him for his impertinence, as the Colonel had brought it on himself by his indiscreet remark. As regards the trouble a Jail Officer experiences in preventing malingering I may here mention an incident connected with some juvenile offenders. About twelve of this lads had got into Hospital suffering from diarrhœa, and as soon as two or three of them were discharged as cured, they would be back again the next day suffering from the same complaint, until the Medical Officer, Dr. McCrae, a most patient and painstaking officer, was puzzled how to account for it, and asked me if there was anything wrong with the food. I told him he saw the rations for himself every day, and that if they were bad, the adult male and female prisoners would also have been affected. I asked him to leave it to me, and that I would get to the bottom of the mystery. He thanked me and expressed a hope that I would, for, said he " I don't like this constantly recurring diarrhœa." I selected two turstworthy convict maistries, and after giving them the necessary instrutions, placed them in the same ward as the juveniles. About twelve o'clock the same night, two of these lads who were to be discharged the next day commenced wrangling in regard to the distribution of some pieces of croton oil seed which they had concealed in the fringe of their "cumblies," or native blankets. There were only three seeds left, one of which was cut up for distribution, and one of the lads complained of the smallness of the share that fell to his lot, hence the quarrel. One of the maistries, who was wide awake and listening to the disturbance, jumped up and seized both the two whole seeds and the broken pieces of the other, and there was a considerable flutter in this cote of innocent doves. Dr. McCrae was greatly pleased when told of it the next morning, and so were the Superintendent and I, for it should be remembered that the health of the prisoners is a very important detail in the successful administration of a jail, and both the Medical Officer and the Superintendent are held responsible for any preventible outbreak of disease. The croton oil plant at the time I am writing of, was very common in Madras, and bushes of it were gowing on the banks of the Cooum, and, as most of my readers know, the seed of the plant is a most powerful purgative.

CHAPTER XXXVII.

The Madras Penitentiary—(*Continued.*)

A Dream and a Government Order.

In a former Chapter I related how two dreams I had were realized in a somewhat peculiar manner. In this Chapter I purpose mentioning the circumstances connected with a similar experience I had shortly after, in which Colquhoun was concerned. The dream and its realization may have been a mere coincidence, or it may not, I leave it to my readers to form their own conclusions, and will proceed to relate the facts. Owing to the kind offices of his good genius the Apothecary, Colquhoun became a fixture in the hospital which was a haven of bliss to him compared to his cell among the rest of the European prisoners. The Apothecary to give him a better opportunity of carrying out his little schemes to enable him to send out and receive letters to and from his friends, represented to the Medical Officer, Dr. Cockerill, that he (the Apothecary) found the work in the hospital in the morning much more than he could cope with single-handed, and asked for the assistance of two Medical Students. Accordingly two Native Students from the General Hospital were appointed to his duty, and used to attend the Jail Hospital every day from 7 to 9 A.M. I saw through this little manœuvre which increased the difficulty of preventing letters passing in and out of the jail, but of course, it would have been unwise of me to protest in the face of the Apothecary's plausible excuse for additional aid. However I bided my time which was not long in coming as I knew Colquhoun would commence his writing again before many weeks had elapsed. It was given out that Colquhoun was dangerously ill with asthma, and that the Apothecary was doing his utmost to pull him through, but there was very little hope of his recovery. The comedy was enacted I believe with the sole purpose of hoodwinking the Jail Officials and lulling our suspicions in regard to Colqubun's little games. The Senior Warder, Daniel Steele, a Scotchman, who although entirely innocent of all collusion in Colquhoun's schemes, had yet a lingering pity for his countryman and believed all these stories, came to me with a long face one evening after locking up, and told me that "Colquhoun, poor fellow, would not live throughout the night, as the Apthecary had said his death was very near." I took this with a little "*cum grano salis*," as I knew from his physical appearance, Colquhoun had many years yet to live, although I must confess it, this death, if it had occurred at the time, would have been a great relief to the Jail officials. Shaw, a convict, whose jail history I have given in a former chapter, was in Hospital along with Colquhoun about this time, but was discharged, leaving Colquhoun in sole occupation of the European Ward. Shaw was of course much put out at being discharged from Hospital where he had been in receipt of better rations and doubtless some of the good things intended for Colquhoun. I had a strong suspicion that Shaw's discharge meant something and awaited events. Colquhoun was thus left in solitary glory to carry out his schemes, and no one could get near him at night, for, as I explained before, every key of the Jail was locked up at night in a box, the key of which was in the custody of the Head Constable of the guard. I would have given half my month's pay to have caught a glimpse at what Colquhoun was doing, but of course under the circumstances I have just mentioned, this was impracticable. I was worried in mind when I retired for the night, and possibly my last thoughts before I dropped asleep may have been of precious stones, which as stated in the earlier portion of this narrative I was much interested in, for I dreamt that I was walking to and fro in front of the entrance gate of the jail and picked up two or three small diamonds, which, on examining, I found to be genuine stones, but not of much value on account of their small size. By a sudden transition, I then found myself in the Egmore Police Court, and I heard my name called as a witness. On going up the steps into the witness box, these oscillated so much that I felt myself falling, when I awoke. After inspecting the prisoners and marching off the different working parties to their respective duties for the day, I went outside the jail and walked to and fro on the spot where I had been walking in my dream, chewing the cud of bitter reflection, and wondering what game Colquhoun would be up to next, to my annoyance. I paced up and down for nearly an hour, till the Head Constable of the guard wondered what had possessed me and whether I was going off my head. It then occurred to me that it was time for the two Medical Students to be leaving the jail, and I knocked at the entrance gate. As I entered I saw the two Medical Students approach the gate from the inside. I stopped them between the two gates, and directed the Head Constable and Deputy

Constable to search them thoroughly. The two young men protested loudly, and wanted to know by what authority I had ordered them to be searched, threatening at the same time to report my conduct to the Inspector-General. I paid no attention to these threats, and told the Police to proceed with the search. Some one must have conveyed the news of what had happened to the Apothecary, for he came rushing up the guard room in hot haste. He was a very dark man, but his countenance was gray with rage. On seeing me, he threatened me with all kinds of dire penalties. I took no notice of his ebullition, but merely told him to go away, or I would search him as well. The students were stripped of all their clothing, but nothing could be found either on their persons or in their apparel until their sandals were examined, when in the inner soles of the sandals of one of the men were discovered two letters, and in one of the sandals of the other man was found a third letter. The Apothecary must have got wind of this fact also, for again he rushed up to the guard room, shouting out to me, but in an altered tone of voice, to come and search the surgery, as he was not safe in the jail. I told him to go on with his work, and that I would search the surgery when I thought fit to do so. I sent for Mr. Simpson, the Reserve Inspector of Police, who was in charge of the Police guarding the jail, and reported the case to him. He took the two Medical Students to the Police Station where they were duly charged, and allowed bail on the condition of their appearing before the Chief Presidency Magistrate the next day. The case however did not come up for hearing till two days afterwards, as the two pleaders employed by Mr. Colquhoun for the defence asked for and obtained an adjournment from the Court to allow of their gaining more information regarding the case. When the case eventually came on for hearing, I was called up as the chief witness for the prosecution, and as I was going up the low flight of four wooden steps leading into the witness box, I inadvertently stepped on the side of one of them, instead of in the middle, and nearly brought the whole concern toppling over and myself with it. I was duly examined and related all that had occurred. Colonel Weldon, the Chief Magistrate, had the three letters placed before him. After reading them he asked me but one questions, and that was whether Colquhoun's Christian name was Adam. I replied in the affirmative. Both the pleaders for the defence asked me a few questions, but they found it difficult to shake my evidence, and soon let me alone. Neither attempted to question my authority in the matter of searching the accused. Mr. Jeremiah, one of the Pleaders, however, wanted to know why I had searched them on that particular morning rather than any other. I thought of my dream, and smiled within myself; but dreams don't count in a Law Court and I merley replied that I had my own reasons for it. He then wished to know whether I had read the letters. I said " yes, and I advise you to read them also." Had he read that one of them, *viz.*, one to Mrs. Coleman, he would not have been so ready to take up the defence. Had it been published, I doubt whether there would have been one among Colquhoun's sympathizer's who would have pitied him. Although affectionately worded it was the most filthy production I had ever seen. It was full of obscene suggestions and clearly showed how utterly depraved both Coluquhoun and Mrs. Coleman must have been, if that was their usual style of corresponding with each other. The Medical Students were found guilty, and received the maximum sentence in such cases, *viz.*, two months' rigorous imprisonment each, and the Magistrate although appealed to by the Pleaders to substitute a fine of Rs 50 each, in lieu of the imprisonment, declined to do so. On the following day, the two young men were both working in a convict gang outside the Jail, with fetters on their legs. They had doubtless been well bribed for their services, and deserved no pity whatever. But Captain Hallet and the Inspector-General (Colonel) Tennant) were immensely pleased at the result of the trial, and commended me for my action in the matter. Captain Hallett made a strong representation to Colonel Tennant relative to the intrigues that were going on between Colquhoun and those who were helping him, and forwarded at the same time, copies of the three letters which were being smuggled out by the students. One of these was intended for the Press, another for Mrs. Coleman, and the third was to Mrs. Colquhoun urging her to do her best to get him released by memorializing the Government herself. Colonel Tennant forwarded Captain Hallett's letter and its enclosures to Government with a strong representation of his own. The outcome was a Government Order couched in very severe terms. The Apothecary was removed from his appointment in the Jail Department, and sent back to Military duty, and the Medical Officer was severely censured. I was extremely sorry for Dr. Cockerill, for he was the last man to connive at the evil doings that were being carried on amongst the prisoners, but he took too many things for granted, and placed too much reliance on the Apothecary who was a broken reed, so far as rendering support to his superior's went. My readers will learn something more of Mrs. Coleman before I conclude my reminiscences. As for Colquhoun, I should state that during my absence on the occasion of my appointment by the Duke of Buckingham and Chandos to act as Superintendent of the Fort Jail at Palghat, he was transferred to the Central Jail at Salem, where, I subsequently learned, he had been employed writing petitions for those prisoners who had appeals to make to the High Court. His ability was so marked that the Judges of the High Court could not help but being struck with it, and wrote to the Superintendent to ascertain who it was that was the author of these appeals as they appeared to emanate from one person. This put a stop to Colquhoun's petition writing. Some years after this, he died at Ootacamund where he was in charge of an estate consisting of land and houses belonging to a well-known Law Officer who had befriended him in the olden days, that is, when he first get into trouble.

I may mention how regarding dreams that I have had that, when dreaming of snakes that appeared to attack me in my dreams, something was sure to happen. On one occasion, I dreamt that two very large black snakes, coiled themselves round my neck and lifted me up into the office which was 20 feet above the place where I was standing in my dream. On the following morning the Jail Superintendent (Captain H. Hallett) came to the Jail, when two block warders (the highest rank given to convicts), made a request to see the Superintendent. I obtained permission to place them before him, when they commenced to vilify me in strong measured terms, which seemed so plausible to the Superintendent that he almost believed them, but on further enquiry found that these statements were entirely false.

CHAPTER XXXVIII.

Madras Penitentiary—(*Continued*)

Prisoners I Have Known.

I am afraid my readers must think that I have the temperament of the Fat Boy in Pickwick who delighted in making people's flesh creep ; but a Jail officer's duties are such that he sees the seamiest side of life, and I must, if I wish to make this a truthful narrative, relate incidents which may shock people with weak nerves. This Chapter deals with a gruesome subject, and I advise those of my readers who have delicate sensibilities to skip it and go on with the next.

Ragavan was an under trial prisoner awaiting trial at the High Court of Madras for the murder of two women whose throats he had cut with a razor borrowed for the purpose from a barber. Preparatory to his trial he was confined in the Penitentiary, and here he had made the acquaintance of a number of Jail birds under trial who had thoroughly primed him as to what he should say in the Court. The case was absolutely clear, and the man was found guilty. When asked to state if he had anything to say why sentence of death should not be passed upon him, he admitted the justice of his sentence, but at the same time begged His Honor, the Chief Justice, Sir Walter Morgan, on behalf of the other prisoners in the Jail to issue an order to remove the Keeper, and that if His Lordship did so, the prayers of all the prisoners would go up to the throne of grace to save his immortal soul from any punishment hereafter. He said that he had been handcuffed, which as an under trial prisoner he should not have been, and that he had also been given ragi conjee to eat, when he should have had a rice ration. I was present at the trial and so was the Superintendent who was seated not far from the Judge. The man spoke so earnestly, and in so touching a manner that the Jury, and the Law Officers present looked at me askance as if I were nearly as bad as the accused himself. The Chief Justice listened quietly to the prisoner and merely remarked, "if what you state is true, why did not you report the matter to the Superintendent who would certainly have rectified any complaint you had to make against the Keeper." He replied that it was hopeless to do so, as the Keeper had it all his own way, and he again said that the prayers of the poor men in Jail would assuredly go up to the throne of grace for His Lordship, if he would only pity the poor prisoners, and relieve them from the tyranny of the Keeper. He also informed His Lordship that I had refused promotion, in order to stay at the Penitentiary to get the old offenders punished.

Like everything else his harangue came to an end, and he was sentenced to death. I was asked no questions by the Court, nor was the Superintendent, and I could not help smiling at the prisoner's statements, for I really thought that the man's perilous condition had driven him crazy. Two of the Madras Papers however took up the matter, and commented very severely on the conduct of the Keeper as revealed by the prisoner. I certainly never expected that an enquiry would have been ordered in the matter by Government, for a number of prisoners had before this asked the presiding Judge on receiving their sentence to be transported to the Andamans, rather than be sentenced to do their terms in the Penitentiary, and I remember once hearing Mr. Justice Holloway say to a prisoner who had made such a request to him "I am very glad you don't like the Penitentiary." At any rate the Superintendent, Colonel Waters, an old Mutiny Officer, who had been wounded in the Sepoy War, and who was acting for Captain Hallett then doing duty temporarily as Chief Presidency Magaistrate, was asked to enquire into, and submit a report as to the truth or otherwise of the prisoner's statements. Colonel Waters was equal to the occasion, and in reply stated that he had been present in Court, when the prisoner had abused the keeper, but there was not a particle of truth in the man's statements, and that he (Colonel Waters) had himself ordered the prisoner to be handcuffed for refusing to be vaccinated, and that the handcuffs were removed from the man's wrists as soon as the inoculation was over. Also that the vaccination of all under trial prisoners was performed in accordance with the orders of Government. Colonel Waters, moreover stated as regards the man's complaint about being fed with ragi, that he only received what he was entitled to under standing orders, and that he was a weak minded man who had been instigated to make his complaint by a number of old offenders who had promised to pray for the welfare of his soul if he did what they wanted him to. He kept up his spirit of bravado up to the last day, and then memorialized the Government for a mitigation of his sentence and I should here state that no execution is ever carried out in such circumstances until the final orders of Government are received. He made a most abject appeal for mercy, and withdrew every lie he had told against me, but as the authorities declined to interfere, he went to his execution in a very penitent frame of mind. It may not be credited by the outside public, but every word the man had stated against me actually redounded to my credit. While on the subject of executions, I will here relate a most gruesome incident with which I as Keeper was concerned. The condemned man had murdered two wemen by cutting their throats in Triplicane and afterwards attempted to commit suicide by cutting his own throat. His trial had to be put back to the next Sessions as the wound had not healed and when the trial came off he had only just recovered. He was found guilty and condemned to death. When the man was executed, it was one of the most revolting sights I had ever witnessed. The drop fell. the wound opened out and bled copiously, and his head seemed half off. But I must get on to other and more pleasant subjects. I had all up-hill work in putting a stop to Jail irregularities, but I must confess, I received the most loyal assistance from Warder Mansell of whom I have made mention in a previous part of this history. It was not, however, till Mr. Edward Dean was appointed Warder, that I really obtained valuable aid. Mr. Dean had before this been employed in the Municipality in which he had done some good service in detecting cases of smuggling in Madras, and the old offenders soon found out that in him was a man who thoroughly understood them and all their pleasant little ways. With two such Assistants as Warder Mansell and Mr. Dean I soon got the Jail into proper working order. It is a great pleasure to me to state that Mr. Dean is now doing well in the department in which he was risen to the position of Jailor at Trichinopoly, and as the Senior Jailor, he now receives a salary of Rs. 250 per month, the highest drawn by any Jail subordinate. He has moreover lately acted as Superintendent, Tanjore Cellular Jail. Subsequent to this Messrs. Henry and William Septimus Upshon were both warders in H. M.'s Penitentiary, and through their excellent services, have both risen to the rank of Superintendents in the Department. Mr. S. Upshon who was my Jailor at Connanore is now Superintendent of the Jail at that place.

One morning I was going my rounds to inspect the European and Eurasian prisoners when I heard a loud laugh proceeding from the European yard. The European Warder on duty, a man of the name ot Studdart, was probably not aware that I was close by, or he would not have allowed this irregularity. His duty was to have fallen the prioners in for my inspection, and not allowed any hilarity among them. I called upon him for an explanation, but could get nothing satisfactory from him. I accordingly told him that I would place his conduct before the Superintendent. I also warned the European convicts that I would bring them up for punishment next day, when one of them who had been awaiting the order to fall in, blurted out the reason for the laughter. They had been talking he said, of Mrs. Coleman's death which had recently occurred, and one of the late comers had stated that there was a rumour that she had either been poisoned or had poisoned herself. Another of the recent arrivals who had been present at the inquest stated that she had grown immensely fat and that when her body was dissected at the *post mortem* examination she was found to have died of fatty degeneration of the heart. Convict Jeremiah whose name occurs in a previous portion of this narrative as having been the last man to see Shaw alive, on seeing me approach, then remarked " I should like to see that fat b—— dissected" which immediately created a roar of laughter. Warder Studdart was duly punished for neglect of duty, and Jeremiah was sentenced to receive thirty lashes. He told Mr. Symonds, the then Superintendent, that what he said was merely in a joke and he really meant no harm to me; but Mr. Symonds told him that jokes were not allowed in Jails. Jeremiah was a well known character in Madras and was a confirmed toper. He was a very thin and emaciated man, but notwithstanding his weak physique, he went through his punishment like a man.

CHAPTER XXXIX.

Madras Penitentiary—(*Continued*).

Prisoners I Have Known.

The fundamental principle of the penal system adopted in recent years by the Government is not to inflict pain upon offenders against the Criminal Law, as many ignorant persons may be led to think, but to make the punishment deterrent, and to induce a reformation in the criminal. With this object in view the underlying idea in a Jail Rules is to combine rigour with humanity, and they have been so drawn up as to afford a well conducted prisoner better treatment in Jail with an eventual remission of his sentence. I mention this fact here so that my readers may not imagine that a Jail officer's life is one of systematic harshness to the convicts. With this little explanation which I trust may not be out of place, I will continue the prison history of some more convicts I have come in contact with.

At the commencement of my career in the Penitentiary there was brought into it Mr. Turnbull, a Subordinate Officer in the service of Government, who had absconded with a large sum of money belonging to the State, and had left the country. He had flitted about London and Paris where he spent large sums of money freely, and enacted the gay Lothario, but Nemesis was close on his heels, and he was run to earth in England, arrested and brought back to India. He was tried at the High Court, received a long sentence, and sent to the Jail at Ooatacamund. He had fitted himself out with a most expensive and elaborate wardrobe, with which no doubt he had been enabled to enter and shine in fashionable society of a certain class. In taking an inventory of the three large trunks of clothes that had come out with him, I found the list a very long one indeed. However our acquaintance was of short duration for he was soon despatched to Ootacamund.

The next case I have to relate is that of four troopers of the 18th Hussars who were accused of having committed a double murder in the Dhobie's Parcherry in Bangalore. It was the "cause celebre" of the time, and created a considerable stir both in Military and Civilian circles, for the regiment to which the men belonged, was a popular one in the Madras Presidency. It was on a Christmas day, when a report was made to some men of the Regiment, that a comrade of theirs was assaulted and severely beaten by some Natives in the Dhobies' Parcherry, and four of the men mentioned, who were all on guard at the time, sallied forth to go and avenge the injury done to their comrade. They must have been the worse for liquor, or they would not have vented their rage on a harmless old man and woman who were the natives killed. The sword of one of the men was taken from him by a Sergeant of Artillery, and was found to be stained with blood. This was used in evidence against the men, in addition to which there was the evidence of their absence from the guard-room. The son of the Regimental Sergeant-Major of their Corps was also called in to give evidence against them. In cases of this kind, there is generally much obstruction shown by the Military authorities to Police enquiries—witness the recent case of outrage on a Burmese woman in Rangoon; and this was no exception to the general rule. The enquiry by the Magistrate at Bangalore was a long one and resulted in the men being committed to take their trial at the High Court at Madras. Thus the accused came under my charge in the Penitentiary, and were for some time there awaiting trial. They were all young soldiers, and were always spick and span in their uniforms. Mr. Whillie Grant, their Solicitor, had visited them twice with a view to obtain instructions for the Counsel for the defence, John Miller Esq., Barrister-at-Law. On the opening day of the Sessions I placed the four men in the dock, and Mr. Grant, on seeing me do this, remarked to me with a smile on his face. "You never had four such good looking fellows there before, had you?" They were dressed very neatly as if for parade and caught the eye of every one in Court. A special jury was empanelled to try the case, but as the defence raised objections to some of the members, other jurors were appointed in their place and the trial proceeded. Mr. Miller had one or two Junior members of the Bar to assist him and contested every inch of the ground taken by the Crown Prosecutor, Mr. Cunningham, and on hearing some points urged by the latter gentleman against the accused, electrified the Court by saying "Here are the Crown Officers crying for blood." This shocked Mr. Cunningham who seemed cut to the quick, for I actually noticed a tear glisten in his eye, while he replied that he did not want any one's blood, but was only trying to do his duty in laying the case plainly before the jury. It was well known that there was no more humane man than Mr. Cunningham. The trial lasted four days, and I knew that Mr. Justice Kernan would have sentenced them to death if they had been found guilty, for I noticed that he had brought his "black cap" with him on the last day of the trial. Colonel Prettyjohn who commanded the regiment, and the Captain of the men's troop, Captain Yeldham, of the "Lays of Ind" fame, were both present in the Court throughout the trial, and were anxious for the honor of their Regiment that the men should get off. Indeed the Colonel had to be called to order very severely by the Judge for some remarks he had make during the progress of the trial. During the lunch hour on one of the days of the trial, Colonel Pettyjohn came up to me while I was standing in the verandah of the Court House, in order to get a breath of sea air, and asked me what I thought of the case. I told him that from the evidence I had heard so far, I thought the men were guilty—"I'll be d—d if they are" said he, and walked away. Captain Yeldham had a lengthy conversation with me about the case, and seemed to take a more rational view of it. On the fourth day of the trial the jury declared one man to be not guilty, but could not come to an agreement with regard to their verdict as to the guilt of the other three. The man, who was found *not guilty* was released, and his three comrades were ordered to be tried a second time. A fresh jury was empanelled and a further trial of three days occurred. The Assistant Superintendent of Police at Bangalore, Mr. Hewetson who had arrested the men and who was rather a nervous witness, was browbeaten in true "Old Bailey Style" and every action of his in connection with the prisoners, was magnified into an enormity, one particularly was severely commented on by the Counsel, namely, that he had separated the prisoners in the "Ball Alley" and examined each man apart with the view of making him confess. Inspector Killman of the Bangalore Police who was another witness for the prosecution, was also put through a very severe cross-examination by the Counsel for the defence. After the speech by the Crown Prosecutor had closed, Mr. Miller made an elaborate defence, making the most of every point in the prisoner's favour. Mr. Justice Kernan's summing up of the evidence was very clear, and from his charge to the jury it was evident to most of those present in the Court, that matters were looking very black indeed for the three men, but the jury, after being absent for some time came back with the verdict of "not guilty." Although there were a few of them who did not agree with this verdict, the majority were for acquittal, and the men were released. Captain Hallett who was a gentleman of rare ability had been appointed to act as Chief Presidency Magistrate, and while holding this office, had received a letter from Sir William Rose Robinson, the Senior Member of Council and temporarily Acting Governor of Madras, informing him that he (Captain Hallett) would be appointed Sheriff for the City for the ensuing year. Captain Hallett showed me the letter, and told me that I should act as his Deputy Sheriff. This did not happen, for three days afterwards Sir William wrote again to say he was extremely sorry that the appointment of Sheriff could not be held by a Military Officer under the rules, and that it would have to go to a Civilian. However, some time after this, a Jail Conference was directed to be held in Calcutta with a view to improving the administration of Jails in India, and an officer from each province was appointed to it, Captain Hallett being selected to represent the Madras Presidency. Before the time appointed for the Conference to meet, I had obtained two months' privilege leave as I was anxious to visit the Bombay House of Correction, the Central Jail at Jubbulpore, and the Presidency Jail at Calcutta, or as Colonel Tennant used to call it "No. 1 Chowringhee," and look into the methods of working in these institutions. Captain Hallett gave me letters to the several Superintendents, and I was able to bring back copious notes of all I had seen at these places in regard to discipline, manufactures, and in short every thing connected with their interior economy. The Jailor at each place gave me all the information he could regarding his Jail. I stayed two days at each of the stations, and made the most of my time. I found that the three institutions I had visited were worked on quite different principles from ours and that the Jail subordinates in the Madras Presidency were receiving much lower rates of pay in comparison. The Jailor of the House of Correction at Bombay was receiving Rs. 300 a month, while the Jailor at Calcutta, a Pensioned Serjeant-Major, received Rs. 350. I observed also that nearly all the clerical work in this last Jail, including the keeping up of the various registers, was performed by native convicts, a thing which was never permitted in the Madras Presidency. I made a note of everything I had seen, and on my return made over all I had recorded to Captain Hallett. After the Conference was over, and he had returned to Madras, he told me that my notes had been of much use to him. He related an incident to me that occurred at the Conference in connection with a difference of opinion that had taken place among some of the members. He had had, he said, received valuable assistance from a young Medical Officer of the Bengal Presidency, who was at the Conference and who took a very practical view of matters. Some of the older officers who were present gave it as their opinion that some of the cells which came under discussion were of a certain size, while he (Captain Hallett) and the young Medical Officer took a defferent view. The discussion went on until Captain Hallett to end it suggested that the whole of them should go personally and measure the cells for themselves. This was done, and Captain Hallett was found to be correct. This incident he mentioned to me to show how even in such trifles a man is likely to err.

In 1877, Captain Hallett left the Jail Department for good on his appointment to the Judge Adocate-General's Department, Madras, in which he rose in a few years to be the Head of his Department, and was afterwards appointed Judge Advocate-General at Army Head-quarters, Simla. Before leaving the Penitentiary, I was the happy recipient of the following testimonial from him which he recorded in his Journal.

H. M.'s PENITENTIARY,
4th December, 1877.

Extract from Superintendent's Journal.

Before handing over charge of the Jail, and leaving the Jail Department for good, I wish to place on record my opinion of the subordinate officials :—

Jailor—Of Mr. Tyrrell it gives me much pleasure to speak in the highest terms. He is the best subordinate official I have known, and Government has no more willing, capable and honest servant.

If the recommendation of the late Jail Conference, that in each Presidency and Province there should be two or three Superior District Jails under the charge of picked Jailors, who will combine the offices of Superintendent and Jailor, be carried out, I am sure Mr. Tyrrell should be the first selected for such promotion. I have but two regrets in leaving the Jail Department, one of which is that I shall be saying "Good-bye" to Mr. Tyrrell. I sincerely hope that he will soon get a better berth.

(Sd.) W. H. HALLETT,
Supdt. of Prisons, Madras.

Captain Hallett had on a previous occasion written to Government that I had performed the varied and exacting duties of my post with such ability as to give him entire satisfaction and that the best thing he could say of my worth was that he did not know whence I could be replaced. There is no doubt that my promotion to a First Class Central Jail was due to Captain Hallett's high opinion of me.

CHAPTER XL.

Madras Penitentiary—(*Continued*).

Prisoners I Have Known.

It seems to me from long experience of the shady side of human nature, that, although most men I have met, even amongst the convicts, had some grains of gold hidden away somewhere deep down in their hearts. There have been others with a natural propensity for evil, who regarded lenient treatment as a sign of weakness, and with whom neither kindness nor severity would avail in turning them away from their objectionable ways. One such of these was a prisoner of the name of DeVarney, who had been a soldier in the 43rd Light Infantry, an Irish-American by birth, and a downright ruffian in character. He had been sentenced to a term of seven years' imprisonment by a General Court-martial, and commenced giving trouble from his first admission into the Penitentiary. He had been awarded "seven days' cells" for insubordination, and when brought into the office, he handled Warder North (afterwards Keeper of the Penitentiary and who died as such in Madras) in a most brutal manner. In fact, the man was such a brute that Warder Mansell's description of him to me was that he was a cross between a man and an alligator. Captian Hallett wished to give the prisoner a chance, and warned him that the next time he interfered with or used violence to Warders in the execution of their duty, he would be flogged. Although well guarded he managed to break through his escort in an instant, rushed to the office table on which Captain Hallett was writing, seized it and nearly turned it over that gentleman, but however, only succeedeed in upsetting the ink over Captain Hallett's clothing. He was seized and secured, and I was ordered to remove him from the office. Half an hour afterwards I was directed to bring him in again, but on this occasion, he was thoroughly secured to prevent his making a second treacherous rush. Captain Hallett had meanwhile recorded this last offence in the Punishment Book and sentenced him to receive "fifty lashes." The Apothecary had been sent for to report medically upon him, and passed him as being physically fit for corporal punishment He was tied to the triangle, and I selected Warder Dean, a very powerful man, and the best we had to handle the cat and tame refractory characters; DeVarney however took his flogging without a murmur, or the quiver of a muscle. It seemed to us that we might just as well have flogged a log of wood for all the signs of feeling he exhibited. He was then locked up in a separate cell. Eventually he was sent home to England by the Military authorities to finish his sentence there, and we were very glad to be relieved of his presence in the Penitentiary. There was another prisoner of the name of Thornton, who although not a refractory ruffian, had his own idiosyncrasies. He had also been in the army, but was sentenced by the Civil power to a long term of imprisonment. He was punished on two or three occasions for breaches of Jail rules, either by reduction of diet, or by getting "cells," but he took his punishment good humouredly, and always had a smile on his face. He had gone on this way for some time, when he suddenly conceived the idea of feigning madness, with a view to getting into hospital. The Medical Officer had him closely watched, and used to visit him every other day. One morning the Warder, whose duty it was to take him out for his daily bath discovered him eating a piece of his own dung. I have read in Holy Writ of such things having occurred in ancient times, but it was the first and only case of the kind that came under my own observation. When asked for an explanation of his conduct, he merely smiled idiotically without replying, which led the Medical Officer to the conclusion that the prisoner was really insane and a representation was made to Government, on the Doctor's recommendation to have Thornton sent to the Lunatic Asylum in Locock's Gardens. This was sanctioned, and we got rid of him on his removal to the Asylum. It had been a habit of mine on leaving my quarters at day-break to go for a short walk outside the Jail, up to the General Hospital bridge and back again several times, after which I would proceed with the work of unlocking the prisoners. One morning not quite two months after Thornton had been transferred, I met him on the bridge coming from the direction of Black Town, where he had apparently been for the most part of the night on a long ramble and was now proceeding on his way to the Asylum. On observing me, he gave me one of his usual smiles and a cheery " Good Morning " and went on his way. His absence most likely had been discovered at the Asylum for I heard afterwards that a better watch was maintained at the institution. As for Thornton, I believe, he could have been safely allowed out every night, for he was not a man of violent character, and would return to his ward when he had finished his nocturnal ramble.

Among other prisoners I have known, were two Brahmins who hailed from the Vizagapatam District and were in custody in the Penitentiary awaiting their trial on a charge of forging Government bank notes. These men had been carrying on the manufacture of false notes on an extensive scale, some of which they had succeeded in circulating in Madras, and had then gone on to Benares and Calcutta and other stations, " foisting " the notes on the public, as they visited the different places. They had been tracked from place to place by Colonel Weldon and Inspector Simpson, both of whom received great *kudos* for their clever capture of the two forgers whom they had some difficulty in running to earth, and in whose possession there was still a large quantity of the notes. These had been manufactured in the good City of Madras, and some lakhs of rupees of them had been impressed. They were such clever imitations of the genuine article, that only an expert could detect the difference. The two men were brought back to Madras, examined magisterially, and committed to the High Court for trial. On admission to the Jail as under-trial prisoners, they at once refused to eat the food prepared for them in the Jail although cooked by a Brahmin, stating, that as members of the *sect* of Brahmins to which they belonged, they would lose caste if they ate food prepared by any other class of Brahmins. Captain Hallett was at first a little perplexed as to how he should act in the matter, for it ought to be remembered that the Jail Rules are very clear in maintaining the caste rights of prisoners in the matter of food. He however, gave them as under-trial prisoners permission to cook their food in their own yard, and I was put to a great deal of trouble in attending to this matter. I, moreover, had to detail a European Warder specially to restrict them to prevent any communication between them and the rest of the prisoners. The trial came off at the High Court, and a very interesting one it proved. Colonel Weldon and Inspector Sam Simpson were examined at great length, and Mr. Barren, the Government Lithographer, was also called in as a witness and questioned. He stated how the accused had obtained some of the plates on which the notes were engraved, and how that not suspecting their designs for a moment, he had given the articles to them. The case was so palpably clear that they were found guilty and transported for life. Shortly after their conviction, they were sent with a batch of other convicts to the Andaman Islands, and one of them, on the voyage out, jumped *over-board* and was drowned. During the whole of my tenure of office as Keeper of the Penitentiary, His Grace the Duke of Buckingham visited the place only once. He was accompained by his Staff, and went very minutely into every thing he saw, asking me many quentions. On inspecting the cooking shed in which the evening meal for some hundreds was arranged, he examind the curries, and the ragi puddings, all of equal size and weight and made in wooden moulds, and had a few of the latter weighed and found them all of equal proportions. He then looked at the cooks, and said smilingly, "These cooks look in fine condition. Is it possible for them to get any extra food." "No doubt of it your grace" I replied, at which he seemed amused and laughed quietly to himself. While on the subject of the Penitentiary, I should add that during the ten years I was in subordinate charge of it, viz., from 1869 to 1879, there were no outbreaks of cholera in the Jail, except on two occasions and these were only sporadic cases of the disease introduced into the Jail, by prisoners who had been sent out under the Prisoners' Testimony Act and who had brought back the disease with them on their return. Even on these two occasions, the number of deaths were but few, and the disease did not assume an epidemic from, whereas prior to 1869 cholera prevailed frequently in the institution, when the diet consisted of rice, the staple food of most of the prisoners, and they were able to get many little comforts smuggled in from outside. From 1869 however when ragi became the staple prison diet, the health of the prisoners was remakably good, and this can hardly be said of most of the Jails in the Presidency, notwithstanding the fact that Madras was notoriously unhealthy at this period, and cholera, small pox, and other diseases were very prevalent in the town. Shortly after his visit to the Jail, His Grace the Duke of Buckingham appointed me Superintendent of the Fort Jail at Palghat, which had been opened two years before this, during the famine, for the reception of the surplus prisoners from the more crowded of the Jails in the Presidency. The appointment was held at the time by Mr. Grimes, an ex-Lieutenant of the 56th Foot, and a brother of Mr. H. Grimes, the Superintendent of the Coimbatore Central Jail. I was appointed to succeed Mr. Grimes Junior at Palghat under the following circumstances. There had been an *emeute* in the Central Jail at Cannanore, of which Colonel Beauchamp was Superintendent, and one or two of the convicts had been shot down from the central tower where the Superintendent and the Jail subordinates had taken refuge. An enquiry was ordered by Government, and Mr. Henry Grimes, who was then Acting Inspector-General of Jails, was deputed to investigate the matter. Mr. Grimes reported that the outbreak was partly due to the *laches* of Colonel Beauchamp who had not acted in accordance with Jail rules. Under these rules a prisoner's offence must always be recorded in the Punishment Book before he is punished, Mr. Grimes said, that Colonel Beauchamp, instead of doing this, had flogged them first and made the entries afterwards. Colonel Beauchamp who had been injured in the eye by a stone thrown by one of the prisoners, was removed from the Jail Department, and his services were placed at the disposal of the Military authorities. Mr. Grimes from Palghat was sent to take charge of the Central Jail at Cannanore, and I was appointed Superintendent of the Palghat Jail, of which I assumed charge from Mr. Ebenezer Sewell, the Assistant Magistrate. This was my first appointment as Superintendent of Jails. The Palghat Fort is known to those who have made a study of Indian History, as having been besieged and captured by the British. Before it was converted into a Jail the Tahsildar's Cutcherry and other Government Offices were located in it. At the time I took charge, four or five of the prisoners were in hospital, dying of dysentery, and others, suffering from the same cause, were in a fair way of following their example—and I am sorry to say soon afterwards succumbed. From my personal observation, I could not but see that there had been a lot of mismanagement before, but I must leave this for a future Chapter.

CHAPTER XLI.

Palghat Fort Jail.

As I mentioned at the end of the preceding chapter, there had been gross mismanagement in the Palghat Fort Jail with its four hundred prisoners, chiefly men from the Coimbatore and Malabar Districts. The unhealthy condition of the prisoners was therefore not to be wondered at, for even of the milk drawn for the patients in Hospital, half was diverted to private uses. An Apothccary of the Subordinate Medical Department was in sole Medical charge of the Jail Hospital, but the poor man was easy going, with no force of character and wanting in the energy necessary to root out abuses in the department of the Jail of which he was the head. I had thus my work cut out for me, but I proceeded cautiously. Although I had been some years in the Department, it was my first appointment as Superintendent, and I had to feel my way to avoid any pitfalls. The convicts were chiefly employed in gangs digging pebbles from the bed of the river and carting them to the roadsides for the repair and upkeep of the roads. The convict labour on these was, however, paid for at a low rate by the Municipality of which the Assistant Magistrate, Mr. Sewell, was the Chairman. In addition to this work, there was a small garden between the moat which surrounded the fort and the fort wall. On Colonel Tennant, the Inspector-General's return from furlough, four new barracks were ordered to be built for the better accommodation of the prisoners. The walls of the barracks were ordered to be of "pisa" work, a method of construction which I have not seen adopted anywhere else, and which I shall describe for the informotion of those who are not acquainted with it. A mixture consisting of wet clay and gravel after being well kneaded is compressed into wooden moulds of about six feet in length, and proportionate thickness, and after the mixture is dry, the moulds are withdrawn and placed higher up Mr. Henry Grimes had done a lot of this kind of work in the Coimbatore Jail, and sent me the necessary wooden frames used as moulds, and under the orders of the Inspector-General, came down himself for three days to give me detailed information as to the plan of the buildings, and the method of their construction. I must confess that he gave me most valuable aid. The buildings at the best were of rough workmanship and were roofed with wooden planks, thickly thatched with palmyra leaves. They were completed before the outbreak of the Monsoon, for such work is obviously impossible during the rainy season in Palghat, where, during my first year of residence, I have known it to pour without cessation for twenty three days and nights, after which there was a break of seven days with cloudy and threatening skies, and there was a wet spell of eighty-two days with rain more or less every day. The rainfall was so great, that I began to wonder to myself where all the water came from, for within thirty miles to the East on the Coimbatore side, there was in all probability scarcely a shower of rain during all the peried, and nearly the same might be said of Ootacamund which is only forty miles to the North from Palghat, as the crow flies. There is no road from the hills North of and close to Palghat, but there is a jungle tract to Ootacamund. Probably a few numbers of the jungle tribes inhabiting these hills may have travelled through these jungles, but it must have been a terribly risky thing even for them, for the jungle is infested with tigers, cheetas, bears, and other wild animals. I enquired from Mr. Sewell, the Assistant Magistrate, and three or four other gentlemen, whether gold was obtainable in the neighbourhood, and they told me that they never heard of its being discovered in the locality although I mentioned to them that I had read of its being found here in an old Indian Gazetteer. At any rate I was determined to find out for myself, and I ascertained that even at this time, there were three or four very old natives residing in the place who made it a means of livelihood to search for and obtain gold in the jungle ; but the average value of their daily find was between four and five annas, and never at any time exceeded eight annas. I sent for the men and offered them the full value of any gold they might find, which was much more than they could obtain in the bazaar. They agreed to deal with me in future, and on some days I would pay them as much as eight annas for what they brought In the course of two months, I amassed a Cockle's pill box full of gold dust. A quantity of it I sent to Messrs. P. Orr and Sons with a sapphire I had with me, and asked them to make me a ring out of it. My next door neighbour, Mr. T. Elsworthy, the Principal of the Palghat High School with whom I was on very friendly terms, was as eager in this question of the existence of gold as I was, and both of us decided to go one morning and see the spot were the gold was found. We took two of the gold seekers to make sure of its being the right place, and Mr. Paton, the Railway Permanent Way Inspector, very kindly took us on his trolly about two miles down the Railway Line towards Coimbatore. Here we got out of the trolly, and wended our way into the jungle for about another two miles before we came to a halt. We were uneasy at finding the imprints of a cheetah's foot near a small but very deep pool of water in which were some very large fish. There were some cultivated patches of open ground close by where the jungle tribes grew their paddy, and it was on one of these, our gold seekers commenced operations. There was a small shallow rill of water running by this patch which emptied itself into a small pit about seven or eight feet deep, and then ran off again in a shallow stream about an inch or two in depth. It was at this little pit or hole that the gold seekers started work. They got out quantities of the sand and pebbles from the bottom and with a common native winnow which did duty for them as a cradle, they separated the pebbles and coarse gravel until there was nothing left but very fine sand. After an immense expenditure of time and trouble, there would perhaps remian a few grains of gold in the residue at the bottom. This operation was carried on several times while we were there, but during the whole of the time not more than five annas worth of gold was obtained. There was no doubt that the soil about here is auriferous, and that he statement contained in the old Gazetteer was perfectly corrtect. Many years before this the locality had been visited by a European miner, a German, I think, who commenced prospecting for gold in a business-like manner, with the latest improvements in gold mining implements of the period, and probably he did find gold in several places, but could not carry on mining on any large scale, as he was stricken down with fever, poor fellow, and had to be sent home, leaving some of his plant behind him in the jungle. Of the gold dust I had amassed, Mr. Elsworthy got four or five gold rings made, and had them set with garnets, several of which I found in the river at Palghat, and had had polished by a native lapidary so that the (Mr. Elsworthy) could safely aver that the rings were entirely the products of Palghat. He gave one of theses rings to a Mrs. Tomlinson, a lady living at Palghat at the time, one to her daughter Mrs. Du'Pen, and one or two to other friends. These rings are probably still in existence, although the owners may not be aware of their origin. There was nothing extraordinary in our finding cheetahs' imprints near the pool we had visited, for prior to this a cheetah had actually been killed in the Church compound, in which place it had sought shelter after visiting the garden of Mr. Gay, a contractor living near the Palghat Railway station. On the Coimbatore side, the Wallajah station was in the old days noted for tigers, a driver having been known to have actually shot one of the beasts from his engine in the Wallajah jungle. At the Wallajah Station, the Stationmaster and porters had on one occasion to rush into and bolt themselves in the office, as a tiger had taken possession of the points. His wire to the District Traffic Manager for guns and assistance is probably the most unique on record.

The Library and Reading Room at Palghat was at this time very low for the want of funds and the Assistant Magistrate, Mr. Sewell, together with two or three others who were anxious to get it out of debt and on a good footing again, called a meeting at which several suggestions were made, among which my suggestion to hold either a theatrical performance or a penny reading, was adopted. The Tahsildar and two or three other Native gentlemen who were members of the institution exerted themselves strenuously to assist Mr. Sewell. Of course even those who took part in the performance gave their ten rupees each towards the fund, and all the Native gentry followed suit, and this brought up the collection to over three hundred rupees which put the Library on a sound financial basis. Some of the ladies sang and several gentlemen gave readings, while I gave a couple of recitations but the gems of the evening's entertainment were a couple of humourous readings by Colonel Dance, a son-in-law of Mrs.

Tomlinson which pleased the audience very much. The entertainment was held in a large room in Mr. Sewell's bungalow where light refreshments were also provided. I was shocked on seeing some of the Native gentlemen come into the room dressed in their semi-transparent mull cloths tied around their waists, which caused them to have a Rontgen or "X-" Ray appearance. One can admire this sort of thing in a music hall dancer, but in a Drawing-room, and in the presence of ladies, it was outrageous. One must draw the line somewhere and I drew it at that. These gentlemen were quite unconscious that they were transgressing the laws of decency. Indeed I may say they seemed as if they were quite proud of themselves. "You may look and you may admire, but you must'nt touch." That was the sort of look they had on their faces. I remarked to Mr. Sewell "surely these gentleman should not come in such dresses where ladies are." Mr. Sewell, who was rather of a serious turn of mind smiled, and replied "why, don't you know this is full evening dress for the Native gentlemen of Malabar?" The concert was a perfect success, and the Library was in a flourishing condition again. As to Colonel Dance I may say that his son was quite recently Collector of Malabar.

CHAPTER XLII.

PALGHAT FORT JAIL.—(*Continued.*)

Compared to Madras, life in Palghat was of the most humdrum character. The community was a small one and chiefly consisted of the official element. After going through the usual daily routine of duties, we had to depend upon ourselves for any amusement whatever. Among those whose acquaintance I had made was Mr. Theobald, a subordinate of the Forest Department, with his head-quarters at Palghat. He was an ardent sportsman and a deadly shot with gun or rifle, in addition to which he was a good taxidermist, so that he was able to skin and preserve every bird or animal that fell to his gun. He had three splendid guns with him. One a heavy elephant gun, and two lighter ones. He understood photography, and turned his hand to almost anything. Taken altogether, he was a very handy man indeed ; when I first saw him he had about 40 monkey skins properly prepared by himself and these he was making into a carpet for a gentleman in Madras. A wealthy American globe trotter, a member of many learned Societies had been out in the jungle with Mr. Theobald for a little shooting and had bagged his first tiger in Mr. Theobald's company. He quickly discovered that Mr Theobald although a Eurasian by birth, was a man a good deal above the average and one who had a thorough knowledge of the Fauna and Flora of the jungle, and so got him nominated as an Associate of one of the Learned Societies of which he (the American gentleman) was an influential member. On leaving the jungle, he promised Mr. Theobald that he would send him out some young gorillas from the Straits Settlements, and this he actually did. Six young animals were sent out to Bombay, but two of the animals died on the voyage, and two on arrival at Bombay. The remaining two, however, a male and female, reach Palghat safely, and Mr. Theobald was the proud possessor of two very fine young specimens of this species of the Simian tribe. With their wistful eyes, there was something very human and childlike in these animals. They would wrap themselves in their "cumblies," and would go to sleep quite cosily at the foot of their master's bed ; but Mr. Theobald feared they would not survive the wet season of Palghat. The male gorilla was the larger of the two animals, and as young as they both were, I have often seen them on a small tree at the back of their master's house breaking off small boughs and throwing them down in sport at any one approaching the spot. After a short time, the female died, and Mr. Theobald was doubly careful of the male animal whom he use to call "Sonny Boy," and the poor brute appeared as if he understood all his master said to him. A soon as ever the weather grew cold, the brute would wrap itself up in its "cumblie" and lie down. It was fed on bread and milk and plantains, but I doubt whether this was the correct thing to give, considering that in its wild state in Borneo, its chief dietary was probably roots and wild fruit. Compared with its limbs, its head and stomach were very large which gave it a most comical appearance, but there was nothing malignant in its nature, for it would allow the smallest child to play with it. It seemed however to pine for its home and parents like a child, and one day it died. Theobald had both the animals stuffed. One day I heard a loud commotion just in front of my compound and rushed out to see what was the matter. To my surprise I saw Theobald holding a very large cobra by the tail and showing how cleverly he could handle the reptile without allowing it to bite him. Some natives passing on the road had seen the cobra on the roadside, and had raised the alarm which brought Theobald to the spot. He at once grasped the reptile by the tail and held it out, a most risky experiment, but it shows what the man's pluck was. He killed the cobra after playing with it in his foolhardy way for some time. Mr. Theobald was a Eurasian of slight build, but a more fearless man I never saw. Nothing seemed to thwart him. Although I have not had the pleasure of meeting Mr. Theobald since he left Palghat, I have often seen his name in the papers. The cause of his leaving Palghat was rather unfortunate for him, as sometime afterwards some Government elephants of which he was in charge, had died of foot disease, a malady peculiar to elephants, and their loss was ascribed to Mr. Theobald's neglect. For this he was removed from the service. In vain he appealed to the Madras Government and the Government of India for fourteen years, for justice—until at last in despair he memorialized the Secretary of State for India, and was finally, after a long enquiry, granted the pension of his rank and service with arrears to be paid from the date of his dismissal. Meanwhile he had obtained employment as a Ranger in the Forest Department of the Mysore State. Many tigers, cheetahs, and bears have fallen to his rifle, and as for rogue elephants, there was not one that has got " khubber " of, that he did not go for and bring to book. His name is well-known in the Mysore Province and Southern India as a Shikaree and many a shooting party of gentlemen has he ciceroned in the Mysore jungles. I have frequently read contributions from his pen in the public papers under the *nom-de-plume* of " Big Bore " giving particulars of these shooting expeditions. It was the irony of fate that sent the officer who was instrumental in having him removed from the British Forest Service, to be, on retirement from service under the Madras Government, the head of the Mysore Forest Department a few years ago. I should like to have been present when the two met ; but Theobald is still in the service and working as zealously as was his wont, I presume his chief has learned to think better of him. His work in Mysore has been chiefly in connection with " khedda" operations, a most suitable employment for one who understands wild animals and their habits. Quite recently I read in the newspapers that one of the largest Pythons ever seen was captured by him. I may here say that for nerve, pluck, and daring, three essential requirements in a successful Shikaree, Mr. Theobald stands second to none in India, and I speak as a lover of the noble sport myself.

Europeans on their first arrival in Palghat are shocked and disgusted by the treatment meted out to the lower orders by the high caste natives of the locality. This is not so pronounced in other parts of India as in Palghat and in Malabar generally. My friend, Mr. Elsworthy, told me that he had frequently to bring his pupils to task for absenting themselves, and that the usual plea put forward by them was that they were obliged to go in search of their *slaves*, or in other words, their jungle toilers, who had given them the slip and departed elsewhere to better their condition. These people are called " Cherumers," and are the aborigines of the locality, and are regarded by the higher castes as little better than dogs. Their wage is in kind, that is, just sufficient rice to keep body and soul together, and a cloth once a year. It is no wonder then that they frequently desert their masters. Scores of time I have seen men, women and children belonging to this tribe close to a pond at the back of my house, looking up the lane between my house and Mrs. Tomlinson's, watching for an opportunity to get on to the road in front. If a high caste man appeared at the other end while they were half-way up the lane, these unfortuntes had to return from whence they started and this "hide and seek" kind of dodging went on for perhaps an hour until the Cherumers obtained a chance to get on to the road, when there were no caste men about. This dodging was laughable if it were not so pitiful, and yet some of these high caste natives are probably congress men and aspire to a seat in the Indian Cabinet, if their long looked for Canaan, a Parliament for India, becames a certainty. I wonder how they would like a Cherumer as leader of the opposition to lay down the law to them. All this disgusted me with the mild Hindu of Palghat and I frequently gave him a piece of my mind, and told him that in Madrss that these poor outcastes would have just as much claim to walk on the roads as the Governor himself. Low as these Cherumers were, there was another class still lower in the scale of humanity. These poor wretches would never appear on the highways, but would shout for alms from the fields adjoining, and were not allowed even into the bazaar. When purchasing their provisions, they were not permitted to approach a shop, but had to lay their money down some distance away, and retire when the provisions were brought and left for them to take away. Can my readers imagine such a thing being done under the very eyes of a civilized Government in the closing decades of the Nineteenth Century. I was determined that some of these poor people should come into my compound as a practical illustration of my opinion on the subject, and I gave my low caste servants a few annas to give them, but one and all refused point blank to put the money into the hands of the outcaste. They said they would leave the money on the roadside, and that is all that they would do, but I was determined to show them a lesson in charity, and went and put the money in the hands of the poor wretches myself, telling my servants that I cared but little whether they treated me as an outcaste or not. They were several members of the Basil Mission in Palghat at this time who attempted to preach Christianity to these people, and one old Missionary, some years before, was determined to do what he could for them in this direction. Accordingly he started one morning in his bullock carriage for the village, but the old man little dreamt of the trouble he would have on the road. Neither the Scripture reader, nor the coachman would go near the village, much less drive into it. The old Missionary, who know Malayalam well, told them that as they would not accompany him on his Christian errand, he would drive himself, but that they should have to walk home, for he would not permit them to ride back in the coach. He took the driver's seat and drove into the village where he succeeded in getting into conversation a with few of the outcastse. This same gentleman used to be greatly annoyed by a Brahmin priest, when he used to have open air sermons for the benefit of the poorer natives. As soon as the Missionary collected a crowd, and began his sermon, the Brahmin commenced an opposition sermon against Christianity. This nearly led to a disturbance on two or three occaaions, until the Reverend gentleman was fain to complain to the Magistrate, and get out a summons against the Brahmin. When the case came on for hearing, the Brahmin said he was merely praying to his gods. This excited the wrath of the Reverned gentleman who shouted out " But these be no gods." The Magistrate found he could not help the Missionary, and the case was dismissed. To show what a priest-ridden country Malabar is, I should here observe that there are small hamlets where even the Tiers, and other low caste Hindus are not allowed to pass through streets occupied by Brahmins, andthis rule is rigidly enforced. It is said that if the shadow of one of these men fell on a Brahmin, he would have to bathe and anoint himself seven times, before he could retire to rest. In connection with this caste system, an amusing thing occurred near Calicut where British troops are stationed. A Company of British Infantry stationed at Malapuram, a few stages from Caiicut, was returning to Head-quarters on relief by another detachment. On their way back some of the men noticed a low caste man jump over a prickly pear hedge into the field alongside. They asked the cook-boys what it meant, and were told that the man got away to avoid a high casteman who was approaching and whom they pointed out. This tickled Tommy immensely, who thought he saw his way to a practical joke The cooks were told to catch both men and this being done, the faces of the Brahmin and the outcaste were rubbed together, and Tommy went on his way serenely. But for the Brahmin it was eternal damnation, for all the waters of the Ganges could not wash away the pollution.

CHAPTER XLIII.

Palghat Fort Jail—(*Continued*).

My lines were cast in much more pleasant places during the term of my employment at Palghat, for the prisoners were much more tractable, and gave me less trouble than I had experienced at Salem, and in the Penitentiary. The greater proportion of them were in for grain robbery during the great famine of 1877-8, and I believe the majority were ryots who had been driven to crime by hunger. As a matter of fact the *raison d'etat* for the opening of the Palghat Fort Jail was the accomodation of the additional prison population due to the increase in crime brought about by the famine. There were of course a few old offenders, who, as is their nature even now, indulged in intrigue against the authority of the Jail Officials, but without much success, for I resorted to the "cat" with these individuals, and quickly brought them to reason. I was glad when my Brahmin Jailor took leave, for it enabled me to appoint a European in his place, who, although not acquainted with Jail routine at first, quickly learnt his duties and did his work more conscientiously than the permanent incumbent. While on the subject of this Brahmin, it is best, I think, before going on with other matters, that I should relate what eventually happened to him.

On the break up of the Palghat Fort by order of Government, he reverted to his former appointment as writer in the Coimbatore Jail where his sins quickly found him out. He was caught by the Jailor intriguing with the prisoners, and brought before the Superintendent, Mr. Henry Grimes. Whatever may be said to the contrary, there was one thing Mr. Grimes would never tolerate, and that was a breach of discipline even amongst those who were supposed to be in his favour. On this point he was inflexible, and much as he had favoured the Brahmin, the latter had to go—and thus ended his career, in the Jail Department.

One of the Apothecaries who had medical charge of the Jail was a Rajput, a pushing man with plenty of ambition, a laudable thing no doubt at times, but not when it is exercised to the injury of the public service of which he was a member. I was informed one day that he had quietly left the station for Madras without obtaining leave. His object in going to Madras was to see a friend in the Surgeon-General's Office, whom he wanted to make the necessary "representation" on his behalf. In his place came the Hospital Assistant of the Municipal Dispensary, stating that the Apothecary was down with fever, and had asked him (the Hospital Assistant) to take temporary charge of the Jail Hospital and to attend to the other Medical duties. *My* informant regarding the Apothecary's absence was a person I could trust, and I was therefore sure of the fact. I went twice to the Suramangalam Railway Station to catch the Apothecary on his return. On the second occasion the train by which he had arrived stopped about two hundred yards outside the Station near the goods shed, probably to enable him to alight and get away without being observed by anybody at the station. Thus I failed to catch him *in flagrante delicto.* I reported the whole circumstance in a long letter to Mr. H. Grimes, who was then temporarily acting as Inspector-General for Col. Tennant. As I thought the Apothecay's offence was one of the gravest character, Mr. Grimes however seemed to take a differnt view of the matter and wrote me a letter which was anything but pleasant reading. In fact he thought I had been too officious and had acted indiscreetly. This made me very indignant, as I was perfectly sure the Apothecary had been to Madras without leave, an offence, which in the case of its being committed by a Military Officer, would certainly have entailed a Court Martial, and besides, I was but doing my duty in reporting the matter.

A few days after this, the Magistrate, Mr. Sewell, visited the Jail and I mentioned the whole matter to him and showed him the correspondence. "Rather sharp work this" he remarked after reading the letters, "but had I known you wanted particulars regarding the man's absence, I could have given them to you, for, in the same train going to and returning from Madras, the Municipal Contractor travelled with him." Colonel Tennant had meanwhile returned and resumed charge of the Inspector-Generalship from Mr. Grimes and I hastened to place the facts before him together with the additional evidence I had obtained. The reply I received from Colonel Tennant was quit a different one from that which I had obtained from Mr. Grimes. In it he said he approved of the line of action I had taken with regard to the Apothecary ; and here a disagreeable matter terminated. As for the Apothecary, I should say here that he has had his ambition gratified, and the now holds an important position in the Madras Medical Department.

I had hitherto seen snakes of all kinds most common in hot places in India, and I concluded from this that these reptiles would not be so much in evidence at Palghat with its tremendous falls of rain, but I was to live and learn, for never have I seen anywhere so many snakes as at this station. cobras and other venemous reptiles were as plentiful as *black berries.* I had three of the first comfortably living in holes in the wall of my well, and it was in Palghat that I first saw a Russel's viper of whose deadliness I had read of before. It was in a hole in a bank by a hedge, and it was quite by chance that I observed the reptile, while out for a walk with a friend. It looked very innocent and harmless while we gazed upon it and made no attempt to get away but it met with a sudden and untimely death from a loaded shot-gun which we had with us. When a person relates a snake story, the tendency of the listener is to receive it " with his tongue in his cheek," but here is one, for the truth of which I can vouch, and which shows the vitality possessed by the cobra. I always thought it was a cat only that had nine lives, but I think a cobra can run it very close in this respect. About a hundred yards from my house and running parallel with it was a road which was constantly used by country carts. Late one evening, a bandy man, while driving his cart and bullocks over this road, was bitten by a cobra as also, was one of his bullocks. One of the wheels of the bandy had gone over the reptile and cut it into two pieces. By a strange fatality, another native with his cart and bullocks came along this road shortly after, and was bitten, at the same spot, also with one of his bullocks, by this very same snake. I regret to say the two natives and their animals died an hour or two after. Now this is a matter I think which affords food for reflection. I have heard of other kinds of snakes which had been as severely injured, slowly crawl away to die and I leave it to my readers to judge whether the cobra had acted upon any feeling of revenge prompted by the consciousness of its injury being fatal, and had remained behind to do as much execution as possible before it died.

I have heard natives speak of injured cobras tracking a person to have their revenge and I have also been told that if you killed the male or female of a pair, its mate is sure to follow you, but this incident was the first instance of anything of the kind I had seen myself.

I had now been nearly two years and four months at Palghat, and during all this period I had not received a single visit of Inspection from Colonel Tennant, the Inspector-General. Naturally I "laid the flattering unction to my soul" that he had found nothing to complain of in my administration of the Palghat Fort Jail, for he was an officer who would certainly have done so if he had discovered anything wrong. I had however the honour of seeing the Duke of Buckingham again, although it was only at the Suramangalam or Palghat Railway Station, while His Grace was on his way from Madras to the West Coast. On an occasion of this kind all local officers received due intimation, and I, with others, drove to the station to meet the Duke's train. His Grace was in his saloon carriage where he received us, and I was presented to him by Captain Hobart, his Private Secretary at the time. My reception was of the briefest duration possible. His Grace asked me how things were going on with the Jail and I replied "As fairly as can be expected your Grace" and bowed myself out.

As I remarked in a previous chapter there was plenty of shooting to be had in the jungles near Palghat. But fruit was scarce. The only kind that was plentiful was the "Jack," a fruit which is very common in all places where the rainfall is abnormal. There was a description of fruit, however, called the "Sour Sop" which I found to be excellent. I spoke to Mr. Brodie, the Assistant Magistrate (now high up in the Civil Service) about this fruit, and he told me he had never seen it. I answered that there were three or four of the trees growing in his own garden. I met him again and he said that he tasted the fruit and had appreciated it very much. This gentleman gave me every help possible. While I was at

Palghat the first Native Convenanted Civilian to enter the Indian Civil Service, one Mr. Ramaswamy Chetty, was appointed to act as Assistant Magistrate of the Station. The fact of a Native being sent to Palghat as Assistant Magistrate was a thing the local leaders of Society could not comprehend, and it caused a great deal of talk and angry comment, especially amongst three or four of the ladies. One lady in particular gave vent to her feelings on the subject in very strong terms. The "fuss and clatter" made in connection with this matter suggested to one the idea of a hawk swooping down on a poultry yard. Mr. Ramaswamy Chetty however came, saw, and conquered, and the lady who was the loudest in her condemnation of him was driven by him to Church in his turn out, *Verbum sap!* Mr. Ramaswamy Chetty attended Church regularly, and was most popular with the Europeans. He had taken a high place in the list of "Passes" in the Examination for the Civil Service in England. In our private, as well as our official relations with each other, we were the best of friends, and I got to like him very much. He was also a man of wide culture, and had some valuable classical works which he kindly placed at my disposal. There was a great deal of comment in the Madras papers regarding the certainty of his losing caste on his return from England, but he did not seem to care a straw for the opinion of his fellow castemen, for he went to Church, dressed, ate, drank and behaved in everyway like an English gentleman. I must also say that his house was furnished in the English style, in the most elaborate and expensive manner, and could scarcely have been in better taste than if the hand of a lady had had anything to do with it. It was some time after I had left the station that I heard of his tragic death. He had either shot himself accidentally or had committed suicide—the point was never cleared up. He had been to Calicut for "the Canterbury Week," and while there had had a dispute with a planter who had used some strong expressions towards him This, it was said, had preyed on Mr. Ramaswamy Chetty's mind, and led him to commit the deed. I was very sorry indeed to hear of of the occurrence, for I liked him very much and felt sure that, had he lived, he would have been an ornament to the Indian Civil Service. In May 1881, Colonel Tennant wrote to me to say that it was his intention to recommend the closing of the Palghat Fort Jail to the Government of Madras, on the ground of the unhealthiness of the place and the number of cases of sickness amongst the prisoners. This was an indirect slur on my administration which I could not pass without notice, and I replied, after a comparison of the death rates before and after I had taken charge, that the health of the prisoners had improved in a marked degree during my tenure of office. Moreover I compared the death rates of the Coimbatore and other District Jails with that of the Palghat Fort Jail, and showed that they were *charnel* houses in comparison. Colonel Tennant was, however, determined to carry his point and wrote to Government to the effect that the reason for maintaining the Palghat Jail no longer existed, as the prison population in the Madras Jails had decreased considerably and the prisoners at Palghat could be easily accommodated in other Jails of the Presidency. While recommending its abolition he gave me every credit for the manner in which I administered the Palghat Jail while I held charge of it, and the Government in their order closing the institution referred in very kind terms to the zeal and assiduity I had displayed while in charge.

After closing the Jail, I returned to my former appointment as Keeper of H. M.'s. Penetentiary on the 3rd June 1881 ; but I had meanwhile applied for, and was granted privilege leave for three months, and was glad to have a respite from my labours.

Before closing my experiences of Palghat I should like to say a few words about my friend Mr. Elsworthy, who I was sorry to hear had died some years afterwards at that station. He was one of the kindest and most genial of men and a capital *reconteur*, with an inexhaustible fund of humourous anecdotes. He had been an Army School Master at St.

Thomas' Mount, and had some funny things to say about one of the Chaplains in charge in his time, the Revd. Mr. F.— This gentleman had a lisp, and one Sunday morning informed his congregation that "Bawabbas was a wobber." On another occasion, he told his hearers, who were mostly soldiers, the amount of the previous Sunday's collection. There was so much silver, he said, and so much copper (mentioning the amounts), seven brass buttons, and six pieces of tin from the corks of soda water bottles. This caused a suppressed titter to run through the congregation, but he went on to say that although brass buttons and pieces of tin were useful things in there way, they were of no use to him and begged that they might not be put in the collection bag any more. Elsworthy was at one time Editor of "The Western Star" at Cochin, and he told me how often he was at his wit's end for "Copy," and of the difficulties in the way of the Editor of a provincal paper. He would often, he said, write a letter in it himself in one issue, in order that he might be able to pick it to pieces in *the* next.

We were badly off in the matter of our spiritual needs at Palghat, but Mr. Elsworthy who was Lay Trustee acted efficiently in the absence of a Chaplain, and used to take the Services. The Revd. W. Elwes, the Chaplain at Calicut at that time, however, would come down three or four times a year for such essentials as Baptisms and the administration of the Holy Communion. The latter belonged to the same country as I did and I was extremely sorry to read of his death recently.

CHAPTER XLIV.

The Penitentiary Again.

Hitherto my progress in the service of Government had been steady, although slow. But there are "ups and downs" in every man's life, and I was to be no exception to the rule, for, after occupying the position of a Superintendent for a period of two years and four months, I was compelled through no fault of mine to revert to my old appointment as keeper of the Penitentiary, and my *locum tenens* to his former post as Jailor of the Central Jail at Coimbatore. Mr. Symonds was still Superintendent of Prisons for the Town of Madras when I returned, and I submitted through him a Memorial to the Government praying to be given some pay and allowances that I received when in charge of the Jail at Palghat. Mr. Symonds backed up my application strongly, chiefly on the ground of my long and meritorious service under Government. Had he stopped here all would have been well, but he went on to say that my substitute was both young and active, and he thought that the Penitentiary required a young and more energtic man. This was unfortunate for me, for the Government could not understand so strange and vague a recommendation and the order on my memorial stated that it did not appear from my memorial that I was anxious to retire from the service, and the Government trusted that I would continue to serve them for many years longer. I never for a moment thought at the time that I would continue in the service for fourteen years more. It was not long after resuming charge of my old duties that instead of the improvement in the management of the Jail that I expected to find, I discovered that there had been a considerable falling off from the condition in which I had left it, particularly in the manufacturing department which alone shewed a deficit of over two thousand rupees. I drew up a memorandum of all the deficiencies and defects I had discovered, and placed it before Mr. Symonds, who, on reading through the document, told me that I had better write to the late Acting Keeper at Coimbatore and ask him for an explanation. I told Mr. Symonds that such a thing would be useless, for he himself would be held responsible, and I further remarked that it would at least take two years to make good the loss and get the manufacturing department into anything like order again. Mr. Symonds admitted the truth of what I said, and asked me to do my best. It was indeed fortunate for Mr. Symonds that Government had decided upon retaining my services at the Penitentiary, for if the late order of things had continued, matters would have gone from bad to worse, and he would have found himself in a most perilous position in the event of an enquiry being ordered into the state of the Jail finances. However, I went to work with a will, and in course of time by dint of constant vigilance and activity got the Jail into something like the condition in what it was when I left it to go to Palghat. I must say this of Mr Symonds that he was one of the kindest Superintendents I had the happiness to serve under, and no superior deserved more loyal support and to have honest and hardworking subordinates under him than he did; that is to say, men who would work for the public good and not to serve their own selfish interests. Mr. Symonds, however, was not served as his kindly nature deserved.

When writing of the Penitentiary before, I omitted to make mention of a somewhat sensational trial that took place at the High Court when two Officers and two Sergeants of the 21st Foot (now the Royal Scots Fusiliers) were charged with criminal trepass with intent to commit an assault. The accused were committed for trial by the Magistrate at Bangalore in connection with the once notorious *Van Ingen Case*, and Mr. Van Ingen, Junior, was also committed to take his trial for shooting at these officers. As might be easily surmised there was a lady at the bottom of the affair. The High Court was crowded during the trial and I remember Mr. James Gray a familiar figure in Madras at one time and since dead who was one of the jury, asking the witnesses in the case some very pertinent questions which I thought were quite to the purpose. The jury were unanimous in their finding of "not guilty" in the case against Van Ingen. The Officers and Sergeants on the other hand were found guilty of the offence of which they were charged, and if I remember rightly, were fined two hundred rupees each. While the trial was proceeding, search was made for the lady witness for the defence, in fact it was the "Helen of Troy" in the case, but she was spirited away like the Helen of old and was nowhere to be found.

One seldom hears of a Duke being put into *Court*, not a Royal Court for that is their natural element as water is that of a fish, but I mean a regular and proper Judicial Court. This was however the case when the Civil Suit of Messrs. Deschamps and Co. *versus* the Duke of Buckingham and Chandos came on for hearing at the High Court of Madras. The suit was for the recovery of a large sum of money, being the alleged value of a cabinet made by the firm for the Duke. His Grace considered the charge exorbitant and declined to pay it—hence the suit. I was present when the case came on for hearing and so were many of the Madras public and we attentively listened to all the evidence, for it was a phenomenon in Madras for a case to come before the Courts in which a real live Duke was concerned, so much so that the Madras papers were full of it. One of the witnesses examined was Captain Hobart, His Grace's Private Secretary, who gave his evidence in a very straightforward manner—but all the same, the decision of the Court was against the Duke. Whether or not, however, His Grace had to pay the full amount of the claim, I am unable to say now, but therecan be no doubt that if Messrs. Deschamps obtained the full amount of their claim with costs this little bit of litigation was a very profitable transaction for them.

I now come to a rather interesting character, a man who caused some stir in Madras by his threats to subvert the Madras Government (this was when Sir M. E. Grant Duff was Governor) and to be the scourge and terror of those who impeded the good wook. This was a man named Howard *alias* Howarth, and afterwards known in Secunderabed and Bombay under the name of Clive Durant. For the purpose of putting his amiable intentions into execution he called together large public meetings on the Island, but the unsympathetic Police intervened and Mr. Howard's (or whatever his real name was) benevolent designs were frustrated. However it was not long before he put his foot into it. He was tried by the Chief Presidency Magistrate,

Colonel Weldon, on two charges of cheating, convicted on both, and sentenced to six months' imprisonment for each offence. Of course he appealed to the High Court, with the result that the conviction in one case was quashed, while it was upheld in the other. Thus Howard's or Howarth's sentence was reduced to six months' imprisonment. He did not need the aid of a lawyer to defend him, for he undoubtedly possessed a certain amount of forensic ability and was a man above the average in intelligence and education. Mr. Symonds allowed him a great deal of indulgence, not only in writing his appeals to the High Court, but also in writing his memorials to the Government, so much so that the latter had to remonstrate with Mr. Symonds at the great liberty he had given the prisoner. I spoke to Mr. Symonds about this as I thought he was too lenient, but he merely answered that in such cases the liberty of the subject must be considered. Colonel Tennant the Inspector General, however, in speaking of Howarth to me remarked "He is a journalist, Tyrrel." One morning, while I was on my duty of inspecting the prisoners, Howarth neglected to fall in with them and stand to attention. I ordered him to do so, and as he hesitated for some time, I reported him for disobedience of orders and brought him before the Superintendent in the Office. Mr. Symonds on reading my report, asked him what he had to say. He replied that he did not mean any disrespect to me but that he considered it derogatory to be mixed up with a lot of blackguards and scoundrels such as some of the convicts were. Mr. Symonds warned him that he must conform to the rules of the Jail, and I must admit that after this he was very quiet and civil and I had no occasion to find fault with him. The indulgence, however, Mr. Symonds had shown him bore evil fruit for that officer, for he was called upon for an explanation by Sir M. E. Grant Dufl's Government, why he had allowed such latitude to the prisoner. Two letters I believe on the subject from Government were received by Mr. Symonds, to which he sent replies. Those who have known

Mr. Symonds must be aware that he was a gentleman of considerable talent and a gifted writer, and I have heard it said that His Excellency the Governor himself remarked that in Mr. Symonds he had found a "foeman worthy of his steel." Notwithstanding this, however, he was a marked man, for after I left the Penitentiary on my appointment by Sir M. E. Grant Duff as Superintendent of the new Cellular Jail at Palamcottah, I heard that Mr. Symonds was removed from his post as Superintendent of Prisons for the Town of Madras, and transferred to the Salt and Abkari Department on a much lower salary. This must have been a great blow to him, for it not only affected his pocket immediately, but meant a reduction in his pension hereafter.

As for Mr. Howarth, after his release, he proceeded to Hyderabad, where under the name of Clive Durant and in conjunction with the late Mr. Solomon, formerly a Director of the Bank of Madras, he started a newspaper under the title of "The Hyderabad Record" in which he was accused of publishing a libel. For this he got "three months." On the death of Mr. Solomon, "The Hyderabad Record" died a natural death, and Mr. Durant gravitated towards Bombay where he was heard of lately in connection with a charge brought against him of blackmailing, of which by means of his usual cleverness he managed to clear himself.

CHAPTER XLV.

Madras Penitentiary—(*Continued*).

Chubb's Locks.

During my tenure of office as Keeper of H. M.'s Penitentiary, the Inspector General obtained the sanction of Government for the purchase of a large number of Chubb's locks for use in the Jails in the Presidency. and a thousand or more of these were got out from England and given into my custody. The locks were in *suites* as they were called, that is, each set of a hundred locks could be opened by one key, a great convenience, since it obviated the necessity for carrying about large bunches of keys, and also saved time and trouble in opening the cell doors. The locks were issued to the various Jails in the Presidency from time to time. The close prison cells in the Jails were all locked up with these locks which were in four *suites* of a hundred each, with one key to each *suite*. In addition to these keys, there were two master keys one kept by the Superintendent, and one by me, which would unlock any lock of the whole four *suites*. Messrs. Chubb's locks are known all the world over for their absolute security from being opened by any key except the one by which each is fitted. But this was not the case with the *suites* which we received, and which we quickly found to be no safer for our purposes than the ordinary locks, for the key of any *suite* could, by filing off certain of its wards, be converted into a *master key* which would open any lock of the whole four *suites*. This fact was communicated to the Inspector-General who would hardly believe it at first, until it was demonstrated to him by ocular proof. Finding no way out of the difficulty, he wrote personally to Messrs. Chubb's on the subject and that firm sent one of their establishment, a Mr. Chalk, from England to enquire into and report upon the faults discovered by us. Mr Chalk duly arrived and the matter was fully gone into in the Penitentiary Office. Colonel Macleod, the Superintendent of the Central Jail at Vellore, was deputed by the Inspector-General to attend the enquiry. The defects of the "*suite*" method were pointed out to Mr. Chalk, and he was shown how, by simply filing away certain portions of the wards of the key of any one of the *suites*, it could be converted into a master key which would open the locks of all four *suites*. In the face of such tangible proof, Mr. Chalk could not but admit that we were right, but he could do nothing he said without the sanction of the Firm, and he promised on his return to England to explain matters fully to them with the view to the defects being remedied. About a year after this, when I was Superintendent of the Cellular Jail at Palamcottah Mr. Grimes, who was then Inspector-General paid the Jail a visit, and in the course of conversation showed me a master key made in gold which he wore on his watch guard and which he said would open any of the Chubb's locks in any Jail in the Presidency. It was a very pretty ornament, and I could not help admiring it. I was under the impression that he knew every thing in connection with our discovery relative to defects in the system of having locks in *suites* with a master key to open the whole, and I astonished him somewhat when I told him that any of the " suites " keys could be converted into a master key in five minutes by means of a file and I showed him how this could be done. As mentoined in the previous Chapter, I was apppointed in the month of July 1885 by His Excellency Sir M. E. Grant Duff to be Superintendent of the Cellular Jail at Palamcottah. This was chiefly done on the recommendation of Mr. Foster Webster, Chief Secretary to Government at the time. At the same Meeting of the Council, Mr. Cavendish of the Police Department, a nephew of the Duke of Devonshire, was appointed Superintendent of the Cellular Jail at Tanjore. It had been in contemplation some time to construct Jails of this description, and correspondence on the subject had taken place between the local Government and the Government of India. The result was that the Palamcottah and Tanjore Cellular Jails were built. The great advantage of this system is that it provides a separate cell for each prisoner, and thus keeps first offenders, and young prisoners from being further corrupted by old and hardened Jail birds, a thing which was practically impossible under the system of housing them in wards at nights. Moreover, it prevented a nameless crime, one which I shall not define further, than by saying that it is the same for which the late Oscar Wilde and a companion suffered two years' imprisonment in Newgate. Hideous as the offence is and revolting as it may be to my readers to know it this crime is more common among the prison population than is generally known, for it is one of those secret crimes that are not easily discovered. I should like to say a few words on this subject before I proceed further. We see an instance of Divine wrath against this crime in destruction of the cities of Sodom and Gomorrah. The Church has thundered against it and kindred vices, the Law punishes it with penal servitude, and society condemns it by ostracising its votaries, and yet this monster still rears its head, even amongst so-called civilized beings. It seems to me that one might just as well think of altering the course of the planets as to attempt to cure a human being of the depravity that is innate in him and forms a part of his nature. This being so in cases where men have had the advantages of education and the sense to know right from wrong, how much more must it be the case with the lower classes of Natives of India who have little or no moral sense whatever. Flogging does not seem to act as a deterrent for the flogging is forgotten when criminal desires assert themselves, and as for penal servitude with which the Law punishes the offender with the ward system in vogue, it simply places him in a position where he has equal or even greater facilities for committing the offence again. The wisest thing therefore that could have been done was to construct the new Jails on the Cellular System.

For a similar reason, it would be a great advantage if in the interests of morality, a separate Jail or Jails could be established for female convicts with none but women officers to administer them as is done in England at the present day.

A few cases of the offence I have just written of were detected among the prisoners from time time, and were punished judicially, but this did very little towards stopping the practice. I remember one case which was detected in the Penitentiary, and the offenders brought before Major Bloomfield who was then Acting Superintendent of Prisons for the Town of Madras. The culprits were two convict cooks who were let out at three o'clock in the morning to cook the morning meal for the rest of the prisoners. The men were detected by the Warder on duty who brought the matter to my notice. On being placed before the Superintendent, the younger and stronger of the two, who was the "assaulted" party in the case stated that he could not help himself as he was overpowered by his companion. This was an absurd plea when one looked at the physique of the two men, but it got him off. His companion, however, received fifty lashes. Had both these men been placed before the High Court as they should have been, they would probably have got seven years each.

Since the occurrence of the events mentioned in this Chapter, separate cells have been built in nearly all the Jails and a new Cellular Jail has been constructed, *viz.*, that at Cuddalore. Let us hope that every convict will eventually be provided with a separate cell or cubicle, in order that a stop may be put to these crimes. I wrote on this matter very fully in two yearly administration reports of the Jail I had charge of.

CHAPTER XLVI.

An Indian Jack Sheppard.

Shortly after taking over charge of the Palamcottah Cellular Jail, I built a new gallows by order of the Inspector-General, as the old one was in a dilapidated condition. For the uprights and cross pieces of the new structure, I employed old iron or steel rails, and I flatter myself that I made a very good job of it when the work was completed. A new gallows was very necessary, as Tinnevelly was at this time what I may say a "hanging district," owing to the number of murders committed in it and the consequent executions. I had at one time as many as five condemned prisoners under my charge awaiting execution, and in addition, there were two or three condemned prisoners, who were kept for months in Jail before their cases were finally disposed of I wrote to the Inspector-General regarding the latter, and he in turn addressed the High Court on the subject. The men were tried and convicted in connection with two murders in which it was alleged they had taken part. There had been a feud between the Roman Catholics and Protestants of the District, and in all such cases, when sectarianism plays a part, blood ran very high, and they hated each other as cordially as only Christians can when they are at loggerheads on a question of doctrine. The Roman Catholics murdered two or three of their Protestant brethren by throwing them into the sea, and thus two of the latter lost their lives in the disturbance that ensued. A retrial of the case was ordered by the High Court, and the men were eventually released for want of conclusive evidence to convict them of the crime. Palamcottah is noted for the number of its Protestant Church Schools, and other institutions for the conversion of the heathen. In fact, I should call it the stronghold of Protestantism in Southern India. In addition to the two local Protestant Bishops, namely, Bishops Sargent and Caldwell, there were half a dozen Missionaries in charge of the several religious institutions, one of the latter being in charge of Miss Tucker's institutions. These, however, were only as a drop in the ocean, for only a very small proportion of the native population were converted, and these only of the lowest classes, inasmuch as Hinduism has too great a hold on the high castes to permit of their breaking family ties, for what seems to them the doubtful benefit of rubbing shoulders with the pariah castes. Doubtless, Bishop Sargent, whom I knew well and who was an earnest worker in the cause of his Master, was doing his utmost to bring the higher castes as well into God's fold, but in the face of hide bound caste prejudices, I am afraid his success in this direction was doubtful. There was a small Hindu temple at Palamcottah which I used to pass on my way to Church of a Sunday evening. The Hindu devotees would assemble at about the hour and would arrange themselves in two rows, men, women, and children, from the age of eight to seventy years. As soon as the Brahmin priest in charge opened the door of the shrine and the God—a hideous idol besmeared with red ochre and oil, and covered with flowers, met their view, every one of the worshippers would fall flat on his or her face in the dust and dirt in a state of ecstasy, an act of devotion which few Christians would be capable of. I have seen these things myself every Sunday evening, and as Bishop Sargent and his Missionaries took the same road to Church, they must also have observed them. With such gross superstition rampant in the District, I am afraid the good Bishop and his Clergy must have had very up hill work.

I must now proceed to give an account of the doings of a prisoner whom on account of his clever escapes, I have likened to "Jack Sheppard" of Newgate notoriety. This was one Sooba Tevan, a sturdy well built young man of about twenty-three years of age, pleasant featured, and a carpenter by trade. One morning the Jailor, Mr. Beeby, came running to me to say that he could not open the lock of Sooba Tevan's cell door. On visiting the cell, I found that the prisoner had been tampering with the lock, and I had some trouble in opening it. One of the warders had observed him secrete something in the flooring of his cell and when the door was unlocked and a thorough search made a small piece of iron belonging to the handle of his urinal bucket was found concealed in a hole in the asphalt floor; with this he had been tampering with the lock of his cell door during the night. All the cell doors are made of iron bars with sufficient space between them to permit of a man's hand going through, and this had facilitated his design. As according to the Jail registers, he was in for the first time, I only awarded him twenty lashes with the "cat." He had been convicted by the Sessions Judge of Tinnevelly on two charges of house-breaking and theft by night, and sentenced to seven years' rigorous imprisonment. Owing to his youth, and, as I thought, ignorance of Jail rules, I sent for the prisoner, and reasoned with him on his folly in attempting to break out of Jail, an offence which would only enhance his punishment. I explained to him that if he would behave himself properly and in accordance with Jail rules he would get off with about five years and six months, instead of his full sentence. On the following day, he told the Jailor that he desired to see me in the Office as he had something of importance to communicate. I gave him the required permission, and he was brought before me. He commenced by saying that I was the only Officer before whom he had been placed that had spoken a word of kindness to him, and that my treatment had so touched him that he was anxious to reveal his past misdeeds to me. He then asked me if I would listen to him. I told him to go on, and this ingenious youth, characterized as he seemed to me by such an innocent expression of countenance, told me a tale that took me by surprise. But I fear the story will lose in the telling, if I put it in the third person. I shall therefore attempt to relate it as much as possible in his own words rendered into English.

Sir, you think me a first offender, but I must tell you that I am an old Jail bird. The Police of the Tinnevelly District know nothing of my antecedents as there are no previous convictions against me here, yet I have been convicted four times and have received four sentences, two of them very heavy ones, and I have on each occasion escaped either from Police custody or from Jail during the period of my imprisonment. All this occurred in the adjoining or Madura District. But things got too hot for me there, and I made my way into the Tinnevelly District where I was not known. My first escape was when I was doing a sentence of six months for theft. I was employed on extra-mural labour and watched a favourable opportunity when the guards who were watching the gang at work had their attention drawn to something else, and quietly gave them the slip. My next escape was from Police custody. I was arrested on a charge of robbery in the Madura District, and was being conveyed to the " lock up," when I get out from the hands of the Police like an Eel and was off before they knew anything about it; so much for the cleverness of the Police! I was re-arrested some time after this, and placed in a Subsidiary Jail for the night, but before morning dawned, I was off and miles away from the place. It was not till months after this that I was again captured, and this time they had me safely conveyed and lodged in the Madura District Jail ; but it was not long before I broke out of my cel at night, climbed the outer wall of the Jail with some little difficulty, and was again at liberty. You do not know, Sir, how precious and sweet a thing is liberty to a man who has been in confinement. I was at large for some six months after this, enjoying my freedom in my own way, committing a burglary here, and a theft there, until I was again laid hold of by the Police and taken back to the Madura District Jail where I was heavily ironed and kept isolated in a cell at night. "Love laughs at locksmiths" they say, so does a prisoner who has any brains, and is bent upon making his escape. Nothing could daunt me, so one dark night I not only broke out of my cell, but released another prisoner confined in an adjoining cell, who had been doing a long sentence for docoity, and we both proceeded to the Jail store room which we quickly broke open, got the necessary tools out, and had the heavy fetters off our legs in a trice. We then visited the Carpenters' shop where we quickly made a rough sort of ladder which answered our purpose exceedingly well in climbing the outer wall. The tops of Jail walls are generally covered with pieces of broken bottles and other bits of glass which are imbedded in the mortar, and are meant to prevent escapes. But this did not stop us, for we had merely to cover that part of the wall we were going over with our prison blankets or cumblies, and there we were, on the right side of the wall without much difficulty. After a rather hard night's work, we were away just as the dawn was breaking, and I bade "good-bye" to the Madura District for good. I did not make the acquaintance of the Police again until I was arrested in the Tinnevelly District in connection with the two cases of house-breaking for which I am now in. That is all my history,—Sir.

I sent Sooba Tevan back to his cell, and could not but admire his pluck and resource, if all he said were true. If he had not made this confession, it might have taken months before the Police of the Madura District could have ascertained his whereabouts. I wrote to Colonel Kilgour, the Superintendent of Police of the Madura District, giving full details of all Sooba Tevan had said, and asked him if there were any truth in them. He confirmed the statements in every particular. The dacoit he had assisted in escaping was never recaptured to my knowledge. Sooba Tevan was perhaps injudicious in making his confession to me, an Officer who was found to take cognizance of it and give information of it to the authorities of the Madura District. If he thought it would get him off his previous sentences, he was mistaken, for they still held good, and in the aggregate amounted to a good deal more than seven years, for two of them were for long periods. These would have to be worked out as soon as he had finished his sentence at Palamcottah As I left this Jail for the Cannanore Central Jail about two years after this, I heard no more of this prisoner.

CHAPTER XLVII.

Palamcottah Cellular Jail—(*Continued*).

Like most places in Southern India, Palamcottah is infested with snakes. The Brahmin Writer of the Jail who was Acting Jailor at the time of my arrival, had to vacate the Jailor's house which I was perforce compelled to occupy in the absence of more suitable quarters. Before my appointment, the Medical Officer of the Jail was always ex-officio Jail Superintendent, and as he had quarters of his own in the town I had to occupy the Jaior's house until suitable house accommodation could be provided for me by Government. The Acting Jailor had lost a cow through the bite of a cobra in the coach house, and searching the premises, I found that there were two or three of these reptiles lurking in holes in the compound. I thought I would be able to hook these as one would catch a fish by means of a fish hook and a bait, and I accordingly baited a hook with a live frog, their staple food, and waited several nights to see what would happen, but the snakes were too "wary" and were not to be "caught on any account. The Jail garden opposite, was infested by them, and not a week passed but what the convict gang employed therein killed one or more. I was certainly surprised one morning on lifting a large wooden inkstand which was placed on my table standing on small wooden knobs, to see a *kattaveedian* coiled beneath it. I managed to kill it, but was astonished to think it wanted to make so close an acquaintance with me, but these small vipers often drop from the roof of a house on the floor. While on this subject, I may here state that when I was an Inspector of Police in the Nellore District, I had read a good deal about the method of dealing with snake-bites in Australia, and I was struck with the absurdity of tying a ligature (which was one of the things said to be employed) in all cases of snake-bite, for I failed to see of what benefit a ligature could be in preventing the poison from circulating into the system, unless the part bitten was either a finger or toe, and even in this case, the action of the venom is so rapid that unless the victim was very prompt in tying the ligature, the poison would be in his system before he would be aware of it. Where then would be the use of a ligature if the part bitten were an arm or a leg or any other portion of the body? The letters I had read were more or less of a sensational character, but nearly all the suggestions they contained were of little practical value. The most preposterous statement of all was, however, in one which mentioned how snakes were destroyed in Arabia by means of nicotine. The method employed was refreshing in its simplicity and reminded one of the nursery tale of the duck and the old woman—and so would probably the Arab to the snake if he knew English—but as his gutturals were not mellifluous enough to charm the reptile, he merely held out his chibouk or pipe at which it would immedietely strike and be poisoned straight away by the nicotine in the bowl—yet this ridiculous story was probably believed by many. At any rate, I was anxious to ascertain for myself whether tobacco had really any poisonous effect on snakes, and I sent for two snake charmers and asked them to bring me two snakes. They told me I need not go far for them as they would probably be found in my own garden or somewhere about the premises, and in a few minutes, a cobra, and a whip or rat snake were got out, the former from a hole close to the fowl house, and only a few yards away from the back door of my bungalow. I went into the garden with two or three friends, and commenced the experiment by telling the snake charmers to put a small quantity of tobacco juice into the mouth of the cobra, and the same of snuff into that of the whip snake. In a few minutes both were stupified, the cobra had stiffened out until I really thought it was dead, but in about twenty minutes, it had recovered, and was making its escape swimming across the water in the garden channel like an Eel, had not the snake charmers been too quick for it, and brought it back. I had both reptiles destroyed. Another of these of Munchausen fame stated in the letter, that chunam would have the same effect as tobacco on snakes, lizards, and other reptiles, but I did not think the experiment worth trying. I must have passed this cobra's hole near my fowl house many a night, when I was Police Inspector, but as a rule, cobras are not aggressive except in the mating season when they are known to chase any one who approaches them. There are doubtless thousands of people in India who have snakes close to their houses and are not aware of the fact.

Palamcottah is famous for its grapes with are grown nearly all over the Tinnevelly District. There was a very large vine in the Jail garden and Mr. Lee Warner, the Collector, had some very fine ones in his garden. Grapes of course are to be had in many parts of India, but none I think can compare with those grown in Palamcottah which I found to be most enjoyable. The produce of the Jail garden was, however, not meant for the use of the Jail Officials, for I sold it for a good round sum to a contractor and credited the proceeds to Government. There was a large piece of waste land south of the Jail and belonging to it, which I thought it a pity to be allowed to remain uncultivated, and I accordingly had it planted with trees, chiefly the *koorakapilly* a fast-growing one. I calculated that if they were properly cared for, they would in a few years be worth some thousands of rupees if merely sold for firewood. Of course all this was not done by me without reporting particulars to the Inspector-General and getting his approval.

A hill was pointed out to me by the natives of the place from which Hanuman, the monkey god was said to have jumped from the Tinnevelly District into Ceylon when in pursuit of the Rakshasa or Evil One, who had decamped with the God Rama's wife. As the jump was for a matter of a hundred miles or so, it was someting to be proud of, and I do not wonder at the natives bragging about it even to this day. But a leap of a hundred miles was a mere trifle compared with some of the wonderful things the Hindu Gods did when the world was young, and if one felt inclined to doubt it, the hill is there to prove it.

There are many places in the Tinnevelly District, where disciples of Isaak Walton can enjoy their favorite sport to their heart's content, and although there are no "Mahseer" to be had, the Carnatic carp, which Mr. Thomas of the Revenue Board in his book "The Rod in India" has dubbed "the Mahseer of Southern India," are plentiful in all the tanks and rivers. In the matter of fishing, I think the Tinnevelly District can hold its own. In one large tank near a temple, the fish were so tame that they would actually take the food out of the hand of the priest who fed them.

I should have mentioned before, that when I was Keeper of the Penitentiary, this same Mr. Thomas obtained permission from Government to have two of the tanks in the People's Park emptied with the view of stocking them with a fish called *Gourami* which is found in the Mauritius and other Islands in the Indian Ocean, and is said to be one of the most delicious species of fish to eat in the world. One of the tanks in the Government House compound had some of them in it. It took a long time to empty the tanks in the People's Park, although I had a great number of convicts employed on the work. They were full of murrel and other kinds of Indian tank fish, and cartloads were brought out and sold. One of the tanks was on the site now occupied by the Victoria Hall, and on the other north-west of it. Both have now been filled up. While the work was going on, scarcely a day would pass without a visit from Mr. Thomas, who was a keen angler and a good one, and took a great interest in the matter, and would superintend many details himself. The work was at last completed, the tanks were stocked with young Gourami, and an order was issued prohibiting any one from fishing in them for the space of two years. The period had scarcely elapsed when returning one afternoon through the Park after fishing in the tanks near the Salt Cotaurs, I observed the Station Master of the Madras Railway Central Station and a Mr. Davis who owned a small Printing Press in Vepery, fishing in one of the reserved tanks. I remonstrated with them regarding their disregard of orders. The Station Master replied that " it was all right " and asked me " not to kick up a row." While I was talking to him I heard a vioce call out to me from the other reserved tank " come here Tyrrell," and I shouted back " you are just as bad ; you have no business to be fishing there." After a few seconds he called out again " Come here Tyrrell " and I answered " all right I'll come and see your ugly old mug." As I went up to him I heard him mutter to himself " It is not a very handsome one at any rate." I was taken quite aback on going up to find that it was Mr. Thomas to whom I had spoken so rudely. He looked at me and said "Well, Mr. Tyrrell, I did not think you would have spoken to me in that manner." I replied " you may be sure Sir that I would never have done so had I the slightest idea as to who you were." His daughter was standing by his side, and his son who had just come out from England was also fishing not far off. He told me he had a bite and had nearly hooked his fish, but he could not say whether it was a Gourami or not. I sat down close to him while he went on fishing, and he told me how he had hooked a Mahseer in the Bohwani river, I think, not far from Mettapollium, and had to play it for four hours before he could land it, and that if ever his arm ached it did that afternoon. The Mahseer, when weighed he said, scaled 46 lbs. I told him I got many good Eels out of the tanks but he did not care for Eels, and as for the edible fresh water turtle of which I spoke to him, he had never heard of it, he replied, but had written a good deal about the fresh water stinking turtle which one could not go near when caught on account of its abominable smell. I wrote a long letter to him afterwards for his information on the subject of Eel-fishing as well as on the difference that existed between the fresh water edible turtle and the stinking variety. The latter I pointed out was larger than the other, with its back covered with thick horny plates of the true tortoise shell color and shape, its belly being much lighter in color and of the appearance of tortoise shell, whereas the edible fresh water turtle had its back covered with one smooth shell with a uniform dark green color while its belly was covered with a plate of a pretty cream color. I further stated that I had caught one of this species about three lbs. in weight. I had hooked it with a very strong hook which was so fast in its jaw that when I landed it I was unable to get it out, and so had to cut the line and tie the turtle to the bough of a tree while I went on fishing. About ten minutes afterwards when I turned round, the turtle was not there, but the line and hook were. It had managed to rid itself of the hook which was so firmly imbedded in its mouth, without, as I told Mr. Thomas, the aid of the family doctor. Dr. Hackett, who was also an ardent fisherman, often carried home in his pocket a young edible turtle he had caught, to be kept in a well in his compound. He told me that he had given a dinner to some gentlemen who had had the real West Indian turtle, at Aldermanic banquets and large hotels, that he had some turtle soup made of the edible fresh water turtle, and that they could not tell the difference. In fact they declared, Dr. Hackett said, they had never tasted anything better in London.

For many years I paid my fishing tax regularly to enable me to Ash in the People's Park, and one Sunday morning after fishing from daybreak till eleven o'clock in the forenoon without a bite, my float disappeared all at once. I made no attempt to play the fish but hauled in my line quickly and drew out a "Chanos Salmoneus" a fish of the Salmon kind, weighing 14 lbs. I sent two pounds of it to Doctor Hackett, two to Mr. Symonds, and some to other gentlemen. It was the largest fish ever caught in the tank. Dr. Hackett, Mr. Deane of the Penitentiary and my son Fred had each caught two or three of these fish, but none weighed over eight pounds. Dr. Hackett ascertained the name of this fish from one of the kind being stuffed, and on exhibition at the Museum. I should not have remained out so long that morning had I not seen the fish rise two or three times not far off, which made me persevere, particularly as the fish is excellent eating. Mr. Thomas in his book has written a very interesting chapter regarding this fish. He presented me with a copy of the work with all his corrections for the second edition. Colonel Hunt, Superintendent of Army Clothing, was also an enthusiastic angler, but none more so than Colonel Thomson of the Royal Engineers.

But to return to Palamcottah. On a hill about three miles from the Jail, there were a number of wolves that used to commit depredations on the flocks of the shepherds who resided in the village close by. The owners begged me to come and shoot the animals and I with two or three friends went one day to see if we could bag any of them but the rocky nature of the hill afforded them good cover and we had to return without being able to get at them. The shepherds begged us to come again and offered us the pick of their flocks for our trouble, for the wolves would appear when least expected, and would sometimes kill more than they could carry away. The pens in which the sheep were kept at night were surrounded with high fences made of thick bush faggots, and seemed impenetrable, but they were not good enough to keep the wolves out There was some very good shooting to be had here. Hares, partridges and grouse were plentiful besides other game.

CHAPTER XLVIII.

Palamcottah Cellular Jail—(*Continued*).

Those who have studied the reports on the administration of justice in the Madras Presidency in past as well as in recent years, will know that the Tinnevelly District bears an unenviable reputation for heinous crime. Dacoities and burglaries were of common occurrence, as indeed I believe they are at the present day. Two or three of my Jail Officials, houses were broken into quite close to the Jail and the Deputy Chief Warder had nearly everything worth carried away, in the shape of clothing, brass utensils, and other miscellaneous articles stolen from his house one night; a serious loss to a man of his slender means. I was at this time a widower and living alone, my children having been settled in life. Before retiring to rest every night, I took the precaution, after fastening the doors and window shutters, of placing chairs against them with empty bottles on the top, so that if any one attempted to open a door or window the crash of the falling bottles would awaken me. I was afflicted with dyspepsia which affected my rest, and one night I was more sleepless than usual. I got up and took a dose of Chlorodyne thinking it would serve to induce sleep. But it was more restless than ever, only getting a wink of sleep now and again and the noise of the carts rumbling on the metalled road close to my house as they passed, seemed to me louder than usual. After a futile attempt to woo the drowsy god, I at length got up about one o'clock, and went into my sitting room and partook of some cold tea, after which I retired once more to rest. Hearing no more noise I eventually fell asleep. On getting out of bed at daybreak, I opened the front door, put my long arm-chair in the front yard, and sat down for half an hour. Shortly afterwards the Warder who was acting as my Orderly came in, and after reporting himself to me went around to the back of the house. After the lapse of a few minutes he returned somewhat hurriedly with the startling news that the house had been broken into during the night. I went at once with him to the back, and found that a large hole had been made through the masonry wall of the building—the outside of the aperture being quite big enough to admit of a man crawling through, while the inner side was not nearly so large. The burglars after making the breach in the wall had discovered that there was a formidable obstacle to their further progress in the shape of a very heavy piece of furniture placed against this part of the wall, which it would have taken at least four strong men to move. This was an antique combination of chest of drawers, cabinet, and escritoire and contained not only my clothing but some jewellery and other valuables which I estimated to be of the value of about six hundred rupees. The noise that I had heard the previous night was not as I thought that of cart wheels moving along the road outside, but the sound the crowbars made by making a hole through the solid masonary of the wall. The burglars would have got off with a considerable amount of booty had they succeeded in their attempt, but that venerable piece of furniture which I picked up at one of Franck's auctions for Rs. 55 some years before, did me good service. I disposed of it to the Assistant Surgeon for Rs. 50, on leaving Palamcottah for Cannanore. I usually slept with a loaded revolver under my pillow every night, so that even had the burglars effected an entrance into some other part of the room where there was no heavy piece of furniture to bar the way, and had they awakened me by their movements, they would have had to pay the penalty. Shortly after taking up the reins of Government, His Excellency Lord Connemara paid a visit to the Tinnevelly District, and put up during his stay with the

Collector, Mr. Lee Warner. A Levee was held at which, I, along with the other principal officers of the station attended. On the following morning, the Governor attended by the Collector was driven up to the Jail. On alighting at the entrance gate and entering the Jail, Mr. Lee Warner fell to the rear, leaving me to show His Excellency around the place. When we passed the inner gate and got within the Jail walls, His Excellency turned to me and asked " Well, Mr. Tyrrell, how long have you been in the country "? " My Lord " I said " I landed at Calcutta on the 19th of April 1849, when the Marquis of Dalhousie was Governor General." I knew that Lord Connemara had married Lady Susan Ramsay, a daughter of Lord Dalhousie and I informed him that I had seen his illustrious father in-law. " And have you never been home since "? queried he. " No, my Lord " I replied, " nor have I ever been on a hill station," " You look well for a man who has been all these years in the country " His Excellency remarked and walked on. He visited and inspected each separate cell and its occupant, the condemned prisoners and the sick in hospital, asking numerous questions as he proceeded with his inspection. The visit however was over in about an hour.

I should explain here, to enable my readers to understand what follows, that previous to my appointment as Superintendent, the charge of the Palamcottah and other District Jails was held by the District Medical Officers in addition to their other duties, and a substantial charge allowance was allowed for the Jail work. Ostensibly this was an economical arrangement, for it saved the pay of the Superintendent, but in reality it was not. The Medical Officer could only devote a fraction of his time to his Jail duties, and the real management of the Jail was naturally left to the Jailor and his subordinates. If these men were not conscientious, the consequences to the Jail finances may be imagined. This was, probably the reason why separate officers were appointed as Superintendents to the Palamcottah and Tanjore Jails, and the Medical Officers were relieved of all but their Medical duties.

Some time after the Governor's departure, I received a letter from Colonel Tennant telling me he had heard that Lord Connemara had expressed his opinion that it was not advisable for the District Cellular Jails to be under Special Superintendents on account of the extra cost it entailed to the Government. I was aware that the idea of being under the orders of Superintendents who had before been merely Jailors was not palatable to the Medical Officers, besides which, they had suffered a diminution of their jail allowance owing to their being placed in Medical charge only by this arrangement.

Moreover there was always a number of young gentlemen, who had failed to pass at Sandhurst and Woolwich, whose fathers were in the Civil and Military services, to be provided for by a paternal Government. I wrote to Colonel Tennant that I had not heard anything from His Lordship when he was at Palamcottah regarding his intention for reverting to the old arrangement. I also wrote giving figures comparing the cost of the whole Jail establishment before and after I had assumed charge. By this means I was able to prove to his entire satisfaction that the Jail had, notwithstanding that the pay of the Superintendent had formed an additional charge, cost less under my managenent than in any year of the period it had been under Medical Officers. Moreover I pointed out to Colonel Tennant, that when I assumed charge the Jail was anything but a well managed one—that nothing whatever in the way of disciplinary measures had been introduced and that two Jailors had within a short time come to grief and were dismissed for taking bribes, etc. One was tried judicially and convicted and sent to Jail, but was acquitted on appeal. If Lord Connemara had really stated what was reported of him, I felt sure he must have been inspired by interested persons. At any rate he must have learnt the truth from Colonel Tennant, for he would not have appointed me afterwards to be Superintendent of the Central Jail at Cannanore, where his Lordship informed me that he had specially appointed me to the post owing to the Jail being in a deplorable state of indebtedness.

Mr. Henry Grimes, who succeeded Colonel Tennant as Inspector General, inspected the Palamcottah Jail and reported very favourably on my administration. In the following year, Colonel MacLeod, the Superintendent of the Central Jail at Vellore, was deputed to inspect the Jail, and I am glad to say he also wrote in most flattering terms of all he had seen. He stated that my book of punishments of prisoners was the best he had ever read. Mr. MacCartie was appointed Collector of Tinnevelly to succeed Mr. Lee Warner, and resided at Palamcottah. He was a great lover of horses and I have often seen him exercising his mounts on the old Military racecourse. Years before this, Palamcottah was a Military Cantonment, and a rather gay one—but with the removal of the troops to other Stations, its glory had departed. Mr. MacCartie visited, and inspected the Jail officially on Christmas Day 1887, and went over the Jail with me. As he was leaving the Jail, I casually remarked to him that I was to be married the next day. He laughed and said "Yes, I know you are, you old fool, and that to a girl of fifteen." I told him he was misinformed as to the facts, for she would be twenty on the twentieth of the following month. "If that is so" said he "it is all right, and I'll send you a magnum of champagne to drink my health." This he did, and sent me a very kind note with it, in which he stated that he had written to the Chief Secretary asking that my services be further retained by Government. This was a spontaneous act of kindness on his part, for I had only spoken to him but once before. He was a man of generous principles and a most genial disposition and I have his note by me now. On hearing how he had been shot through the heart and killed at Paardberg, and the letters that appeared about him in the "Madras Mail," I thought of sending it to that paper as evincing one more of his many acts of kindness. Although a Civil Servant of Government, he had a fine military instinct, for not only did he take six months' leave to serve as a Volunteer in the Burmese War of 1886-7, but on retirement from the service on a well-earned pension, he left peace and contentment at home, to fight as a Private in the ranks, for his Queen and Country, for whom it may be truly said he laid down his life.

CHAPTER XLIX.

Cannanore Central Jail.

In the month of March 1888, I attained the summit of my ambition in the Jail Department, that is, to be a Superintendent of a Central Jail, an appointment usually given to a Military Commissioned Officer, or an Officer in the Civil Service. This was the post of Superintendent of the Central Jail at Cannanore to which I was appointed by H. E. Lord Connemara. I had been informed that the Jail was in a very backward condition regarding its finances, and that it had cost the Government more for its maintenance than in any other Jail, inasmuch as the average cost per head of the Jail population was the highest recorded. The Jailor was a Parsee, who had held the post for fourteen years at the time of my appointment as Superintendent. He had received the highest character from Mr. G. M. Grimes and other Superintendents who had held charge during the preceding nine years. He was a man of prepossessing appearance, pleasant manners, and of a powerful physique. Few soldiers in the Station could compete with him in feats of strength, for he was a very good athlete. He was also on a good footing with the Military Officers, many of the younger of whom used to visit him at his quarters. Just before I had been appointed to Palamcottah, he had been there on leave, and had gone round the Jail as a visitor. He told the Jailor there that he expected to be appointed Superintendent of the Jail. He was unquestionably well fitted for the position, but unfortunately for him as the sequel will show, he had been studying his own interests and not those of Government during his whole period of service at Cannanore, and had successfully wheeled himself into the confidence of the successive Superintendents, that he had it all his own way with them. I had been told that he was a very hard working man, but I quickly discovered that he belied the reputation. There had been considerable loss in the manufactures, and I had a great deal of trouble in getting matters right again. I also found out that the Deputy Jailor was in the habit of lending packs of cards on hire to the prisoners to play with on Sundays. On searching a store-room in charge of this official, I found a number of packs and was informed that although such packs had been found from time to time with the prisoners, they had never been destroyed. With all these irregularities being brought to light one after another, it quickly dawned upon me that there had been gross mismanagement in the Jail for years. Thus, about this time, the Native Sub-Judge, Kunhan Menon of Tellicherry was undergoing his trial before the Sessions Court on a charge of bribery and corruption, which ended in his being convicted and sentenced to a long term of imprisonment. Kunhan Menon was a very old servant of Government, received a very large salary and was considered a man of great intelligence. In a certain Civil Suit, which came before him, some bank notes were given to him as he was driving home, and unfortunately for him two of these notes were traced and proved to have been in his possession and this and other evidence convicted him. He had tried many thousands of cases in his time, and was said to be a man of wealth. In the course of the trial, a number of account books belonging to contractors, and which were produced by the prosecution as containing evidence of bribes being given to the Sub-Judge, were impounded by order of the Court, as they also contained entries of amounts being given in bribes to the Parsee Jailor and other Jail officials. Some very large sums had been given in this way from time to time, and the

Jailor always received the lion's share. Mr. Cox, the Sessions Judge of Tellicherry, and lately Accountant-General, Bombay, drove into the Jail one day and commenced asking me a number of questions. He examined the Medical Officer's Journal to see what orders had been passed by Mr. Grimes on certain representations made by the former, and evidently came to the conclusion that the Jail work had not been carried out as it should have been. He also directed me to furnish him with certain Jail records. As he was an Official visitor, I did not hesitate about giving him all the information he needed, but as to letting the Jail records go out of my keeping, even temporarily, I could not do so without the authority of the Inspector-General. As the matter, however, was one of urgency and importance, I telegraphed to Mr. Henry Grimes, the then head of the Department, following the wire up with a letter of explanation giving full particulars. I received a reply directing me to give Mr. Cox every information possible. Shortly after this I received an order from the Inspector-General. transferring the Parsee Jailor to the Trichinopoly Jail, and the Deputy Jailor Mr. Hillier to the Salem Jail, both in the same capacity in which they were at Cannanore. A day or two after the receipt of this order, I receive a letter from Mr. Grimes saying he was at a loss to understand why the Government had ordered these transfers without any previous reference to him. I replied that I thought it was due to the report made by the Sessions Judge, but as I really knew nothing more, I was unable to given him any further information. To postpone going to Trichinopoly as long as possible, the Parsee Jailor reported sick and was placed on the sick list. This was an easy matter for him, for he had friends all over the Station. Colonel Porteous who had been appointed Inspector-General of Jails in the place of Mr. Grimes who reverted to Superintendent of the Vellore Jail, was directed by Government to make a full enquiry into the matter, and brought with him Inspector Short of the Nilgiri Police to assist in the investigation. It was a long and difficult task getting the records and other evidence from the contractors and other persons who had given the bribes. One man stated and he had no records to show, as his house had been broken into and all the account books stolen, although it was discovered afterwards that he had smuggled the books out of the district. Mr. Perkins, the Jailor of the Trichinopoly Jail, was sent to Cannanore in the Parsee Jailor's place, and Mr. Locke from the Penitentiary as Deputy Jailor. Colonel Porteous wrote to the Medical Officer, enquiring if the Parsee Jailor was in a fit state to proceed to Trichinopoly. The reply being unsatisfactory, he addressed the Chief Medical Officer, Surgeon-Major Major. He replied that the Jailor was suffering from a trifling indisposition only, and that he would be fit to travel within a week or ten days. The Jailor then paid a visit to Colonel Porteous which resulted in his being informed that if he did not proceed at once to take up his new post at Trichinopoly, he would be dismissed the service But he was determined on remaining at Cannanore to watch the case against him, which he knew was being enquired into, and he either resigned the service or was dismissed, I forget now which. The Native Head Warder of the Jail, the Deputy Chief Warder, the Head Writer, the Remission Writer, and one or two others were all suspended, and I thus got a new staff of subordinates. All the accounts for past years were audited, and the manufacturing accounts chiefly for the purchase of wood, were found to be in a deplorable state. The Deputy Chief Warder Titus must have known what had been going on, although there was no evidence to show that he was a participator. I mentioned this to Colonel Porteous who however thought that he was as bad as the rest, and would have to go, for he was able to give important information if he felt inclined to do so. Hillier, the Deputy Jailor, would no doubt have been reinstated, and sent to some other Jail had he elected to give any evidence at all, but as he determinedly kept silent, and as there was a good deal to his discredit in other respects, he was dismissed the service. The Remission Writer was put on his trial at the Sessions Court at Tellicherry, the principal charge against him being that he was concerned in the release of two convicts long before their term of imprisonment had expired under the remission rules. He did this by manipulating the figures in the remission books, but the Judge held that as these books did not bear Mr. Grimes, the Superintendent's initials, the evidence was not conclusive, and he accordingly acquitted the prisoner. Shortly after this a number of letters were seized by the Sheristadar of the Sessions Judge's Kutcherry, in which mention was made of the fact that prisoners when in Jail, had obtained money from their friends outside, wherewith to bribe the Jailor and the Native Head Warder. Among these were also letters from the Native Head Warder to the friends of prisoners asking for money. In one of these he mentioned that he was sending them some carved cocoanut shells which he thought they would prize very much. For these he received the sum of Rs. 50, as a small return for his kind offices on behalf of the prisoners. The cocoanut shell carvings, which I should here say, were very well done, were the work of Burmese prisoners in the Jail, and therefore cost the Head Warder nothing. The letters from the convicts to their friends mentioned the bitter hardships and trouble they were undergoing in Jail, but that all would be well with them if they would only send the money to the Jailor and the Head Warder. The Jailor and the Head Warder were arrested on a warrant by the Sub-Collector, who after the necessary investigation committed them for trial to the Sessions Court. The Jailor had of course the best legal advice that could be obtained in the District, and both Dr. Kernan (son of the Justice of that name), the Medical Officer, and I were summoned as witnesses for the defence. The trial lasted two days, but the Counsel was well advised in not calling upon either of us to give evidence. Both prisoners were found guilty of each of the two charges on which they were tried, and I think were sentenced to six months' rigorous imprisonment on each charge. The Jailor appealed to the High Court against both convitions, and succeeded in getting the conviction reversed in one case. But as it was upheld in the other, he had still six months' imprisonment before him. Just before the trial, I wrote to the Inspector-General asking him not to send the Jailor to the Cannanore Jail in the event of his conviction. He was kept for a long time in the Subsidiary Jail at Tellicherry, until judgment was delivered on his appeal, and then ordered to be transferred to the Coimbatore Jail, but even then he remained in the Subsidiary Jail for some days longer by going on the sick list. Colonel Porteous on getting information of this, made inquiries, and had him promptly sent on to Coimbatore. Here also he managed to obtain a number of comforts, such good things as jams and jellies, and potted meats, etc., besides getting letters to friends smuggled outside. Colonel Porteous told me that in one of the letters he was referred to as the alligator. Colonel Pickance, the Superintendent of the Coimbatore Jail was greatly put out that such irregularities should have occurred in the Jail without his knowing it, and some of the Jail subordinates who had helped the prisoner were dismissed. Colonel Porteous after enquiry ordered his transfer at once, and saw him off at the station to the Vellore Central Jail, where Mr. Cavendish, the Superintendent, put him to learn weaving as he wrote and told me afterwards. Colonel Porteous was naturally very much annoyed at what had occurred in the Coimbatore Jail. The Colonel's report to Government was a lengthy one, and he did even spare the three officers who had charge of the Jail previously, who were all called upon for explanations. He also pointed out all the offences those who were suspended were guilty of, and showed how, from the Contractor's books and other records he had examined, it appeared that the Jailor during his fourteen years of service had received altogether about Rs. 62,000 in bribes. This he stated probably represented only a third of what the Jailor had received.

This report would be worth reading by any Jail officer at the present day, as it would give him an insight as to how the Jail and his *confreres* had worked for their own ends and how the Superintendents had been hoodwinked. In a local paper, it was stated that the Parsee Jailor had boasted that he would put me in his pocket as he had done the other Superintendents, but this did not turn out as he expected.

I should add that the Deputy Chief Warder Titus was subsequently reinstated by order of Government.

CHAPTER L.

CANNANORE CENTRAL JAIL—(*Continued*)

The pay of the Jail Establishment is aways drawn from the local Treasury on the first day of every month, and I always made it the custom never to delay disbursing the salaries of all the officials. Accordingly on the 1st of May 1888, when the pay was drawn I told the Jailor, who walked with me from the office to the outer gate, that I would pay the Establishment at 5 P.M. that day. He looked at me in alarm, and said "surely you won't do this work, Sir." I told him that I certainly would, as the Inspector-General's orders were explicit that all payments of Establishments should be made by the Superintendent. He replied that he had made payments hitherto to the Warders and that if this duty was withdrawn from him, the men would lose all respect for him. I told him rather sharply that there were many other ways by which he could ensure the respect of his subordinates besides paying them, and that as the Inspector-General's orders very clearly prescribed the Superintendent's duty in this respect, I should carry them out in any case. I also pointed out to him that he should have been the first to assist me to carry out this orders instead of raising objections. He had actually tears in his eyes while urging me to allow him to continue the old practice; but I found out afterwards why he was so solicitous about paying the men himself. Many of the unfortunate Warders did not receive their pay till the middle of the month, and they dared not open their mouths to complain, for fear of the Jailor getting them into some trouble or other. The men had to work hard enough for their pittance, and it seemed to me a piece of cruelty that payment of their salaries should be delayed at all, seeing that men in their position must necessarily be put to much hardship if kept waiting for their just dues for days. This consideration always influenced me in making it a rule to pay them at once when the money was drawn from the Treasury. I also discovered that some of the Warders on entertainment were compelled to " square " a Jail official in proportion to the amount of their salaries, if they expected to rest secure in their appointments. This was a piece of infamous extortion that I could not tolerate, and I quickly put my foot on it Instead of the " hard-working, conscientious official " that he was reported to be, I found that he took things very easy. Instead of being present, as he should have been, in obedience to the Jail Rules, at the unlocking of the cell door in the morning, the Jailor frequently left the duty to the Deputy Jailor Mr. Hillier and the Head Warder.

Kunhan Menon, the Sub-Judge of Tellichrry, of whom I have made mention in the last Chapter, was after his conviction, sent to the Cannanore Jail. I regretted that he had not been sent to some other Jail, for having been a resident of the District, and a man of wealth and position, he had naturally a large circle of friends who would be anxious to help him while in the Jail. Thus I expected attempts would be made to undermine the honesty of the Jail subordinates, with the view of getting illicit articles smuggled in, and the Superintendent would have to be omniscient, who could tell everything that went on in the Jail when his back was turned.

About this time His Excellency the Governor, Lord Connemara, visited Cannanore accompanied by his Private Secretary, Mr. Rees. A large Shamiana or reception tent with a small dais inside was erected at the toll-gate at the entrance to the Cantonment at which His Excellency alighted. A number of the Officers of the Garrison and the Municipal Commissioners of the town were present and presented His Excellency with an address to which he replied in a long speech. Among the private individuals present were the Jailor's daughter, and another Parsee lady, the daughter of Hirjee, the shopkeeper, both very handsome young ladies. They strewed the pathway on which His Excellency walked with flowers and Mr. Rees, who was struck with their appearance, asked me who they were. Of course I told him, whereupon he remained silent. After replying to the address of the Municipality, His Excellency drove on to Colonel Vanderzee's the Station Commandant's house, where he remained for the remainder of his visit. A levee was held in the evening at the Commandant's house at which I was present.

Next morning I received a note from Mr. Twigg, the Sub-Collector, to the effect that His Excellency desired to see me at the Colonel's bungalow and mentioning the hour I was to be present. Also asking me to weigh Kunhan Menon before I came and bring with me a telegram which I had received from the Eliya Rajah of Travancore directed to the prisoner. On arriving at the house, I followed His Excellency and Mr. Rees to the back verandah of the building, so that whatever was said at the interview was between us three. The conversation was chiefly about Kunhan Menon who, I gathered, had got his friends to use their influence on his behalf. His Excellency it appeared had received several communications urging the prisoner's release on the ground of his loss of health and weight since his confinement, and stating that further detention in Jail would be fatal to him. While I was speaking to His Excellencncy. Mr. Rees put me a question which I answered, when he quickly brought me up sharply by saying "you are speaking to His Lordship." This "*nettled*" me and I replied "You asked the question and I answered it." I told His Excellency that Kunhan Menon who had been in Jail for sometime had actually gained in weight since his admission, and that he appeared to be in fairly good health. I then handed His Excellency the telegram sent to the prisoner by the Eliya Rajah, which I had with me for very good reasons. Here was the Prince of a Vassal State of the British Government, condoling with a prisoner of that Government, and cheering him up with the promise of the Dewanship of the State on his release. Such a thing might seem incredible to European readers, but nothing is impossible in this land of Ind. His Excellency returned me the telegram, and directed me to make it over to Colonel Porteous who was shortly expected to arrive at Cannanore for the purpose of making enquiries into the mismanagement that had been going on in the Jail for years. His Lordship futher said that he had selected me for the post of Superintendent of this Jail to rectify all past shortcomings and get it into order again.

On Colonel Porteous arriving I handed him the telegram about which he had no doubt heard from Lord Connemeara. Kunhan Menon to my great relief was transferred to the Trichinopoly Jail where he died some time afterwards. Had Kunhan Menon been sent to Jail before I assumed charge of it, he would probably have been a gold mine which some of the Jail officials would no doubt have exploited for their own special benefit. Even a Jail where discipline is lax, must be purgatory to a man living in the lap of luxury, such as Kunhan Menon did before his fall. The Jail Superintendent's house at Cannanore was probably one of the best in Cannanore, and would have been an ideal residence, were it not that the grounds were swarming with snakes, more especially cobras. There were three lawn tennis courts laid out in terraces close to the house, and to prevent the sides of the courts falling, they were faced with large laterite blocks. The interstices between these places afforded capital shelter for the reptiles, and it was difficult to get at them. I purchased a large number of ducks and fowls, and they were all killed in less than a week by these reptiles. In one night I lost six ducks; but the fowls were pretty safe as they were on perches some feet from the ground. Three or four of the reptiles were killed on the premises and Mr. Cavendish, who acted for me for one month while I was on leave, and who had made a bath-room of one of the rooms downstairs, while going to the room for his evening bath saw a cobra disappear under a commode. He shouted for his servants who came with bamboos and quickely despatched it Mr. Cavendish told me that if he had not seen it in time, he would probably have been bitten the same night while in the act of using the commode.

One night on visiting the Jail at midnight, I found Head Warder Titus and the other Warders going their rounds. Titus showed me a kattaveedian which had been swallowed by a cobra. He cut at the cobra with his sword and it had immediately ejected the kattaveedain which it had partly swallowed. This shows that snakes are cannibalistic in their tendencies. But of course this was known to me before. The tanks all about Cannanore contained alligators but none exceeded five or six feet in length. One of these was actually found in the verandah of the store-room of the Native Regiment. It had probably left its tank for its nightly prowl and could not find its way back again.

Colonel MacDonald Smith, who was Inspector-General of Jails, wrote to me asking if I could send two or three young alligators for his friend Colonel Carter, known to reader of the *Madras Mail* by his letters under the *nom-de-plume* of "Small Bore," who was making an investigation with a view to ascertain the difference between the several spieces. My son, who was with me, shot two of them, which I sent to Colonel Carter. Some of these alligators found in the back-water at Beypore were very large. One Sunday while on a fishing excursion with my son and some others, I saw a very large alligator quite close to us. It was lying motionless on a small rock about four feet from the water. My son out of pure mischief shot at the brute with a double barrelled gun. The effect was ludicrous, for the brute opened its jaws, made a noise, which set us laughing, and plunged into the water. Some of the No. 4 shot must have stung it and disturbed it from its evening nap, for it to make such a peculiar noise. I did not know that an alligator had a voice, but I can now confidently assert that it has, although not quite up to the requirements of a Music hall.

CHAPTER LI.

Cannanore Central Jail—(*Continued.*)

In addition to the inconveniences I made mention of in the previous Chapter, I found the Superintendent's house swarming with rats. I obtained a couple of rat traps and caught several. One of these animals which was caught by the legs in a steel trap managed to escape while the servant was in the act of removing it from the trap. The same night as I was asleep on the cot with my right hand hanging over at the side of one of the legs, a rat bit me on the forefinger. The bite might have been more serious had the teeth met in the flesh of my finger, but luckily the upper incisors had struck the nail, which prevented them from penetrating. The wound, although it bled, was not so severe as it would otherwise have been. A bright light was burning in the room and I saw the rate scamper away from the bed and get underneath a large box about three yards away. It had its tail cocked over its back as if it were quite proud of the achievement, and had performed a righteous act. It seemed to me that it was the same rat that had escaped in the morning and had waited its opportunity for revenge. The wound was painful and annoying, and I made up my mind to clear the place of these vermin. I sent for a bottle of "Rough on Rats" from Messrs. W. E. Smith and Co. at Madras, sprinkled a little of it over some boiled rice which I kept near by for the rats to eat and awaited results. Next morning I found three or four of them dead in the rooms. While on this subject, I may say that I had heard and read of the ingenuity displayed by these rodents when in search of food, but never could I have believed what they were capable of until I had seen some of their efforts in search of food. One morning when I was Keeper of the Penitentary, while going into my dining room I observed a rat on the cocoanut-oil bottle with its tail down the neck of the bottle. On seeing me it bolted with its tail covered with oil. I had been told that this was the usual method which rats adopt in getting at oil in bottles and I could hardly credit it. But here was proof which I could not resist. I should explain that cocoanut oil was generally used at this period for lighting purposes, kerosine being scarcely known. I had missed several eggs that had been kept on the top of the meatsafe and came to the conclusion that the servant had stolen them. But in this I did him an injustice, for on going one day into the dining room which was seldom visited, I saw a sight which quite astounded me. A rat was on the floor on its back clasping an egg with four paws, while two others were hauling it along by its tail towards the bathroom where the tubs and other things could screen them from observation, while they made their meal. I had read something of the kind in a letter which appeared in one of the Madras papers some time before this but put it down as one of the usual tales of the times. Possibly there was something in the air of the Penitentiary, which was not conducive to morality, for like the old offenders the rats were up to all kinds of mischief imaginable. But to go back to Cannanore, I had a lot of tomatoes growing which I had planted in a large bed of pineappels, about a hundred yards from the house. A number of ripe tomatoes were stolen from time to time, which I was convinced was not done by the servants and I could only ascribe the theft to rats. So I mixed some " Rough on rats " with boiled rice and put it out in the ground. On the following morning I found a jackal lying dead close to the spot, and two others by the side of the road between my compound and the Jail premises, a quarter af a mile away. This was shooting at the pigeon and killing the crow with a vengeance, for jackals, however noisy and troublesome they may be at night, are very useful scavengers, and I regretted that they should have met with so painful a death. I must say though, that jackals were too numerous in the locality where I lived and used to make the night hideous with their howls, even before it grew dark.

I had a rabbit warren not far from the house, surrounded by a wire netting of thin and close meshes so as to keep the jackals out. These rabbits had been bred from a number of tame ones purchased by the Superintendent, Mr. Symonds, had relieved and the latter should by right have paid for them. They bred very fast, and Mr. Symonds had rabbit curries, stews, and roasts on his table at which I was a guest on two occasions. I am no lover of rabbit no matter how nicely it may be cooked. Mr. Symonds on transfer to Coimbatore took a number of them alive with him, but I had to pay the bill nevertheless. After the Jailor's conviction, the Superintendent, Mr. Symond's predecessor, whom I have just made mention of, wrote asking me to make over the wire netting and two large bisons' heads, which were over the entrance door of the house, and which he had left behind, to Mr. Brown, the wood contractor of the Jail and a friend of the Jailors, as they had been borrowed by the Jailor from that gentleman. I wrote back to say that Mr. Brown could remove the articles as soon as he wished, but that there was only one bison's head when I assumed charge. Mr. Brown accordingly took them away, but had I known that they belonged to him, I should never have allowed them to grace the Jail premises. In addition to the rabbits, which I distributed as presents among my friends there was large Sambur doe, the doe of a spotted deer, and a male antelope. On two occasions, the antelope injured both deer and sambur and ran at a prisoner, one of a gang employed in the compound. So I sent for a butcher, and had the animal killed and dressed, sending portions of the carcase to some of my friends. I had a leg roasted for my own use, and found it better than any mutton I had ever eaten. Sometime after this the Sambur was bitten by a snake and died, and as I feared the same fate for the spotted deer, I presented it to the detachment of the Norfolk Regiment then stationed at Cannanore, who took it with them on relief to Wellington, where it became a pet of the Regiment. It met with an untimely end, however, owing to an attack of indigestion brought on by its having partaken of two or three newspapers and a table cloth for breakfast one morning. Apparently civilization had engendered a depraved taste in the animal.

I frequently joined in theatricals at Cannanore where I usually gave recitations, and on one occasion Mrs. Barton, the wife of the Captain commanding the detachment of the Royal Scots Regiment stationed there, wrote beseeching me to come down to the Barracks and assist the men in getting up an entertainment for the evening as they were always glad to here me recite.

Sunday was the only day I could call my own, although even on that day I usually visited the Jail for a short time. Many a good day's fishing have I had in the Beypore back-water. My bungalow was a half-way house between the seashore at Cannanore and the back-water at Beypore, the distance between the two places being about six miles. Captain Applewaite of the Suffolk Regiment usually accompanied me on my fishing excursions, and was up at my quarters before day-break on Sunday morning. After "Chota Hazree," we would drive out to Beypore where we hired a large boat and went up the back-water towards the sea. We were generally successful, and would bring home a good basket of fish. We would also throw out lines for Eel fishing, and I was very much amused once at an argument between him and my son regarding and eel the latter had caught. The line was balted by my son and put out and while he was getting another line ready with live bait the Captain pulled in the first line with the eel on. The eel was exactly eight feet long and weighed eight pounds. Captain Applewaite took it home with him to ascertain its exact length by means of a measurement he had made on the wall, and found it exactly eight feet long. He kept two pounds for himself and sent the remainder to three of his freinds in equal shares with a chit saying that there were "two feet of eel two pounds." Captain Applewaite like most ardent anglers was full of his own exploits with the rod. He told me once in all seriousness that he always caught the biggest fish with the smallest tackle possible. Although I had no reason to doubt his statements, some of his fishing stories really staggered me. But there are many more anglers with a special gift in this direction. I also used to go out of a Sunday with Captain Garnet Radcliffe of the 29th Regiment M. N. I., and on these occasions Lieutenant Staunton of the same Regiment would accompany us. Captain Radcliffe was a first rate angler and knew how to handle the rod and line. He was, moreover, a good shikaree, an unerring shot with both gun and rifle, and altogether a good all-round sportsman. Many a pleasant hour have I spent in his company. May he live a thousand years! as the Spaniard would say. On leaving Cannanore he was appointed to the Command of a Regiment in Burmah.

Captain Massey of the Norfolk Regiment and a relation of "Redan" Massey, used also to join our fishing parties occasionally. He was also a very kneen sportsman. Cannanore is noted for its snipe during the season, but my duties did not allow me many opportunities of indulging in this sport. Many a time Captain Barton and Dr. Bean, the Cantonment Medical Officer sent me snipe after a successful day's shooting. I joined the Volunteers at Cannanore, and although I did not go to drill, I used to attend target practice, and won a prize at the rifle matches at the 200 yards distance. On account of my weight "which was sixteen and half stone then," and corpulency, I could not lie down and was therefore not much good at the long distances. But at the annual rifle meeting, I made a bet of five rupees each, with Captain

Barton and Dr. Bean, that I would make a better score than either of them at the 500 yards range if they would allow me to sit on a chair and use the back as a rest while shooting. They agreed and I scored one centre and four bull's eyes out of five rounds in this position, beating them easily, although both were good shots. There was of course a good deal of laughter and chaff at my novel position in the match.

I visited the old and disused Jail at Tellicherry on one occasion, and came across an interesting relic of old times. Behind one of the Jail buildings there was a lot of old iron and other articles, among which was a cage made of hoop iron large enough to hold a man, with places for his legs, arms, neck and head when standing upright. On the top, was fastened an iron ring by which the cage could be hung up to the bough of a tree where the unhappy man whose lot it was to receive this punishment was made to swelter in the noon day sun and shiver in the cold at night. I was told that there had been two of these ingenious devices and that they once belonged to Tippu Sultan, that fiend in the art of torture. I wrote to the Inspector-General about the cage and suggested its removal to the Madras Museum where it would appear to advantage as a relic of the barbarous times of Tippu. I heard afterwards that it had been removed by the Department of Public Works, but whether it was ever sent to the Madras Museum I am unable to say.

CHAPTER LII.

Cannanore Central Jail—(*Continued*).

The Cannanore Central Jail had a bad reputation on account of the high death-rate of its population ; but this was chiefly due to the effects of the heavy rains during the Monsoon Season, and probably not to any want of care and attention on the part of the Jail officials. A large proportion of the prisoners came from other parts of India, where they were accustomed to a much drier climate, and the wet weather at Cannanore naturally told upon them. At the time

I assumed charge, there were a hundred very old prisoners who had been transferred from time to time from Jails in other part of the Presidency, and I pointed. these men out to Colonel Porteous, the Inspector-General, as being themselves likely to cause a high death-rate. After inspecting each of them, he directed their re-transfer to other Jails. One of these men, a man named Madhava Tevan, came from the Tinnevelly District and was a noted dacoit. He had no less than six life sentences against him, all for dacoity with violence, and was the leader of a large gang of dacoits (Maravans). At his request, I submitted a memorial to Government praying for a reduction of his sentence, but it was useless, for Government declined to interfere, the man's crimes being two notorious. Even had the Government remitted three of his life sentences it would not have been of much use to him, as he would have had three more to work out each for a term of twenty-five years. It may not be generally known that a life sentence for dacoity is twenty-five years, whereas for culpable homicide it is twenty. These in the case of well-conducted convicts can be reduced under remission rules to nineteen and sixteen years, respectively, so that this convict, even had the Government listened to his appeal, could not under any circumstances get off with less that fifty-seven years. We had in Jail about three hundred Burmese convicts, and these men were troublesome at first. There was some trifling alteration made in their diet by order of Government which roused their ire and I feared an outbreak. I explained matters to them fully, but several of them were dissatisfied still and were ripe for a revolt. I had thus a very unpleasant time of it and for a whole week scarcely left the Jail from early morning till it was time to lock up. I was compelled to lock up some of the prisoners and confine many others to their wards, which had the effect, fortunately for the prisoners and confine many others to their wards, which had the effect, fortunately for the Jall officials, of quieting them down. One Sunday morning, a Burmese prisoner struck another Burmese prisoner on the head with a piece of wood that he had secreted the day before while working in the Carpenter's shop. The injured convict was taken to the Hospital by the Jailor and his assailant locked up. I had just left the Jail when I received the Jailor's note reporting the occurrence and stating the Hospital Assistant had mentioned to him that the injury was not a very serious one. So unconscious was the Hospital Assistant of the serious nature of the hurt that he even omitted to report the matter to the Medical Officer, but about 5 o'clock in the evening the injured convict sank and died. Nothing of course could be done for the man as it was discovered after his death that he had bled inwardly, although at the time he declared that he would be all right. I reported the matter at once to the Assistant Superintendent of Police, who held an enquiry into the matter. The case was enquired into magisterially and the Burman was committed for trial at the Sessions Court at Tellicherry on a charge of murder. Here he was tried and sentenced to death. There being no gallows in the Cannanore Jail, he was removed to the District Jail at Calicut where he was executed. I was sorry for the man's untimely end for he was a quiet, well-behaved prisoner, and must have received great provocation from the man he had struck who was a ruffian of the worst description and had actually bullied this man in the Carpenter's shop the day before. Owing as I said to the want of a gallows in the Cannanore Jail, executions were carried out in the District Jail at Calicut, but as it was in contemplation to close this Jail, I was ordered to construct a gallows at Cannanore. This I erected at the back of the Jail with the assistance of the Department of Public Works.

About this time, Doctors Lethbridge and Walker, the heads of the Medical Departments of Bengal and Bombay, who had been deputed by the Imperial Government to make an inspection of all the Jails in the Presidency, arrived at Cannanore. It was in contemplation to close some of the Jails and this caused a flutter among the Jail officials in the Presidency, as many would be affected materially by the change. They visited the Cannanore Jail two days in succession and the Medical Officer of the Jail, Dr. Thummon Singh, who was put through a crucial examination in connection with the sickness prevailing among the Burmese prisoners, had a very trying time of it. These Burmese were suffering a good deal from scurvy and Mr. Thummon Singh was put some very pointed and unpleasant questions regarding his diagnosis of the disease as he was under the impression that it was not scurvy.

Doctor's Lethbridge and Walker then visited the Jail Hospital where they closely examined each patient. One man, a Burman, was in a very low, anæmic state, so much so that Dr. Lethbridge thought it would be a wonder if he recovered at all. He said that he had received a letter from a Medical Officer in charge of a jail in Bengal for whose opinion he had great respect, stating that he had discovered a remedy for anæmia. This Dr. Lethbridge declared would, if true, quickly bring down the high death-rate prevailing in many Jails. He mentioned the name of the remedy to Dr. Thummon Singh who said he had none of it in his surgery, nor did he think it was kept in stock in the Medical Stores at Madras. I told Dr. Lethbridge that I had a bottle of the stuff with me which I had got down from Bombay. The Burman, however, in spite of all prognostications, recovered in time. While talking of medicines and Medical Officers, both Doctors agreed that some members of the profession were the greatest faddists out. My Jailor, Mr. W. S. Upshon, was rather struck with this remark. I am glad to say that he is now Acting Superintendent of the Cannanore Central Jail.

A very lengthy report was submitted by them to the Government of India, a copy of which was of course sent to the Madras Government and one of their recommendations was that the Cannanore Central Jail should be closed, and the District Jail at Calicut retained after certain alterations had been made in it, those prisoners for whom accommodation could not be found in the latter institution being transferred to the Coimbatore and other Jails. No doubt their recommendation for this step appeared conclnsive to them; but it was well known to the Inspecter-General of Jails, the Sanitary Commissioner, and the Surgeon-General, Madras, that the Calicut Jail was any thing but a success. I wrote at great length to the Inspector-General, giving my views regarding the proposition, and pointing out the great expense it would entail on the Government if the Cannanore Jail were abolished. Able as Doctors Lethbridge and Walker were they could not obtain a real knowledge of the state of things in a two days' visit. The nearest large Jail to Cannanore is that at Coimbatore, nearly two hundred miles away but as that Jail was frequently overcrowded, its surpuls population had to be accommodated in Jails further away still, and the proposal to send the prisoners at Cannanore to Coimbatore and other places just as likely to be overcrowded, was absurd, leaving out of consideration the cost of transfer which reaches a high figure even at ordinary periods, when all prisoners sentenced to twelve months' imprisonment and over have to be sent to Central Jail. In such cases not only has the cost of travelling for the prisoners to be taken into account, but the traveling expenses of the Police escort has to be reckoned for. Besides this, the prisoners on the expiry of their terms of imprisonment have to be provided with subsistence allowance and train fares to their homes. Dacoities and other gave crimes were of frequent occurrence on the West Coast. If Cannanore Jail were closed all offenders would have to be sent hundreds of miles away. What would happen then if there were any serious outbreak in the District, and where could the disturbers of the peace be lodged with insufficient Jail accommodation at hand. All this and more to the same effect, I pointed out to the Inspector-General. and I am glad to say that the Madras Government took no action on the proposals made by the two doctors. Had the Inspector-General of Jails, Madras, and the Surgeon-General of the Presidency also been appointed on the Commission, the recommendation to close the Cannanore Jail would not have been heard of. Some time afterwards, the Surgeon General visited the Cannanore Jail, and on my speaking to him about the report made by the two Medical Officers, he said it was very easy to find fault, and probably had he been deputed to examine some of the Jails in Bengal and Bombay he would have found a great deal to complain of, and this was strictly true, for the some of the Jails in those Presidencies had been much neglected even by Medical Officers who were in charge, and from what Doctors Lethbridge and Walker wrote about them they were in a far worse condition than the most backward Jail in the Madras Presidency. Some time after this, as if to prove the truth of my contentions, there was an outbreak among the Tiens, or toddy-drawers of the district, and great numbers of them were made prisoners. The Subsidiary Jails were overcrowded, and accommodation had to be found for many in the Central Jail. The outbreak was due to an additional tax being put on toddy trees which the men resisted. I pitied the poor men who were sent to the Central Jail, for they generally belonged to a peaceable and law-adiding class. What the weight of each prisoner was on first being sent to Jail was not known, as prisoners are not weighed in Subsidiary Jails. After being kept a month or so in those Jails, many of the men were transferred on the arrival of fresh prisoners, to the Central Jail at Cannanore. Doubtless they had lost a great deal in weight during their period of imprisonment in the Subsidiary Jails, for they were put on a diet they were unused to, and a great number of them also lost weight in the Cannanore Jail, where the prescribed diet consisted of Ragi, with only two meals of rice a week. Such food would naturally be distasteful to men whose daily fare consisted of large meals of rice with as much toddy as they wished to drink. The Inspector-General (Mr. Cardew) on inspecting the Cannanore Jail at the end of March 1893, could not understand how so many men, all recent admissions, could have lost so much in weight. He casused a number of prisoners who had been working in the shops for some years to be weighed and found that these men had gained a little ; but they were not toddy-drawers, who were chiefly the only prisoners who had deteriorated. He also considered that the death rate during the three months, *viz.*, fourteen, was abnormal, and after the conclusion of his inspection wrote me two demi-official letters which animadverted on these facts, and which were anything but pleasant reading to me. Of course, I replied to him demi-officially and showed him that his conclusions as to the fault lying with the administration were erroneous, and that in this case the Jail officials were neither responsible for the high rate, nor for the loss in weight of the prisoners. After this I obtained three months' leave, April, May, and June of that year and Mr. Mills from Trichinopoly acted for me during my absence. I knew Mr. Mills was no friend of mine, and that he did his best to show that the Cannanore Jail had been mismanaged. I took chagre from him again on the 1st July and had not been many days at work before I received from the Inspector-General, an order of Government appointing me Superintendent of the first-class Central Jail at Rajahmundry and directing me to hand over charge to the Medical Officer Dr. A. O'Hara. The Inspector-General wrote strongly in praise of my work to the Government and stated that if he could not find a suitable officer as Superintendent of the Cannanore Central Jail, he would take charge of it himself in addition to his own duties. He letter to Government of which he sent me a copy, was a revelation to me considering what he had written to me before demi-officially, and I said to myself " Tyrrell, there are more things in heaven and earth than are dreamt of in your philosophy."

He actually did take charge of the Jail and found out for himself that Mr. Mills who had acted for me had not carried out his duties in an upright and conscientious manner. He reported the matter to Government and Mr. Mills was dismissed the service. During the period he was in charge of the Cannanore Central Jail, Mr. Cardew was quickly to discover for himself that what I stated as to the causes of the sickness amongst the prisoners was correct, for he lost 14 prisoners in one month through disease, and he very kindly wrote to me and told me so. He also gave me a lot of information of what had been going on in the Rajahmundry Jail for which I was very thankful.

CHAPTER LIII.

CANNANORE CENTRAL JAIL—(*Continued.*)

In some of the Chapters dealing with my experiences in the Penitentiary, I have given accounts of certain convicts who by reason either of their peculiarities, or the nature of their crimes, had brought themselves more prominently to the notice of the Jail authorities. In this Chapter I purpose relating the exploits of three such men who were in the Cannanore Jail during the period I was in charge as Superintendent, each of whom had distinguished himself in his own peculiar way.

The first of these was a man named Itharsa Nair, an ex-Police Inspector, who had been arrested for shooting the Public Prosecutor at Calicut. He was tried on the capital charge and after a lengthy trial condemned to death. Owing to the responsible positions held by the victim and the murderer and the aggravated nature of the crime, the case caused an immense sensation at the time. The sentence was confirmed by the High Court, and, as is usual with men in his situation, he memorialized the Government. He was a fine looking, stalwart man in the prime of life: but he gave the Jail people all the trouble imaginable in connection with his diet. By order of the Medical Officer, he was given a special ration consisting of rice, milk, sugar, etc., all of the best quality and not the usual jail diet of ragi. But even this did not appear to satisfy him, for he complained to the Inspector-General who was down at Cannanore at the time on inspection duty, that the milk given him was sour and that the rice was obtained with the special object of poisoning him.

On one occasion speaking to the Jailor, Mr. Wheeler, he told that official loftily "neither your Government, nor your Superintendent, nor you will ever be able to hang me, for something will happen to all of you, if you only attempt to execute me." His memorial to Government so far as I remember ran to a length of a hundred and forty-four pages; but I had quitted Cannanore for Rajahmundry, before the orders of Government were received, and I left him, as well as a female convict under sentence of death, an undesirable legacy to the Medical Officer, Surgeon-Major A. O'Hara, who took charge, pending Mr. Cardew's arrival. Mr. Wheeler, however, afterwards wrote telling me that Government had declined to interfere in Itharsa Nair's case, and that the "Indian Lion" as he called him on account of his idle boasts, was completely cowed and walked to the gallows as calmly and quietly as any one could have desired. Also that he (Mr. Wheeler) had "helped the unhappy man on his long journey with as much despatch as possible and with about twelve inches extra drop."

Itharsa Nair's extraordinary boasts led me to think that he had a deep-rooted conviction that nothing could happen to him that was not prescribed in his "book of fate" as Pope calls it. It is not generally known that every Hindu child has its horoscope cast at birth by a Brahmin astrologer employed for the purpose, which is implicity believed in, and which regulates the course of action in life of the child when it has grown to manhood, or womanhood. Possibly Itharsa Nair was promised a long lease of life in his horoscope, and acted accordingly. The next case was one of the determined suicide, of which Mr. Cardew wrote and gave me some particulars shortly after my arrival at Rajahmundry. The prisoner in question, a Moplah of the name of Marakal, had in a fit of desperation, ripped open his stomach with a shoe-maker's knife, drew out his intestines, and cutting them piece by piece threw them away one by one, just as a conjuror would bring out small pegs and other articles from his mouth and show them to his audience. The man appeared to be in a frenzy, and no one cared to approach him. The Jailor, Mr. Wheeler, however, rushed upon and overpowered him. The man, however, had fatally injured himself, and he died a couple of hours afterwards. Mr. Cardew in his letter to me commended Mr. Wheeler in very high terms for his pluck in securing the man, when others were reluctant to go near him. The case was a peculiar one, and as Mr. Wheeler wrote a detailed account of it to me I cannot do better than give it as nearly as possible in his own words.

"Marakal had two sentences each of 14 years' rigorous imprisonment for the murder of his mother, his sister, and his brother-in-law; both sentences were confirmed by the High Court, but were to run concurrently. On memorializing the Government however the prisoner made the matter worse for himself, for it was ordered that the sentences should run *consecutively*, thus raising the total period of his imprisonment to 28 years. This preyed on the man's mind, and he kept continually asking why he should do twenty-eight years, when the High Court had ruled that he should only do fourteen. All was explained to him fully, but to no purpose. He grew sullen and refused to eat his food, and as Mr. Cardew had just taken charge, he had evidently made up his mind to murder him and then commit suicide. I had my eye on him, but to me he was extremely respectful, and gave me no chance to report him. At inspection he asked Mr. Cardew to have pity on him, and give him an opportunity of telling his grievances privately in the office, and Mr. Cardew was about to allow the interview, when something flashed across my mind and I said to Mr. Cardew 'Sir, if I may be allowed to speak to you, please don't allow that prisoner his request now. After inspection I will explain why.' And it was good for Mr. Cardew that my feeble and simple voice was heard, for so sure as Marakal had got Mr. Cardew in the office upstairs, he could have made a mess of him in quick time for the same knife with which he had cut his bowels into thirty-six pieces, he had in his possession, and was only waiting for a fairly good chance to attack Mr. Cardew. I never spoken of this, and what I did as regards securing the convict was only my duty. Marakal had been employed in the shoemaker's shop where he had seized his chance of securing and hiding on his person one of the small knives for cutting leather." This concluded Mr. Wheeler's letter, but what seems strange to me in the affair is that a man should have lived two hours after the best part of his bowels had been removed. I have heard of such a thing happening with a wild beast, but it was the first time I had known it to occur with a human being.

Turning now to the next case with which I shall conclude this chapter. Iruman Kutti, whose extraordinary escapes from Jail I shall describe, had formerly been in the service of the Moplah Rajah, or Chief at Cannanore, whose residence had been broken into, and a great quantity of jewellery and other valuables stolen. Some time after the burglary, Iruman Kutti was apprehended at the Railway Station at Calicut for a burglary committed there and among the property on his person was found some of the jewellery stolen from the Rajah. For the offence committed at Calicut, he was duly tried and sentenced by the Sessions Court at that place, and was brought on to Cannanore with a view to the burglary committed in the Rajah's Palace being enquired into. After the case was investigated by the local Sub-Magistrate, he was committed for trial at the Sessions Court at Tellicherry. The jewellery was kept in the Sub-Magistrate's Office until required by the prosecution. One night, however, the box was stolen, the jewellery removed, and the empty box thrown over the cliffs into the sea. It was found next morning by two European Soldiers who made it over to the Police. In the absence of the stolen property, the trial could not be proceeded with and Iruman Kutti was remanded, but he saved the Sessions Court at Tellicherry the bother of trying him by making his escape from the Subsidiary Jail there. He was at large for some time after this, and when re-arrested, it was at a village not far from Calicut. He was sent up to the Cannanore Jail along with a number of other prisoners under Police escort, and before reaching Tellicherry, he persuaded the Head Constable in charge of the guard to let him see one of his wives who was living about half a mile from the high road. The constables were directed to march on and stop at an indicated spot while the Head Constable with Iruman Kutti were to go on to the latter's wive's house for a short time and then return and catch up the rest of the party. Doubtless the Head Constable had been heavily bribed, for Iruman Kutti had numbers of friends in well-to-do circumstances ready to help him. There had been much delay in this day's march and it was getting dusk at the time. When within fifty yards of the house, the prisoner begged to be allowed to go on alone to see his wife saying he would not be away more than ten minutes, and that as he had handcuffs on, it was not likely he could escape without being easily caught, nor was it, he said, his intention to escape. The Head Constable foolishly permitted this and Iruman Kutti went away never to return, leaving his friend the Head Constable to mourn his loss. The latter who was a very young and inexperienced man was much affected, for he knew what was in store for him on his return to Calicut. He was tried for neglect of duty, got twelve months, and died of cholera a few days after his release. The remainder of the prisoners were of course brought into Cannanore all correct. It was some months before Iruman Kutti was again captured, but this time he was safely escorted to Central Jail and committed to my charge. He had sentences aggregating eight years against him and his wonderful exploits were the common talk of the District. Like Jack Sheppard he was a middle sized man, fair, with a persuasive manner, but he was a source of anxiety to me on account of his slipperiness, and I had him placed in the close prison cells to make sure of having the pleasure of his company, at least as long as I remained in charge of the Jail. In accordance with Jail Rules I visited his cell every day. Finding me inexorable, he wormed himself into the confidence of one of the Medical Subordinates, and frequently got on the sick list by employing the usual dodges prisoners adopt when they wish to avoid work and get into hospital. But in Iruman Kutti's case, he was treated for some time in his cell. I spoke to the Medical Officer on the subject, for I was perfectly certain that the man was malingering, and warned him that Iruman Kutti had many friends outside the Jail who had stolen property of his, and who would go great lengths to effect his escape, and that it would be risky to remove him from his cell to the Hospital but the Doctor was a gentleman who believed that the centre of all wisdom lay in his own brain and that the rest of the world were fools, and ordered the prisoner to be taken to Hospital. Of course in matters where the health of prisoners is concerned, the Medical Officer is responsible and his word is supreme and I had to give in with as good a grace as I could. Mr. Wheeler was as much concerned as I was about the man, for escapes from Jail are regarded as very serious matters both by the Inspector-General and the Government, and I continually made enquiries from the Hospital Assistant as to the prisoner's condition both morning and evening. The replies at first were that the man was suffering from Diarrhœa, then for some time he was bad with Dysentery, and the Hospital Assistant would no doubt have had him down with cholera next had not Iruman Kutti saved all further concern about his welfare by making his escape one night. The time he had spent in Hospital he had utilized in concocting measures to effect his escape. The roof of the Hospital Verandah was very low down and he found no difficulty in making a hole through it and he had friends waiting outside the Jail wall who knew the very hour he was to break out, the neeessary ropes and other material were in readiness. The outer wall of the Jail was quite close to the back verandah of the Hospital in the roof of which he had made a hole to break through, and on the outside of the wall not far from the Hospital was the Jail burying ground and the gallows, an uncanny spot without any roadway, and only visited by jackals at night. It was at this place that he got over. Thus every weak spot was taken advantage of by this slippery scoundrel. Next morning traces of betel and nut were discovered at the spot where the prisoner's friends waited for the signal, which went to show that every thing was prearranged, and that the prisoner must have communicated with his friends while in Hospital. I was so incensed at the man's escape that I nearly forgot myself in speaking to the Medical Officer to whose wilful obstinacy I attributed the escape, for, had the prisoner been kept in the close prison cells, this could never have happened. He had not been away many days however, before he was again caught by the police, and had he been brought straight to the Central Jail all would have been well, but with their usual perspicacity, the Police merely handcuffed him and kept him in a country Police Station lock-up with two Constables on guard as sentries. Next morning the bewildered Policemen found their little cage empty and the bird flown. The dysentery he was said to have suffered from had apparently not grown worse for the complaint had interfered but little with his activity. Only a few months ago, I read an account in one of the Madras Dailies of this very man being tried and sentenced to death on a charge of dacoity with murder, but the capital sentence was not confirmed by the High Court. The man was a professional burglar and dacoit and was living on the proceeds of his crimes. His exploits and his marvellous escapes from Jail and Police custody would, I have no doubt, fill a large volume and make more interesting reading than many so-called romances of crime. As for the unfortunate constables who had charge of him at different times no less than six of them were in Jail at one time for neglect of duty in allowing him to escape.

CHAPTER LIV.

Cannanore Central Jail—(*Continued*).

Among my experiences at Cannanore was one connected with a case of riot in which I was called upon to give evidence. The Native Infantry then located at the station was far from being a pattern corps in the matter of good conduct, owing to the rowdy character of some of its members. Some of the Sepoys had a quarrel with the inhabitants of the village close by, that is, between the Cantonment and the Jail, which ended in a free fight, and which I observed as I was driving into the Cantonments. Several of the villagers had received a severe beating and before I reached the Native Infantry bazaar, three or four of them made a report of their having been severely handled by the Sepoys. Then a Sepoy in undress, a Mussulman, came up to my bullock coach and complained that he had been cruelly thrashed by the villagers. There was no doubt of this, for the man was covered with blood. I advised the man to go at once to the lines and report the circumstance to the Jemadar Adjutant who would take the necessary steps to have the men identified and brought to justice. Had he acted on my suggestion, the disturbance would have been nipped in the bud, for from the spot where he had been beaten to the lines the distance was not more than ten miuntues' walk, but he had apparently told his grievances to his comrades and aroused their indignation, hence the serious nature of the riot which ensued. On visiting the Jail next morning, a report was made to me by several of the Warders that a number of Sepoys had not only entered their houses and ill-treated them, but had thrown their things out and did as much damage as possible to their little belongings. One Warder was so severly beaten that he had to be sent to Hospital where he was kept nearly a month before he was declared fit for duty. The Police were brought on the scene by the reports made by the villagers and several of the Warders, and a general investigation followed some days afterwards. My son, who was with me when the reports were made, and I, besides the Warders who had been assaulted were requested to go down to the lines and pick out those of the Sepoys whom we could recognize I identified two men, and my son three, while the Warders also picked out two or three more of their assailants, but it is a wonder that any were identified at all, for it is one thing to see a man rushing about in loose undress clothing at one time, and another to recognize him in spick and span regimentals paraded with hundreds of others similarly clothed, who had had nothing whatever to do with the affair. My son and I were kindly requested to enter a room in one of the Regimental buildings in order that we might not observe the men who were being identified by the villagers, but this I flatly refused to do, as I considered it a reflection on my sincerity. About a month or thereabouts after the riot, Mr. Twigg the Sub-Collector came in from Tellicherry for the trial of the rioters. My son and I were of course both summoned as witnesses, and on my way to the bungalow where the Court was held, the Acting Adjutant of the Regiment with whom I was on friendly terms asked me, although not in so many words, not to be too hard on the men. I replied that I had no such intention but that I should merely speak the truth when called upon to give my evidence. I also told him that I was put to a great deal of trouble myself in writing letters in connection with the case, besides other annoyances, and that the men richly deserved punishment for they had actually made their way without a shadow of provocation into some Warders, huts situated close to my house. The trial lasted two or three days, on each of which the Court was crowded. The best legal advice was engaged for the defence, *viz.*, Mr. Rozario from Tellicherry, an intelligent and learned practitioner, who put the witnesses for the prosecution through a searching cross examination. On being called upon to give my evidence I found some difficulty in recognizing the men I had identified at first on the occasion of their being paraded for the purpose, for now some of them were in plain clothes and some in uniform, and as the men were in shadow, I asked the Magistrate to be allowed to see two of the men whom I could hardly recognize in the dull light in the verandah, in order that I might examine their features more closely. This was readily granted and I had no difficulty in identifying the men I had first picked out My son was more puzzled still, for after he had given part of his evidence, the Court adjourned for lunch, and on its re-opening, some of the accused who were dressed in uniform before the adjournment were now in plain clothes. But he was allowed by the Magistrate to go near the men, and inspect them closely, after which he succeeded in identifying the three men he had picked out on parade. The trial ended in the conviction I think of eight of the accused. They were charged on two separate counts, and were found guilty of both and sentenced, if I remember rightly, to two months' rigorous imprisonment for each offence. Thus were these rioters committed to my special care. The Sepoy whom I had first seen when covered with blood, and who made the report to me of having been assaulted by the villagers was acquitted. I was glad of this because in the severe thrashing he had received, he was adequately punished for molesting the villagers. This regiment I was informed was guilty of similar acts of molesting village people when it was stationed in Burmah, prior to its transfer to Cannanore. It was afterwards broken up by order of Government and a Burmah battalion recruited in its place. These disturbances between the Military and Civil population are at all times a nuisance and a source of anxiety to the authorities.

I omitted to mention while relating my experience of Police life in the Nellore District of an high-handed proceeding on the part of a Military Officer. A detachment consisting of details from various regiments, all under the command of Captain Bowen, 19th M. N. I., had marched a long distance from up-country and had camped at Nellore on its journey down to Madras. I was Reserve Inspector at the time, in addition to being in charge of the Jail guards, while the Town Police Inspector was an old pensioned Subadar in the sere and yellow leaf, whose knowledge of Police work was not up to modern requirements. About three o'clock in the afternoon of the day on which the detachment had marched into camp at Nellore, a report was made to me that one of the European Soldiers from the camp had entered the Native pensioners lines which was quite close to the Police office, and had struck an old pensioned Havildar in a most brutal manner. I at once proceeded to the spot with two or three Constables and saw the old pensioned Havildar. The poor old man was bleeding profusely, and as it was evident that he had been very roughly handled, I arrested his assailant, a burly European Soldier who was in an advanced state of intoxication. The man it would appear had been in search of a daughter of Eve but had gone to the wrong quarter. I locked the Soldier up to the Town Police Station and reported the matter to the Native Treasury Deputy Collector who was the only Magistrate in the Station at the time, the Collector and his Assistant being out on "Jummabundi." The Superintendent of Police, as it happened, was also absent on Inspection duty. I wrote a note to the Officer Commanding the Detachment informing him of the arrest, and the offence for which the Soldier was in custody. About 5 p.m. he sent an escort with a note to me to hand the prisoner over. I wrote in reply that I was unable to comply with his request, as the Native Magistrate had directed the man to be brought before him in the morning. About three hours later, a Constable came running to me with the information that the prisoner had been forcibly released. I at once proceeded to the Station, and met a guard of about twenty men fully armed with the prisoner in their midst and the Officer Commanding (Captain Bowen) on horse back. On my approaching the party, Captain Bowen asked me if I was the Inspector. I said I was. "Well" he replied "I have been and forcibly released the man as you failed to hand him over to the escort I sent for him," I said "you have committed a very grave offence in taking out a prisoner by force from the Station and had I been present I should not have allowed you to do so." He did not reply to this, but merely gave the command "Quick March" to the party, and away they marched to the Camp. I wrote a letter and sent it by a special Constable to Captain Gordon the Superintendent, who was forty miles away, informing him of what had occurred. A report was at the same time made to the Collector of the District, and both these officers took a very serious view of the matter. But meanwhile the detachment had departed on its march towards its destination. A report was made to the Military authorities in Madras, and a summons was issued by the Collector to Captain Bowen to appear at his (the Collector's) Court at a given date to answer the charge made against him by the Police. I was one of the witnesses for the prosecution examined by Mr. Dykes the Collector. The accused was anxious to prove that he was not armed, that is to say, he was without his sword, but I soon set that point right. He was not aware that I had seen him with his Regiment when I was in the 43rd and both Corps marched together and encamped near each other, day by day, till we arrived at Banda to take part in the campaign in Central India. Had he known this, he probably would not have put such foolish questions as "on which side he wore his sword" and "on which side of his horse was I standing" and others of a like nature. He was found guilty and fined Rs. 200 or in default one month's rigorous imprisonment. But the Nellore District had not done with him yet, for another summons against him was issued by the Sub Collector to answer a charge of having flogged two or three of the villagers at Khandepore, one a rather important personage in the village. It would seem that his grass-cutters while in camp had trespassed on village limits for the purpose of cutting grass. The villagers resisted and I believe took the grass away, whereupon Captain Bowen ordered two or three of them to be seized, tied to a cart-wheel and flogged. For this little frolic, he was also fined Rs. 200, or in default another month's imprisonment. At each Court he was allowed time to pay the fine, but I afterwards heard that another representation had to be made to Madras before the money was recovered.

CHAPER LV.

Cannanore Central Jail—(*Continued*).

I have mentioned in a previous Chapter that I had received two unpleasant demi-official letters from Mr. Cardew, the Inspector General, while I was on leave prior to my taking up my appointment at Rajahmundry. In writing this, he had evidently been misled by Mr. Mills my *locum tenens* as to the state of the Cannanore Central Jail otherwise he would never have written to me as he had done, while Mr. Mills was in charge. He had reported to Government most favourably on my administration of the Jail and written in the highest terms possible of me and pointed out to the Government that my services might still be retained as Government would benefit by my remaining in the service for a few years longer. I omitted to mention in one of the previous Chapters dealing with my private life in Cannanore, that Mr. Green of the Revenue Survey (afterwards Head of his Department) and Mr. Twigg, the Sub-Collector, gave a "Cinderella" to which I was invited. Before the ladies arrived, the gentlemen decided on having a little practice at "Barn Door" dance which was then coming into vogue. Mr. Twigg who was a very active man pulled me out of my seat, and said "come! come! Tyrrell and have a "Barn Door" dance with me." I did not wish to refuse, but considering that I was sixty three years of age at the time, and weighed Sixteen Stone, Six Pounds, I must have gone through my evolution with the playful grace of a rhinocerous. Mr. Dumergue, the Collector, had just arrived in Cannanore and would have attended were it not for his wife's indisposition. At any rate we had a glorious night of it. The ladies left the dance about one o'clock in the morning, but we remained on till day-break, having a most enjoyable time of it with a supper and a "sing song," until day light warned us to take our departure. I drove direct to the Jail in my bullock coach, a distance of three and half miles, never thinking of going home for a moment, for it was my custom when out very late at an enterainment to go straight to my work as I could never lie in bed after day-break. Mr. Dumergue visited the Jail quite early, and told me the reason of his non-attendance at the Cinderella the previous night. He went all over the Jail and seemed highly pleased with everything that he had seen during his inspection. He also spoke to me on the subject of fishing for *Bar Meen*, a variety of fish found close to the Bar at Calicut and others places, and on his return there, he wrote me a most humourous letter about his luck when angling for this fish in the back-water at Calicut. One day the fish were at school and could not be found, he said, and another day they were not at home, but he expected better luck next time. The Mussalman fishermen catch this fish with a cord instead of line, thick enough to hang a man with and a hook big enough to catch a shark. A piece of white rag is attached to the hook and this is thrown out to a distance, after which the line is hauled in as rapidly as possible. The Bar Meen seize the hook with the white rag on it and are immediately drawn out, no time being allowed them to play, a wise precaution as the fish has very powerful jaws and strong teeth. It is known to anglers on the West Coast, that the Bar Meen when hooked is a perfect fiend. On one occasion, Captain Radcliffe, hooked one of these fish in the back-water very near Cannanore and felt sure of landing it. He had the best of tackle and a spoon bait with three double hooks. The fish readily seized the bait, made a rush through the water and jumped out to a great height, made another rush and another jump when the line slackened and the fish was gone. On hauling in the spoon bait and the hooks, the latter were found to have been drawn out quite straight as if they had been hammered out on an anvil. Captain Radcliffe was exasperated and damned his tackle, but I rather think he should have damned the fish for its "cussedness" in not allowing itself to be caught as a respectable fish should have done. A fish from twelve to sixteen pounds in weight is very seldom landed with English tackle. Mr. Thomas in his "The Rod in India" mentions how destructive these fish are to English tackle and relates many instances of such experiences as he had while fishing at Mahe and in the river not far from Tellicherry.

The Medical Officer of the Jail at this time was Dr. Kernan, son of the Justice of that name. One Sunday he went out with a friend to fish for Bar Meen at the bridge across the river not far from Tellicherry. The following morning he came to the Jail on his usual weekly inspection. Before leaving, he informed me that the heat rather distressed him. On the following day he wrote me a note saying that he did not feel well, and that he would pay his usual visit to the Jail on Wednesday, but as he did not turn up, I concluded that he was still indisposed. The next day (Thursday) I received a telegram from the Secretary to the Surgeon-General enquiring where Dr. Kernan was and I at once drove to his house in the Cantonment to ascertain the reason of his extraordinary message. While going into the compound, I met Apothecary Shunker who had been in attendance and who informed me that Dr. Kernan had just expired. I was terribly shocked to hear this and sent off a telegram at once to the Secretary to the Surgeon-General in reply to his wire. Probably the note Dr. Kernan wrote to me on Tuesday was the last he was fated to write. Dr. Currie, the Cantonment Medical Officer, had died on Tuesday and Dr. Kernan had been in attendance on him a few minutes before he expired but found he could do nothing. Their deaths following so closely were ascribed to influenza, and both Officers were in harness within twenty-four hours of their deaths. Both were splendid stalwart men in their prime and were true sons of Erin. Their deaths caused a great loss to the public service. I shall always have the kindest recollections of Dr. Kernan, for not only did he help me in every possible way with my Jail work, but was the best Medical Officer I ever had, although I have had many good ones, among whom I may reckon Dr. Poynder who aided me materially, and whose father the Revd. Mr. Poynder I knew as Chaplain of Cawnpore in 1850. Among those whose names I shall remember with gratittude for their valuable co-operation, the following come prominently to my recollection :—Colonel Hyde, Surgeon-Captain Robertson, Surgeon-Major A. O'Hara and Dr. Bain (now Principal Medical Officer at Mercara in Coorg). At Rajahmundry Major Evans also helped me in every way. I take this opportunity of expressing my gratitude to these gentlemen, for it was in a great measure due to their valuable assistance that I was able to make my Jail administration the success it was acknowledged by the authorities to have been. Looking back on my Jail career I must confess that the majority of the Medical Officers I had were conscientious and upright gentlemen, although I must say that there were who were not absolutely a success so far as their Jail duties were concerned. Men who had their peculiar fads and cared nothing at all for the Superintendent's wishes in regard to the maintenance Jail discipline.

I got into disfavour with some of the good people of Cannanore for reporting Dr. Da'Costa who had been appointed to the Medical charge of the Jail and who worked with a will against me. In the space of six weeks, he had failed to visit the Jail for seventeen days exclusive of Sundays. After this he wrote to me one Sunday to say that he would not be able to come up for inspection the following day (Monday) as he was down with Dysentery, but would probably be able to come on Wednesday. I was sorry to hear of his Illness and as I had occasion to visit the Cantonment, I drove down in my bullock coach with a view after finishing with my own business to enquire as to how Dr. Da'Costa was getting on. On approaching Hirjee the Shopkeeper's gate-way, I was astonished to see the worthy Dr. Da'Costa riding out of the shop compound looking as lively and cheerful as he could possibly be. He was not at all disconcerted on seeing me, but

I thought his writing me such a note as he had done that morning was really too bad of him. So I hesitated no longer, but sent in a statement of his visits to the Jail to the Inspector-General. I did not, however, mention the circumstances of his having written me the note he had done, nor how he had committed himself in other ways, but merely confined myself to pointing out his non-attendance on week days. This led to his removal from the Medicial charge of the Jail by order of Government who called upon him for an explanation of his conduct. I doubt if he was ever able to give a satisfactory one. But some of the ladies in Cannanore with whom he was a favourite, considered I had used him very ill for he had led them to believe that he was a noted ladies' Doctor, so I forgave them for their anger against me, the more especially as he had told them that I had reported him for being merely absent on Sundays. Dr. Poynder, who was still in Cannanore, kindly enlightened me as to what was being said against me, but it troubled me very little, for I was conscious of having done no wrong. I had two other Medical Officers for a short time, who certainly attempted to work me as much harm as they could, but they went about it more discreetly than Dr. Da'Costa.

CHAPTER LVI.

Dieting of Prisoners.

The following remarks on this all-important subject in Jail administration are meant chiefly for the information of Jail officers generally and the younger and Junior class of Jail officials in particular.

Ragi on the whole is a more nutritious and substantial food grain than rice and is the principal cereal now used in all Jails of the Madras Presidency. The prisoners in addition get a small quantity of dhall three days in the week and rice instead of ragi two meals in the week, while five ounces of meat without bone is allowed three times a week. Of course vegetables, curry stuff, ghee or gingelly oil and salt are issued daily. Each article of diet is weighed before issue and the most scrupulous exactness is observed in this respect. The scale is ample, *e.g.*, the weight of ragi flour issued for each man, viz., 24 oz., suffices for any healthy man. Four ounces of the flour is boiled into a gruel in the morning with sufficient water to fill a quart pot. At twelve o'clock in addition to curry, ten ounces of ragi are boiled and made into a pudding which when cooked weighs from 2 lbs. 4 oz. to 2 lbs. 8 oz. a large quantity to be eaten by one individual. At 5 P.M. after the day's work is over and the prisoners have bathed, another ragi pudding of the same weight is supplied with curry, vegetables and dhall, after which the convicts are locked up for the night. On a meat day, the mutton is cooked separately into a good curry with vegetables and dhall added. Thus it will be seen that the allowance of food is ample, and the quantity of salt, viz., one ounce per diem, is more than enough for each man, for outside the Jail, he would scarcely consume one-fourth of the quantity. The diet of European prisoners is ample. In all these matters, the Jail regulations are very explicit, but a Jail Superintendent cannot be too cautions in making his purchases of grain for Jail use, for this is now a part of his duty. When I first joined, it was the rule to give the dieting of prisoners out on contract at so much per head and I have known many prisoners to die of complaints brought on by eating food made from blighted or damaged grain. Ragi and other grains when stored in pits is liable to get damp, and if not promptly dried in the sun become mouldy and unfit for consumption, even when thoroughly washed and dried in the sun. Such grain, if eaten, sooner or later produces bowel complaints and in some cases causes death. It is exceedingly difficult for one not acquainted with the difference, to distinguish damaged grain when washed and dried, from good grain, but as all Superintendents of Jails are naturally anxious to prevent sickness and keep down the death-rate among the prisoners, they cannot be too cautious in their purchases of grain for Jail consumption if they would wish to maintain their reputation as good Jail Officers. Even experienced Jailors are frequently deceived by damaged grain which has been washed and dried, being palmed off on them as good grain.

The weight of every prisoner is recorded twice a month and falling off in weight is not only noted by the Superintendent, but is also reported in a monthly return for the Inspector-General's information.

Many of the outside public are probably of the opinion that such matters should lie within the sphere of the Medical Officer's duties, but as the Superintendent is responsible to Government for any deterioration in the health of the prisoners, this duty is considered to more rightly belong to him, although the Medical Officer in some measure shares the responsibility. At the Penitentiary there is always a European Medical Officer of experience in Medical charge, but this is not the case in all the Mofussil Jails. I am sorry to say I have often asked the Medical Officer to condemn grain brought by contractors, which I did not think up to the standard required and which I subsequently buried. Many a time also I have got contractors fined for bringing inferior meat and milk not up to the required standard. At the Penitentiary about thirty years ago, I had a great deal of trouble with the mutton butcher and got him fined several times. I was much amused one morning when Dr. Cockerill, the Medical Officer of the Jail, told me that while he was driving home from the Jail and when passing along the Mount Road, the Jail butcher had thrust a leg of mutton into his carriage, evidently as a bribe to the worthy Doctor.

On one occasion in Cannanore during a suspicious outbreak of sickness, the Medical Officer was asked to explain the causes of the disease. Many of the so-called cases of sickness were, in my opinion, nothing more than malingering on the part of some of the prisoners whom I knew to be skulkers. The Doctor stated as his opinion, that it was due to the ragi not having been sufficiently ground, sifted and cleaned. On this, Surgeon-Major Walker from Ootacamund, a Medical Officer of wide experience, was deputed by Government to enquire into and report on the matter. I knew nothing of this until the Jail Doctor drove him up in his bullock trap to the Jail one Sunday morning and took him straight to the ragi grinders' and cleaners' room. I was fortunately at the Jail when Surgeon-Major Walker arrived. After examining the whole process of grinding and cleaning of the grain, he looked at some flour that had been issued for the day, after which he proceeded to the cook-house, saw some of the puddings that had been cooked for the day and tasted them. On the following day he again came up with the Jail Doctor and went around the Jail with me. After looking at the patients in the Hospital, he went into the question of the ragi flour fully. The Jail Doctor pointed out that he thought the flour issued was neither so fine nor so clean as it should be. This rather tickled me, because the flour had been run through the finest of muslin sieves and probably at that time there was no other Jail in the Presidency, where so much trouble had been expended in cleaning, grinding and sifting the flour as in the Cannanore Jail. It came as a surprise to him, when Surgeon-Major Walker told him that we had been sifting away the best parts of the grain, *viz.*, the inner coating which would have tended to keep the men in health. He got some puddings boiled both of the coarse flour and the fine, and after tasting some of each, said that those made from the coarse flour were more palatable. He picked out half a dozen prisoners and got them to taste the two kinds of flour puddings also, and they all coincided with him and preferred those made of the flour cointaining the inner husk. As a matter of fact all Natives who eat ragi never take the trouble of cleaning the flour to the extent we did, but cook it in a coarse state. I myself have often tasted the puddings supplied to the prisoners and found them very palatable, and I also relished a spoonful or two of the curries made in the Jail when prepared by a cook who knew his work well. All the ingredients used in the manufacture of the curry were of the best description and were mixed in proper proportions. Although I was not aware of it until after he had arrived, I was pleased that Surgeon-Major Walker had visited and inspected the Jail. At any rate the Jail Doctor who had been doing his best to thwart me obtained very little satisfaction from his report, for had the report resulted in what he expected it would, I might have been called to account very sharply. Another Medical Officer I had was an Assistant Surgeon who was also led away by his subordinates into believing that the Tapioca or Cassava root issued occasionally to the prisoners in lieu of vegetables was detrimental to the health of the prisoners. This as well as the *Rozelles* he condemned and he made an entry in his journal to the effect that they were not to be issued to the prisoners any more. Of course I stopped their issue, although we had large quantities of each growing in the Jail garden. One Medical Officer got the notion into his head that tomatoes were not healthy. With such faddists has a Jail Superintendent to contend. Of course a good deal can be said on both sides, but this I may say of the Cassava or *Manioc* root, that this vegetable which is something like a sweet-potato in appearance, is boiled and sold on the road-ways in bazaars and is eaten in quantities by the poorer class of Natives on account of its exceeding cheapness. Any one who has read Stanley's "Through Darkest Africa" will know that his eight hundred odd followers lived on nothing but flour made from this root for a matter of about two years, and that the only time it had any injurious effect on them was when the root was not properly washed before being made into flour. All that wants eliminating is a milky juice that exists in the root when raw and this completely disappears when it is boiled. This same Medical Officer I regret to say proved himself anything but successful in a number of cholera cases, although he appears to have deserved credit for his success in curing 85 cases of Influenza without a single death. But I have heard it stated by competent Medical Officers that the slightest cold is sometimes put down as Influenza. If however all these 83 patients had really the true Influenza, he certainly deserved all the praise imaginable, for two very able Medical Officers had succumbed to the disease in a couple of days, as mentioned in my last chapter. The experience I have related above will instance some of the annoyances a Jail Superintendent has to put up with, but there is shadow and sunshine in every walk in life and I have had my share of one as well as of the other.

CHAPTER LVII.

RAJAHMUNDRY CENTRAL JAIL.

The journey from Cannanore to Rajahmundry is a long one, the greater part of it is however by rail. On arrival at Rajahmundry, I took charge of the Jail on the 29th of July 1893 from Mr. G. D. Grimes who was transferred by order of Government to the Cannanore Central Jail, a less important charge. He was *retired* shortly afterwards on a very small pension. Rajahmundry Jail, I was informed by the Inspector-General, was in a very bad way, especially in the matter of its finances. The general health of the prisoners was anything but satisfactory, the prisoners had deteriorated in physique—that is to say, they had lost in weight, the Jail expenditure was heavy, the manufacturing department was in a deplorable state and peculation was rife among the Jail subordinates. Thus at the outset, I had a fromidable task in cleaning this Augœan stable single-handed, for the Acting Jailor and the Deputy Jailor were utterly incompetent for the duties they had to perform. I had to suspend the former on account of some very questionable transactions in which he was concerned, and he was transferred. A Mr. Wills, the Jailor of the Bellary Jail, whom I knew formerly as an Acting Warder in the Penitentiary, was sent in his place. Wills had originally been a Sergeant in a Cavalry Regiment and was an excellent Jail officer, and a man of experience. He quickly discovered all the trickery and peculation that had been and was going on, and by personally attending to the issue and cooking of the rations, a marked improvement was observable in the periodical returns of weight of the perisoners. The chief trouble I had, however, was in the manufacturing department, the books of which had been very badly kept, and which showed a considerable balance on the wrong side. Material and stores for this department were charged for, which were never purchased, and the manufacturing Store-Keeper had been having it all his own way for a long time past, and no proper check had been kept upon the expenditure. After a great deal of trouble and heavy work in going into the accounts, I submitted a report to the Inspector-General, which he sent up in turn to Government. I received in reply an official letter from the Chief Secretary covered by one from the Inspector-General desiring me to call upon the Store-Keeper for an explanation of certain serious discrepancies in his account. Had the man been tried probably there would have been some difficulty in obtaining a conviction, although he was clearly unable to give a satisfactory account of his Stewardship. He, however, cut the Gordian-knot by sending in his resignation which under instructions from the Inspector-General I accepted. The Store-Keeper of the Guntoor Jail was sent in his place, and this man, although not very efficient strove honestly to do his best. Of course all extra expenditure was stopped and by the end of the year I managed to evolve something like order out of the chaotic state in which I found the Jail on assuming charge. Not only was there an improvement in the manufacturing department, but the dieting, etc., of the prisoners was in a much better condition. I must here acknowledge that in regard to this matter, I was much indebted to the Medical Officer, Dr. Evans, who gave me every assistance, and told me how things were going on before I assumed charge. I was rather amused, however, to discover one peculiar method of making money adopted by one of the Jail officials, which I had never heard of before. This was in connection with the purchase of sheep and goats to stock the Jail farm which was maintained for the purpose of supplying mutton for the prisoners regulary. Animals which were in good condition would be exchanged for poor attenuated beasts and of course to the benfit of this particular individual's pocket. I thought I was cognisant of all the ways which were resorted to by Jail subordinates, but this was the first time I learnt of this ingenious way of "raising the wind," and like Captain Cuttle, when found, I made a note of it. All this tended to convince me that there had been a great deal of corruption and trickery going on among the Jail subordintes, and that it needed an iron hand without the velvet glove to bring them to a sense of honesty. Probably it was not much better in this respect than the Cannanore Jail had been when I first took charge of that institution. Lord Wenlock had visited the Rajahmundry Jail some months before this, and was considerably annoyed at not being able to obtain satisfactory replies to the enquiries he made regarding certian matters in the Jail, and was obliged to question the Jailor and the Head Writer to obtain the required information. Moreover there had been an escape from the Jaii of four long term prisoners the night before His Excellency's visit which was rather unfortunate. One of these was the notorious Pulney Andy, who threw his breakfast gruel over Lord Wenlock some months before at the Penitentiary when His Excellency visited that institution. Pulney Andy was in one of the close prison cells in the Penitentiary at the time, and when asked by His Excellency if he had any complaints to make, threw his gruel at Lord Wenlock through the iron bars of his cell door, for which Mr. McCready sentenced him to fifty lashes after His Lordship's departure. The other prisoners were I believe recaptured a short time afterwards, but Pulney Andy is still at large. Even if this escape had not occured, the very backward state of the Rajahmundry Jail as reported by the Inspector-General afforded sufficient reason for Mr. Grimes' removal to a lower appointment. The Writer, a Brahmin, named Ramaswamy Iyer, worked with real good will, and with his assistance and that of the Jailor's, I was able to get everything on a more satisfactory footing. The Jailor I regret to state has joined the great majority but the Writer is now the Jailor of the Civil Jail, Madras. The Jail wall extended for a mile round, and just outside was a large garden and somewhat extensive areas of waste land. Wild pigs were numerous and caused us a lot of trouble by the damages they would do the garden produce, while only a few years before this, Panthers and Leopards were very frequently seen between Rajahmundry and Dowlaishweram, a distance of eight miles, the country around being covered with low brush wood, thus affording them excellent cover. Good fishing was to be had in the Godavery and alligators were also numerous in the river. Small pieces of agate are plentiful enough in the District and can be picked up by any one who is able to distinguish the stone, and more than one diamond was found in the river. One lucky individual, a cooly of the Public Works Department, was so fortunate as to find a good sized ruby close to the Dowlaishweram anicut, while bringing out pebbles from the river.

A close prison was being built by the Public Works Department when I assumed charge, and on its completion I soon had it fully occupied by such of the prisoners as needed a severer discipline.

A small quarantine prison consisting of four good sized wards which had just been constructed outside the Jail gate for the purpose of detaining new comers for ten days before their admission into the Jail proper, with a view to prevent any infectious disease being introduced into the Jail, was brought into use after my arrival. We had two or three bulls and several cows on the Jail farm, which were kept for the purpose of supplying milk for the Hospital, butthere had been no sales effected of the surplus milk. So, in order to set an example, I at once commenced purchasing the milk obtained from these cows for my family. In addition to this, I purchased not only such vegetables as I needed for my table from the Jail garden, but also grass and fodder for my horse and pony. Mr Cardew was rather surprised when he visited the Jail and examined the Bill book to see the amount. I credited to Government for milk, vegetables, and grass supplied to me, for such a thing had scarcely ever been done before at this Jail, but I had made it a rule to pay for all these things in whatever Jail I happened to be, and I would never allow a contractor to approach my quarters. In this I was actuated not only by a desire to avoid scandal, but because I considered it the correct thing to do.

We had several executions at Rajahmundry, but the gallows was one of the old style of structure, *i.e.*, merely a ladder leading to a wooden platform with uprights and a cross bar, the platform having no raised earthwork upon which the official could step off in case of necessity. An unruly convict on such a drop could if he chose cause a sensation by bringing down one or two of the officials with him. I wrote to the Inspector-General about this and a more suitable structure was ordered to be built. As usual executions took place at 6 A.M. and the body was cut down at 7 o'clock. As soon as the condemned man had dropped, the Medical Officer usually retired on the plea of his having office work, and would return again at 7 o'clock in order that he might answer my usual enquiry as to whether the man was dead or not. This part of his duty was most distasteful to the Doctor, who relieved Dr. Evans but of course either he or his Assistant had to be present at executions to pronounce life to be extinct. As a matter of fact the man was dead almost instantly after the falling of the drop, but routine in this matters had to be strictly observed, for it had to be stated on the warrant ordering the execution, before its return to the Court which issued it, that the execution had been carried out without *contretemps* of any kind, or if anything unusual happened, it had to be noted in the warrant also. At Rajahmundry I had on one occasion no less than three men in the condemned cells awaiting execution.

CHAPER LVIII.

Rajahmundry Central Jail—(*Continued*).

During my fifty-two years' residence in India, I have been in some very hot stations, but one of the hottest during the months of April and May is Rajahmundry. During the latter month, the heat was so stifling at night indoors that I was compelled to sleep out in the open air on a camp cot with two coloies to fan me all night, although my bungalow was one of the airiest and best in the station. In my back verandah which faced the east I have known the thermometer to register 120° Fahr. one particularly hot day, and outside at 10 o'clock at night it stood at 100. On this day, the Inspecting Post Master, a gentleman whom I had seen only a few days before at Rajahmundry in the best of health died very suddenly in the Travellers' bungalow at Ellore of heat apoplexy, not a soul being near him to render aid, and a Railway Officer of some standing also had a stroke about the same time and died in a few minutes while waiting at the Railway Station. Indeed the heat on this day was so terrible, that as many as fifty flying foxes dropped dead while hanging from Tamarind trees, their favourite places for roosting during the day. It seems to me a most astonishing thing how these unfortunate featherless birds can stand the heat day after day in the hottest weather, particularly as their black skins would absorb the heat rays more than if they were covered with light colored feathers. This species of the genus "bat" live entirely on fruit, and are often shot and eaten by many Europeans as well as Natives. The taste, however, is an acquired one, for the bird is anything but a pretty object to look at. In this connection, I shall here relate an anecdote of an officer who had a partiality for the flesh of these birds. The gentleman in question was a Colonel occupying a high position in the Public Works Department, who had a friend, a Member of Council, paying him a short visit in camp while on his way to the Hills. At dinner the conversation turned upon flying foxes, and the Colonel spoke in high terms of these birds when properly cooked. The Member of Council, however, declared that he could never think of eating them, no matter how nicely they were cooked. The Colonel said nothing and the dinner progressed, the Member of Council relishing the curry and a stew which he declared were excellent. On the following morning, the Colonel adroitly brought the previous night's conversation into question on the subject of flying foxes, when his friend, the Member of Council said, he had never eaten them and never would, whereupon the worthy Colonel dryly remarked " well you ought to know the taste of them now for you had them for dinner last night." The Member of Council admitted that they were certainly very palatable, but that he would never have touched the dishes, had he known what they were composed of. It is the general belief that the flesh of the flying fox is beneficial in cases of consumption and they are killed and eaten even to the present day in the suburbs of Madras, *i.e.*, at Pallaveram and Poonamalee, and other places. Like the taste for green frogs and iguanas, the fondness for flying fox must be an acquired one. As for iguanas, I may say with perfect truth, that I often saw Native Officers of Regiments bargaining keenly for these reptiles in the old Market of Madras about thirty years ago.

There is one redeeming quality in the climate of Rajahmundry. Although frightfully hot in the months of April and May, the first few showers in June bring down the temperature sensibly and the place becomes cooler, and the climate more bearable than it is in Madras and other Coast Towns during the corresponding periods. The most trying month, however, is May, and while lying on my camp cot in the open with two coolies fanning me, I have drunk as many as a dozen bottles of ærated water each night, and as these were brought by train from Madras, and the empty bottles returned in the same way, this proved rather a large item in my expenditure. Like many other Indian stations, Rajahmundry was infested with snakes. I killed a cobra and two other poisonous snakes in my bungalow. A cobra was once coiled on a window sill in my bath-room, and in the half light of the dawn, I took it for a piece of rope and was on the point of touching it with my hand, when it escaped through the venetians. I preserved two small snakes, one a small black one with white spots, the size of peas, in a bottle of spirits. These together with a centipede of unusual size and color, and two large black scorpions which I also preserved I presented to a gentleman who is I believe now in Madras, and who made the collection of them a hobby. The year 1894 was my last full year in the service, and I worked with a will to get the Jail into perfect working order. Just about this time however the Jail at Guntoor was closed, and a large proportion of the prisoners were transferred to the Rajahmundry Jail. These men were declared by Dr. Evans, the Medical Officer to be a most unhealthy lot, and this naturally increased the daily average number of sick in Hospital, but on the whole the report was more favorable than we hoped for, and the death-rate not so high as we feared it would be.

There was a great saving in the cost of rations, and the cost per head for diet was much below the normal. In regard to manufactures, there was a net profit of Rs. 8,000, a gain which had never before been effected since the time the Jail was built, and I am glad also to say that there were no escapes during the year, although there were many thorough-paced scoundrels whom I was obliged to make acquainted with the "Cat." The Medical Officer, who succeeded Dr. Evans was of far too generous a disposition for Jail work, and the Hospital bill for Medical comforts, in the shape of liquor, etc., amounted to a considerable figure. Prisoners who had never tasted anything better than country liquor in their lives were given Exshaw's and Hennessy's brandies, when country rum would have been just as efficacious for all practical purposes.

One Superintendent, a Medical Officer in charge of the Vizagapatam Jail, wrote complaining that two of the convict maistries sent to him by my predecessor to teach weaving to the prisoners in that Jail knew nothing whatever of the business, and as they were, moreover old and sickly, and inclined to give trouble, he obtained permission from the Inspector-General to send them back to the Rajahmundry Jail. These men had been selected by the late Acting Jailor who had recommended them to Mr. Grimes as being skilled in the trade. On their return I recognized one man named Aligiri as having been one of the greatest scoundrels in the Penitentiary while I was Keeper there and capable of every kind of villainy imaginable. He had several previous convictions against him and was an out-and-out skulker. He had not the least knowledge of weaving and should never have been sent to Vizagapatam. On returning to the Rajahmundry Jail, he got on the convalescent list, and nothing in the shape of work could be got out of him. While in the Penitentiary, he made a surprisingly clever escape which puzzled the Jail officials. He was discharged from the Hospital wearing a truss belonging to Government, and was one of the first prisoners to be placed in the new close prison cells. He was not missed when the men in these cells were counted next morning for he had dressed up a lay figure to look like a man asleep in the cell, and by means of some wood which he had stolen from the Carpenter's shop he succeeded in getting over the Jail wall. His escape was not discovered until all the prisoners had fallen in. Had the beat constables gone their rounds eight times every hour as they should have done, the man could not have succeeded in getting away As it was, he cleared off, truss and all. He was a considerable time at large and used to act the part of a Catechist, frequenting Toddy and Arrack shops at night, preaching the Gospel to his benighted brethren, and was actually believed by them to have been a very saintly man, most enthusiastic in the cause of his Master. At the end of 1894, when grain was cheap, I obtained the sanction of the Inspector-General and laid in large stocks of it sufficient to last the Jail population for the whole of 1895, and thus effected a considerable saving during that year, for prices had risen again after I had made the purchase. I was not relieved from Jail duties until the 8th of April 1895, when Mr. Young assumed charge from me. I expected to have been relieved on the 1st of April, *i.e.*, at the commencement of the official year, and I was anxious to get away from Rajahmundry as the hot weather had set in, in real earnest; but Mr. Young was detained on account of the illness of his wife. Prior to this in the month of February His Excellency the Governor who had been on tour to Vizagapatam and other Stations, returned to Madras, *via* Rajahmundry. On the day before His Excellency reached Rajahmundry, Mr. LeFanu, the new Collector, paid a visit to the Jail while the Medical Officer and I were holding our usual weekly inspection, and was shown to the block where we were engaged. I never had the pleasure of seeing this gentleman before, but it seemed to me that he was in a very bad temper, finding fault with everything that he saw. His mood was so captious that the Doctor who was rather a nervous man hardly knew what to reply to him. He pointed to a scab on one prisoner's leg and then on another's until the worthy Doctor was inclined to believe that fetters should be discarded altogether. But I took matters more coolly and smiled to myself at some of the trivial things that the Collector seemed to make such a deal of. On going around the other blocks he cooled down a little, but found fault with the buildings and said that they should be plastered with cement in order that all might be of a uniform color. Before leaving the Jail he passed some severe strictures on the Jail management in the official visitors' book, remarks which he would certainly not have made if I were a near relation of his. After he had left the Jail, the Head Warder of the guard told me that Mr LeFanu had come walking up to the Jail with a cigar in his mouth. On being told that he could not go inside smoking, he declared he was the Collector of the District. The Head Warder politely however insisted upon his removing the cigar from his mouth, and this seemed to have aroused the Collector's ire. This piece of enormity on the part of the Head Warder in stopping him, the autocrat of of the District, from doing as he liked, was unpardonable and terribly offended him. Hence his irritability and captiousness in the morning. I don't suppose there is another Collector in the Presidency who would have allowed a trifle of this kind to disturb his equanimity. After he had left, all the chief officials of the station received notice that His Excellency Lord Wenlock would be at the station next morning. Accordingly all the District Officials, myself included, were present to receive His Excellency who was accompanied by Mr. McCartie, his Private Secretary, and Aide-de-Camp, and Mr. LeFanu, the Collector. The whole party came over from the Vizagapatam side in a steamer to where we were all standing to receive them. After shaking hands with all. His Excellency asked each officer a question or two. Turning to me he enquired how things were going on at the Jail. I replied that there was considerable improvement in every direction. On which he asked if there were any more escapes. I replied that I was glad to say that there were none. After leaving the Jail the previous day Mr. LeFanu had probably gone straight away to meet His Lordship, and even had he made any disparaging statements to His Excellency regarding the condition of the Jail, he would have discovered that Lord Wenlock knew more about the Jail than he did and that His Lordship had specially appointed me to it in order to rectify previous mal-administration. Moreover he would have found no sympathy from Mr. McCartie who knew me in Palamcottah and had recommended in the strongest terms my further retention in the service on public grounds.

I forwarded a copy of Mr. LeFanu's remarks to the Inspector-General and at the same time wrote him a demi-official letter relating the episode of his attempting to come into the Jail smoking, but even had he not done this, I should have been able to reply to every one of his strictures satisfactorily. But my readers will see how easy it is for an Officer in his position to make criticisms on the work of those who happen to be in a less responsible position than himself. Surgeon-General King, the Sanitary Commissioner of Madras visited the Jail on two successive days shortly after this and made a minute inspection of everything. What he said with regard to my management was quite different from what Mr. LeFanu had written and he gave me great credit for my careful administration. Of course the Sanitary Commissioner thoroughly understood how to inspect a Jail and knew what he was writing about.

CHAPTER LIX.

Rajahmundry Central Jail—(*Continued*).

While I was in the Penitentiary, I joined the Eurasian and Anglo-Indian Association and my Certificate of Membership was signed by the late Mr. D. S. White, the President of the Association who was an old friend of mine. There was a branch of the Society at Rajahmundry under the Chairmanship of Mr. Robert Weaver, another old friend of mine, a man of great histrionic ability, a genial soul and now Officer in Charge of Pensioners in Madras. He is a well-known man and one whom I hope to see flourish to a green old age. The Treasurer was Assistant Surgeon Lychlander, who I am glad to say was also an energetic officer and succeeded in establishing the Branch on a firm basis. I became a member of the Branch Society as well and presented the Society with a sum of Rs. 125 in all, for entertainment, etc. On my leaving the Station, the members got up an entertainment in my honour. During the course of a very pleasant evening some of the more vigorous spirits decided upon "chairing" me and carrying me shoulders high around the compound. It was no joke to do this for I weighed about sixteen and a half *stone* and I was in a state of perturbation, lest the gentlemen who took upon themselves the duty of carrying me around should not be able to bear my weight. With the prospect of broken bones before me, the ride was anything but an enjoyable one. However, everything passed off pleasantly. The District Judge after my departure also joined the Association, which benefited by the valuable aid an officer of his high rank was able to give it. His predecessor, Mr. Ross, had to be sent Home on a furlough on account of an unsuccessful attempt to commit suicide due to his having heard that Mr. Clark of the Revenue Survey had been appointed to take charge of the District Mr. Ross had been Registrar of the High Court at Madras and was afterwards appointed Civil and Sessions Judge at Calicut, and it was while in the latter position that he became involved in the once famous "Ross-Morgan" case. The case is so well-known to my readers that I need not dilate upon it. The affair commenced at Calicut where Mr. Morgan was employed as Disirict Forest Officer. The High Court had not only this trial on hand, but the equally notorious divorce case of Ross *versus* Ross and Clarke. As the proceedings were very fully reported on in the local papers of the day I must refer those unacquainted with the details of the case to the newspapers of the time. I had some correspondence in connection with an objection Mr. Ross had rasied as to the quality of the wood and in the manufacture of certain almirahs in the Jail for use in his Court House. He was thoroughly versed in the Law and judging from certain of his remarks regarding the way the almirahs had been made, he appeared to know something of carpentry as well. He studiously avoided visiting the Jail although as an official visitor he should have looked us up at least once in six months. At the time of his attempt at suicide, Mr Ross was engaged in trying the great succession case in which a son of the Rajah of Venkatagiri claimed the estate and title of the Rajah of Pittapore, deceased, on the ground of his being a son by adoption. Mr Ross and his successor were in favour of the claimant. But one of the deceased Rajah's wife claimed the property for a child of hers, although the evidence showed that for years the Rajah's state ot health had been such as to preclude his being able to obtain any offspring. The witnesses examined on both sides were legion and among them were Mr. Lychlander and other Medical men, while the best native lawyers were brought down from Madras After some lakhs of rupees had been spent on the case, it was decided in favour of the Plaintiff by the District Judge. An appeal was made, however, to he High Court, which reversed the decision of the Sessions Court, and found for the Defendant. The case was then brought before the Privy Council which upheld the decision of the High Court and thus ended one of the most celebrated Civil Suits of recent times. Mr. Ross had, I believe, written a very able judgment in the case, and the worry and trouble he had gone through in sifting the evidence, may have contributed equally with Mr. Clarke's transfer to the Godavery District to disturb his mental balance, for he succeeded afterwards in his second attempt at self-destruction. Mr. Ross was a man of great talents and it is a matter of great regret that he should have been driven to this awful deed.

On the day of my retirement from the service, *viz.*, the 8th April 1895, I had been serving Government for a period of forty-eight years, seven months, and fourteen days, with never a furlough to Europe, nor a residence in a Hill station, a record which I do not think has ever been beaten in India. This fact in itself will convince my readers that the Government was perfectly satisfied with my administration, for, had it been otherwise, I should have been pensioned on attaining the age of fifty-five. I do not think there is any other Public Servant who has been allowed to remain on for so long after he had attained the official age of retirement. I do believe that it was the saving of over half a lakh of rupees to the State which I was instrumental in bringing about by my careful management of the Jail finances, which mainly influenced Government in their desire to retain my services.

I have frequently been amused to see accounts in the newspapers of how certain officers have obtained a well-earned furlough after serving the Government for a period of perhaps less than ten years, and thus probably in a total service of thirty years, seven of it would be spent in England. Of course it is but just and proper that Officers should enjoy all the privileges that a paternal Government allows them, but there are hundreds of Europeans in India whose means will not allow them a furlough to Europe, nor even a trip to the Hills, and yet these enjoy fairly good health when they take proper care of themselves. I have quite recently seen some old veterans who have borne the heat of the Indian sun wonderfully well. One old Sergeant-Major I saw lately, was 88 years of age, but then he was probably one in ten thousand. He had been over seventy years in the country and had never been to a Hill Station during all that time. This frisky young dog when spoken to would always cheerily reply what " fine sunny weather it was." Several other European pensioners have I seen with ages ranging from 79 to 83, who have borne the heat of the Indian sun remarkably well, although forced by circumstances to live in small houses without any punkahs at all. Few of these men ever trouble a Doctor, and it seems as if death had forgotten their existence! A friend of mine, a Warrant Officer, who served with me in the Mutiny is now seventy-nine years of age and yet looks much younger than many a man of fifty-five. Another, a brother Sergeant of mine in the 43rd Regiment is now living at Poonamallee and is 93 years of age. The reason of this is that they have been blessed with a good constitution which they have taken care of. Nearly all the old men I have known were married at a very early age and were spared the temptations which young men of the present day are so little able to resist. It is no use blinking the fact that a great deal of the sickness in the European Army in India is the result of these same temptations to which the men have succumbed. I am firmly of the opinion that *married life in India is conducive to longevity, and that many of the obstacles that lie in the way of a soldier's marrying should be removed.*

I have often read of the comfort there is in having a good family Doctor, but family Doctors are expensive luxuries to a man of limited means and such a blessing is denied to thousands of our poorer fellow creatures A Police Inspector in the mofussil when travelling in his Taluq, probably some fifty or sixty miles away from Medical aid, has to be his own Doctor, as I was forced to be some forty years ago, when a man had not only to learn to Doctor himself, but afford medical aid at a pinch to others who might be urgently in need of it, in cases of outbreaks of cholera, dysentery and fevers. And this assistance I was able to render to many who were only too thankful to receive it. In this connection I may add, that Major A. Balmer, the Superintendent of Police at Nellore warmly thanked me for the medical aid I had given to the poor in Naidupett during and outbreak of cholera there, and in cleaning out an old Chuttrum in which a number of cases occurred. The day is far distant before the millions in India will be in a position to have medical attendance within call as is the case in England now. Many Europeans who have been forty and fifty years in India are able to stand the heat even on the hottest day without the Punkahs and *Khus Khus* tatties which are an absolute necessity for the new European arrival, but I regret to say this is not the case with me, for the older I get the less do I feel able to bear up against the heat, although I am only in my seventy-second year. The heat when the temperature in the shade has ranged from 106° to 110° Fahr. has rather distressed me, but my readers will not wonder at it, for a few days of this sort of weather in England would kill thousands of people. I found the use of certain so-called patent medicines when taken in proper quantities very beneficial, although the use of these same remedies is condemned by many gentlemen of the medical profession, and especially the younger members of it, whose dislike to the use of patent medicines of any kind whatever is uncompromising merely because these remedies do not find a place in the British Pharmacopœa, but

I have known many of these young medicos to learn from experience as they grow older and prescribe the very remedies which they had condemned years before. Faith acts, I admit, a prominent part in these cures, for example, note the astonishing cures performed by Captain Fred. Burnaby by the simple use of Cockle's Pills, during his ride to Khiva. Dr. Collier one of the leading members of the noble profession in London himself placed it on record that they were the best made pills in the kingdom, although I will not go so far as to say that they are a panacea for all diseases. Thirty years ago in Madras, I would have been willing to lay a wager of fifty rupees that I would take two of these pills every night, and would weigh some pounds heavier after I had been doing this for a month. I had done this before, more especially during the hot weather and always gained in weight. This is but natural when it is considered that one would consume more food and sleep better at night after taking this medicine. I have not taken any of these pills for years, but as for condemning them one might with as much logic condemn Dr. Furnell's Pills which have the greatest sale of any pills in Madras. Yet only a few years before Dr. Furnell was Surgeon-General to the Government of Madras, and probably prescribed these very pills in the ordinary course of his practice. Even Warner's Safe Cure Pills was patented by a European Medical Officer in Bengal. It is easy enough for young Medical men to find fault with patent medicines merely for the reason that their prescriptions are not disclosed, but if they take the trouble to ascertain for themselves, they will find that nearly all patent medicines are manufactured by experienced members of their own profession. Dr. Collis Browne's Chlorodyne is no exception to the rule, and there are thousands who swear by Beecham's Pills, which are now procurable even in Regimental Coffee Shops. While I am on this subject, I will mention a few tonics which I found very beneficial. The best preparation of Iron I found to be " Fer

Bravais," while some French remedies, and Stearn's Wine of Cod Liver Oil and their widely known patent remedies would all be classed as quack nostrums, but I have nevertheless derived great benefit from them ; so much for blind unreasoning prejudice. Even now the words of those two distinguished Medical Officers, Surgeon-General Walker and Surgeon-General Lethbridge, the Heads of the Medical Department in Bombay and Bengal, occur to me and there is a great deal of truth in the opinion they expressed that some members of the Medical Profession were the greatest faddists out.

CHAPER LX.

Rajahmundry Central Jail—(*Continued.*)

Before I leave the subject of my experiences of Jail life at Rajahmundry, I should like to mention a circumstance which occurred there before my arrival and assumption of charge of the Jail, a circumstance connected with the burial of a lady who died at the Station, a matter sufficiently mournful in itself, but rendered more so by the peculiar circumstances which attended the interment. Mrs. Lever, the wife of the Deputy Collector of the Sub-Division, a very young woman, died very suddenly while her husband was out on duty at Ellore, some eighty miles away. A telegram was sent to him announcing the fact and he wired back that he would be in by the first train that evening, and he was expected in before the actual interment took place. The Burial Service had been read over the deceased lady by the Officer in Medical charge of the Station, but the grave was kept open by his permission until Mr. Lever's arrival. My friend, Mr. Robert Weaver and the Clerk of the Church remained by the grave side, but as was often the case in those days, the train was late and did not arrive till long past the hour it was due. The Medical Officer had also kindly allowed the coffin lid to be left unscrewed in order that the bereaved husband might take a farewell look at his wife. After darkness had set in, the

Church Clerk went home for dinner and the grave diggers went outside the cemetery gate, leaving Mr. Weaver alone with the dead. He sat for hours on a tomb-stone close to the open grave with nothing to disturb the silence of the night but the moaning of the wind through the trees and the howling of the jackals in the graveyard ; and it was not till past midnight that Mr. Lever came to the cemetery nearly frantic with grief. He got down into the grave, the lid of the coffin was removed, and he took a last fond look at the face he loved so well. Bowed down with sorrow, he was helped out of the grave and the lid of the coffin was screwed down. The grave was then reverently filled in, and it was not till one o'clock that the party left the cemetery. A circumstance such as this is, so rarely happens in civil life that I felt a thrill of sympathy pass through me as my friend Mr. Weaver related the facts.

I left Rajahmundry on the 9th April 1895 for Bangalore and the journey was far from being a pleasant one on account of the dreadful heat. At the Ellore Railway Station, I bade " good-bye " to my friend Mr. Weaver, who was at the time paying the Pensioners there. At Bezwada, a place hot, if not hotter than Rajahmundry, I had to remain for some hours waiting for the train to take me on to Guntakul where I arrived the following evening From thence I went on by the usual route to Bangalore. Although Bangalore is far from being a cool place in the month of April, I found a considerable change in the temperature from what I experienced of it in Rajahmundry. But the Bangalore of 1895, I found to be quite a different kin of place from what I had known it in 1855. Handsome buildings had sprung up all over the Cantonment and I felt Rip Van Winkle after his long sleep, when I surveyed the place after an absence of nearly forty years. The old Infantry Barracks had been converted into Commissariat buildings, spacious Barracks had been built for the Cavalry and Artillery at Agram, and the old Cavalry Barracks had been improved out of recognition and were then occupied by the Dorsetshire Regiment. The Church on St

John's Hill had been errected and Benson and Cleveland Towns, where there had been nothing but a barren plain, had sprung into existence with handsome buildings everywhere. The Railway had not only come into the station, but had gone on to Mysore, and was connected with the Southern Mahaxratta System. A new Market had also been built, a place much needed as there was really no Market at all in 1855. I wrote a long letter to the Resident (the Honourable Colonel Robertson) showing what Bangalore was forty years ago when Sir Mark Cubbon was Chief Commissioner as compared with the present day, and this I am glad to say Colonel Robertson found interesting. There were no fine buildings on the South Parade as there are now.

The Plague made its appearance in Bangalore while I was there and I made it a point to visit all the localities from which plague cases were reported I was thus enabled to furnish authentic infromation to the "Bangalore Daily Post" in letters which I wrote on this and other matters to that paper under the *nom-de-plume* of 'Observer.' This was done with no interested motive for I certainly was never paid for my contributions but merely in the interests of the public health, and I am happy to say my motives were recognized and I was thanked by several people for my contributions. Indeed I was offered the post of Plague Superintendent by the local authorities, but as this would have interfered with my daily drives in and around Plague infected spots, I declined the honor. I never was so much gratified as when I saw that Colonel Robertson fearlessly visited all Plague infected localities in order to ascertain the state of things for himself, for it showed that as a ruler he was awake to the gravity of the situation. The Plague was at its height at this time as I thought no correct account of the number of deaths from this disease had been kept. I used to count the number of corpses that were carried down Tannery and other roads. I forget now the number that were carried down each hour but they were certainly alarming and showed the virulence of the epidemic. I got inoculated with the plague serum twice and so were two members of my family. A few of my friends suffered very severely after undergoing the operation, but I am glad to say that it never affected me in the least, although the maximum dose of the serum was injected into me on the second occasion

My letters to the "Daily Observer" regarding the old and unhealthy looking cattle slaughtered for consumption caused some sensation. Good beef and mutton can of course be had in Bangalore, but most of the meat exposed for sale would be condemned as unfit for human consumption if exhibited in any butchers' shop in England, and bring down a heavy fine on the seller. I have however since found out by several visits I paid to the Moore Market, the old Central, the Smithfield, and other Markets in Madras that for really bad beef Bangalore certainly does not bear away the plam. But the very worst beef I have ever seen was sold in the Pondicherry Market, although I must admit the fairly good mutton can be had there In regard to mutton, the worst I have seen was at Negapatam, although in this respect Pallaveram and St. Thomas' Mount run it very close Probably one cannot expect much in the shape of good meat during the hot weather months in some parts of the country, but something more might be done by Municipalities in respect of suspervision of cattle slaughtered for consumption. Seventy-five per cent. of the meat now exposed for sale in the bazaars would not have been considered fit to be issued to the prisoners in the Penitentiary twenty or thirty years ago.

Writing about the Penitentiary brings to my recollection the case of a prisoner whom I omitted to mention in my reminiscences of that institution. This was a man named Cousins, a reporter on one of the Madras Papers, who had received a long sentence for forgery. Cousins had conducted himself well in the Penitentiary and as a reward for his good behaviour was sent together with two or three other well behaved European and Eurasian prisoners to the Andamans, as a Convict Overseer. There had been some difficulty with the European and Eurasian Convict Overseers there, one men had struck a comrade over the head with a bottle from which both had been drinking and killed him. The guilty man was tried and sentenced. I remember reading the reports of the trial in the newspapers which were most interesting. It was after this that the lamented Earl of Mayo was assassinated by a convict Amir Ali who as some of my readers may remember suffered the extreme penalty of the law. The Convict Overseers we selected were not likely to commit themselves as those from Calcutta had done, as we were very careful in our selection, and all were well conducted men anxious by good behaviour to obtain a mitigation of their sentences, and thus it came about that Cousins was selected. He had married a Eurasian woman in Madras, and I was informed on reliable authority that he was heir presumptive to a Baronetcy, his brother the then Baronet being childless. On arrival at Port Blair he wrote a very entertaining letter to a convict friend in the Penitentiary, descriptive of his experience of the place and of the voyage out. Captian Hallet after reading it handed it to me to peruse also, before giving it to the addressee. It was a most interesting letter and Captain Hallett declared that it could not possibly have been better written. Cousins' wife joined him sometime after, but what became of him eventually I never heard. There are many persons still living in Madras who may probably remember Cousins well. Another remarkeble prisoner whom I knew in the Penitentiry was one W. Seymour Burch describing himself as an M. A. of London. This individual was I believe at one time a pupil of St. Mary's Seminary at Madras. He had obtained a position as Head Master of the Bolarum Grammer School by means of a bogus diploma, from thence he went on to Trichinopoly and Bombay. On returning to Madras he came to grief through forging the name of the Revd. Father Kerr, Domestic Chaplain to the Earl of Ripon, Viceroy of India, whom he personated. By this means, he was able to mulc one or two high dignitaries of the Roman Catholic Church of some large sums of money. He was discovered, tried and received three years' imprisonment. In the Penitentiary he was always well behaved and extremely courteous. In fact his letters were subscribed " Yours very sincerely and most courteously." Sir Charles Turner Chief Justice of Madras, twice visited the Penitentiary and spoke to Burch. On one occasion Sir Charles informed me that he knew Burch's uncle very well, and that he was a gentleman of some position at home. He was sent to the European Jail at Ootacamund and after his release went to Calcutta. But the trail of the serpent was over him and he soon came to grief at the latter place in connection with the fraudulent sale of some furniture which he had obtained from one or two firms and never paid for.

CHAPTER LXI.

General.

During his tenure of office as Commander-in-Chief of the Madras Army, Sir Neville Chamberlain visited the Penitentiary two or three times. He was most anxious that something should be done for poor European Pensioners, a large number of whom were living in a state of wretchedness and poverty in Madras at the time. I had often spoken to Captain Hallett regarding these unfortunate people and gave it as my opinion that no European Soldier should be pensioned in the country unless he had a fair chance of obtaining some employment sufficiently lucrative to keep him and his family in decent comfort, and I also stated this entire pension was not sufficient even to provide him with quarters such as he obtained free when soldiering in Fort St. George. Some of these men, I said who deserved well of their country were forced by sheer poverty to live and mess with the lowest class of Natives, and on receiving their pittance of fifteen rupees a month they would give ten rupees of it for board and lodging reserving the balance for a carouse of two or three days, after which they would lie up till next pension day. A married pensioner with a family was in a still more deplorable condition, for how far would fifteen rupees go towards feeding and clothing a family of five or six, with the prices of provisions rising every year. All this I mentioned in my conversation with Captain Hallett. I remember a Pensioned Sergeant on Rs. 30 per month going about in a disgraceful state of shabbiness but in his case his wretchedness was due to intemperate habits ; but even with Rs. 30 a month a married European would find it difficult to live respectably in Madras what must it be then on Rs. 15. Another instance was that of a pensioned Private of my Regiment of the name of Hopwood who received a pension of Rs. 17 a month. This man lived with a native woman in a hut on the other side of the Chintaripettah bridge close to the Penitentiary. Although I helped this man as well as others on more than one occasion, I could never see him without loathing—the man was such a disgrace to the Eurpean community. He was found dead one morning under a hydrant on the south side of the bridge not far from his hut. Apparently he had gone to it for either a drink or a wash in an inebriated condition and the water had probably finished him In his case, doubtless, death was a happy release. Captain Hallett asked me to give my views in writing as to what I thought should be done for these men, as Sir Neville Chamberlain had had his attention drawn to the subject, and would be glad to give his serious consideration to any practicable scheme that might be suggested for the social and moral regeneration of these unfortunates. I accordingly wrote at some length stating what should be done—but I particularly recommended that a number of quarters should be built for the pensioners in the People's Park north of the present Victoria Hall—the cost which I considered would not be excessive, being recovered by a small monthly rental being charged for each set of rooms. It should be remembered that the People's Park of those days was not so circumscribed as it is now. There was plenty of land unoccupied which could have been utilized for building purposes and water, could have been laid on which would have saved each tenant Rs. 2 per mensem for water, and if they also did their own washing, there would have been the dhobi's pay saved as well. Taken altogether the Pensioners would have benefited not only physically but merally also if my suggestion had beon put into execution, especially in the case of married Pensioners. Many of the poor fellows were living in the purlieus of John Pereira's and other crowded localities where clergymen were unable to find them. Thus were their spiritual wants also neglected. I spoke to two or three clergymen on this matter, but was met with the reply that they did not see what could be done for these poor souls—of course they would be glad they said to do anything that lay in their power.

I omitted to mention while writing my experiences at Cannanore that Colonel MacDonald Smith, the Inspector-General, asked me to forward the usual certificate of fitness for further service enjoined by the Civil Service Regulations when an Officer has attained the age of fifty-five years and it is considered desirable to retain his services for any further period. This occurred after Dr. DaCosta's removal from the Medical charge of the Cannanore Jail and although I asked his successor, a European Commissioned Medical Officer for the usual certificate he did not seem to be in a hurry to give it to me. He had apparently heard from some of the ladies the precious stories spread about me in connection with Dr. DaCosta's removal from Jail duty, but one morning after the usual Inspection he examined me medically and wrote out the Certificate. He had probably mentioned the circumstance to some friends of Dr. DaCosta under whose advice he seems to have acted subsequently, for after inspection the following week he asked me not to send the certificate on to the Inspector-General of Jails, as the Secretary to the Surgeon-General had written to him to say that I was to be examined by a Medical Board. Such a thing was never required of me before and I penetrated the motive which made the Doctor suggest a

Medical Board on this occasion. I therefore placed the matter before the Inspector-General who immediately replied in terse language—" Tell Dr.—that no Medical Boards are necessary. The Certificate he gave you is quite sufficient." This effectually quashed any further attempts of this kind to get me out of the service, and I had no further trouble in regard to Medical Certificates.

This Doctor was the only European Commissioned Medical Officer from whom I did not receive the cordial support that I expected of him. He had listened to a number of tales told to my discredit by a few of the ladies and accepted them as gospel truth. But he is not the only good man who has been thus led away by slanderous tongues. Probably a Superintendent who lost thousands of Rupees to Government through lax management, or even the Parsee Jailor, would have suited some of these ladies better. The year before this, Colonel Porteous, then Inspector-General, wrote to Government recommending the retention of my services and stated " Mr. Tyrrell is hale and hearty " which he considered was ample reason for my continuing to serve the State, and I am quite sure he knew more about me than some of the ladies did. After this matter of the Medical Certificate, Mr. Cardew was appointed Inspector-General, and on one of his visits to Cannanore he dined at the Officers' Mess. Next morning while inspecting the Jail he made a remark to me which I at once recognized as coming from the leading lady in the station and I told him so. He admitted it to be true and thought that she talked too much. Surgeon Captain Robinson who knew me intimately and was a sincere friend of mine, wrote to me from Secunderabad on his transfer to that station, what the same lady would be thought of by Secunderabad Society where her measure would be quickly taken and she would be relegated to a back seat. The same lady had tried to patronize his wife he said. But the most humourous letter he wrote to me was about Dr. DaCosta who he stated had tried to get him out of the station. I am told Dr. DaCosta no longer graces His Majesty's Service.

CHAPTER LXII.

CONCLUSION.

After an absence of sixteen years I am again domiciled in the good city of Madras, and even in this short period what changes have taken place! New buildings every where! Some of them for architectural beauty will compare favourably with any in India. There is not a doubt about it, that Madras is forging ahead and in the near future will probably rival Bombay in the matter of its public buildings, although I must admit that Bombay does possess some very handsome structures. But of course I am speaking of Bombay that I saw for the first and last time twenty-five years ago. My readers should have seen Madras as I saw it for the first time when I came from Calcutta in 1854 and compare it with the Madras of to-day. They would be surprised at the great change that has come over the place. There were no grand shops then on the Mount Road as there are now. The People's Park was a burning ground and not the garden it is now. You would have required a hatchet to cut your way through the awful smell that emanated from the place where the bodies were being cremated. Although the tanks sixteen years ago were stocked with fish and there were some pleasant drives through the grounds, the place was not much to look at. That fine building, the Victoria Hall, now occupies the site of one of the tanks which in a previous part of this narrative I said was stocked with "Gourami." I was in Madras when the building was projected, and I may add that like many other citizens I suscribed my mite of Rs. 10 towards the construction of the building. The remaining tank that was stocked with this fish is still in existence, but is now an ornamental water, and I fear that the lovers of the gentle art will find very few Gourami remaining in it. One cannot help sighing for the past. Not that old times were better, but one loses his capacity for enjoyment as he gets older and pleasures become Dead Sea fruit. One morning I went through some of my old haunts in the Park, and I do not think I shall ever be tempted to take out a fishing license again, for its glory, as a resort for such anglers as Mr. Thomas of the Revenue Board, Colonel Thompson, R. E., Colonel Hunt, Superintendent of Army Clothing, Doctor Luke Hackett, myself and a few other minor disciples of Izaak Walton, having long since departed. Mr. Ellis was then the Superintendent of the Park as he is still now, and long may he continue to hold this responsible position, for it is probably due to his exertions that the Park has became the ornament to the City it is now. While on this subject, I must not omit to mention that fine structure the Moore Market which was sprung up within the last three years. Such a building was a crying want in the old days. I visited it several times during the day and twice after dark when its magnificent lamps were lighted. I measured the site on which the building stands pacing the distance on every side and found it according to my measurement exactly a hundred yards square. The cost of the building I judged must have been tolerably high. On examining the various stalls I found that provisions of all kinds could be had, including fruit, vegetables, biscuits, sweetmeats of all descriptions, oilmansstores and other miscellaneous articles. But what I was disappointed in was the quality of the meat exhibited for sale. I have visited the Market several mornings during the past month and only on two occasions did I observe any good beef or mutton for sale. A visitor new to the place would think there was no good meat to be had in the country, but a Health Officer should surely be able to recognize good meat when he sees it. I would recommend my readers to pay a visit to this Market any morning up to eight o'clock if they desire to see an interesting sight, for on every occasion I was there the place was scrupulusly clean and everything was neat and tidy. Undoubtedly the Moore Market is a fine building and will be an aid to the comfort and convenience of the Madras public in years to come, when Sir George Moore and the writer of these reminiscences have joined the great majority.

Another surprise in store for me was to see the number of buildings that have sprung up between the Park and the Penitentiary. Thirty years ago the whole of the site of these houses was a Jail garden. On the Railway side of the General Hospital is Adam's Park, one of Madras green spots now, but thirty years ago a high mound without a blade of grass and facetiously styled by Colonel Bowen "Mount Blanc." As I stated in one of my Chapters on the Penitentiary, I removed thousands of cartloads of sand which was utilized for the formation of a garden on the Cooum side of the Penitentiary. On visiting Adam's Park it was forcibly brought to my mind that by the removal of this mound of earth I had done my small share towards improving the City, although I little suspected it would become the shady green spot it is now. But what most suprised me was that the waste piece of land east of the Central Station, and not far from the Elephant Bridge had within the past few years become a crowded Mart. Could mortal man have imagined on my first arrival in Madras in 1854, that such a Railway Station as the present Central Station would have come into existence within the space of twenty-five years and that the old ramshackle building, that did duty for the General Hospital, would be transfromed into the magnificent structure that is now the pride of this City?

In 1854 such a sight as a Native driving in a carriage was a rare thing indeed, but the old order has given way to the new, and the Native of India has flourished under the Government of the Crown, while the ruling race except in the case of a few high-placed European officials and merchants of position have been relegated to a position in the social scale which it never dreamt of occupying during the days of John Company Bahadur. With all these fine parks and buildings for the public good, where does the Poor White or Eurasian come in with cheap Native labour competing against him, and the prices of provisions rising yearly? Even twenty-five years ago these unforunates were infinitely better off. At that period duck's eggs could be had at a pie each, hen's eggs ten for an anna, ducks eight for a rupee, while half grown fowls were also obtainable at the same rate. A good sized leg of mutton could be bought for four annas, and rice, flour, etc., were sold for one-third the price they are at the present day. Even European Commissioned Officers with their increased income could not live half as well now as they did when I first arrived in Madras Servants' wages have doubled and three horses could have been kept on what it would now take to maintain one, for the days when forty measures of horse gram could be purchased for a Rupee and 46 lbs. bread are gone for ever. So much for the march of civilization and progress! The British Soldier of forty years ago had not the comfortable Coffee Shops and Soldiers' Homes that are provided for him now, but he always got good value for his money. A substantial supper consisting of bread, fried fish, or meat with a cup of tea or coffee cost only one and half annas. This was the case in Poonamallee more than thirty years ago. On driving round the Fort one evening I was surprised to see the sea so far away as I was always under the impression that the sea ran close up to the walls of the Fort. In 1854 when I arrived from Calcutta the waves when the sea was at high tide, would actually wash over the road close to the foot wall.

And now I must come to the end of these reminiscences of a very nearly forty-nine years in the Public Service. Whether I have taxed my readers' patience or credulity I am unable to guess, but if I have done so I ask their pardon. It is an element in human nature to doubt and it is for this reason that I give them an assurance that every circumstance related in these pages is absolutely true and there are many living now in Madras who could vouch for the truth of many incidents I have here set forth.